Serial Killing for Profit

SERIAL KILLING FOR PROFIT

Multiple Murder for Money

Dirk C. Gibson

PRAEGER
An Imprint of ABC-CLIO, LLC

A B C CLIO

Santa Barbara, California • Denver, Colorado • Oxford, England

Library of Congress Cataloging-in-Publication Data

Gibson, Dirk Cameron, 1953–
Serial killing for profit : multiple murder for money / Dirk C. Gibson.
p. cm.
Includes bibliographical references and index.
ISBN 978–0–313–37890–4 (hbk. : alk. paper) — 978–0–313–37891–1 (ebook)
1. Serial murderers—United States—Case studies. 2. Serial murders—United States—Case studies. I. Title.
HV6529.G534 2010
364.152'32092273—dc22 2009039145

ISBN: 978–0–313–37890–4
EISBN: 978–0–313–37891–1

14 13 12 11 10 1 2 3 4 5

This book is also available on the World Wide Web as an eBook.
Visit www.abc-clio.com for details.

Praeger
An Imprint of ABC-CLIO, LLC

ABC-CLIO, LLC
130 Cremona Drive, P.O. Box 1911
Santa Barbara, California 93116-1911

This book is printed on acid-free paper ∞

Manufactured in the United States of America

This book is respectfully dedicated to the memory of all the victims of serial murder. In addition to those killed by serial slayers are those left behind: their family, friends, co-workers, and neighbors, who oftentimes struggle to cope with the cold consequences of this crime. Law enforcement, criminal justice, and judicial personnel also are frequently scarred by their experiences in serial murder cases. Last but not least, thanks to my special friends for their love and support: Chloe, Crystal, Erica, Kyle, Mitchell, Pink Paws and Sparkles, you know who you are.

Contents

Acknowledgments

There are a number of books, articles and other resources I would like to mention as being especially important to my study. Historical-critical research like mine inherently depends upon the formative research of others. Katherine Ramsland's *The Human Predator: A Historical Chronicle of Serial Murder and Forensic Investigation* (Berkley Books, 2005), Harold Schechter's *The Serial Killer Files* (Ballantine Books, 2003), Peter Vronsky's *Serial Killers: The Method and Madness of Monsters* (Ballantine Books, 2004), and Michael D. Kelleher and C.L. Kelleher's *Murder Most Rare: The Female Serial Killer* (Dell Books, 1998) were all useful in several chapters. Also deserving of mention are Michael Newton's book, *The Encyclopedia of Serial Killers* (Checkmark Books, 2000), Philip Jenkins' *Using Murder: The Social Construction of Serial Homicide* (Aldine de Gruyter, 1994), David Everitt's *Human Monsters: An Illustrated Encyclopedia of the World's Most Vicious Monsters* (Contemporary Books, 1993), and *The Encyclopedia of Serial Killers* (Berkley Books, 1995), by Brian Lane and Wilfred Gregg.

The chapter on the Benders was informed by Robert Adelman's *The Bloody Benders* (Stein and Day, 1970), and William Bolitho's chapter, "Old Man Bender's Orchard," in Jonathan Goodman's *Masterpieces of Murder* (Magpie Books, 2004). Richard Jones' *The Mammoth Book of Women Who Kill* (Carroll & Graf, 2002) was important to the chapters on the Benders and Belle Gunness. Joseph

Geringer's series on Gunness for *The Crime Library* was also quite valuable.

Alexander Gilbert's important series of articles on the Haarmann crimes for *The Crime Library* deserves acknowledgment, as does "Fritz Haarmann—Werewolf in Hanover," by Steven Morris in *New Criminologist* (September 20, 2007). The chapters on Gunness, Marie Becker and Raymond Fernandez and Martha Beck were all enriched by Kerry Seagrave's *Women Serial and Mass Murderers* (McFarland & Company, 1992). Derek Bickerton's *The Murders of Boysie Singh* (Arthur Baker Limited, 1962) was an invaluable resource for the chapter on Singh, as was Annie Hilton's "Boysie Singh 20th Century Pirate of the Caribbean," in *Trinidad & Tobago's Newsday* (August 7, 2005).

Another series by the *The Crime Library*, by Mark Gado on the Fernandez/Beck murders, deserves special mention. The chapter on Blanche Moore was dependant on Jim Schutze's, *Preacher's Girl: The Life and Crimes of Blanche Taylor Moore* (Avon Books, 1993), and Philip Carlo's biography of Richard Ramirez, *The Night Stalker: The Life and Crimes of Richard Ramirez* (Kensington Publishing Company, 1996) was similarly instrumental in the chapter on the Night Stalker. The Ramirez chapter was also enhanced by Anthony Bruno's series for *The Crime Library*.

Irene Pence's book, *Buried Memories: The Chilling True Story of Betty Beets, the Texas Black Widow* (Kensington Publishing Company, 2001) was very useful in the chapter on Beets. The chapter on the Copeland case benefited from *The Copeland Killings: The Bizarre True Account of Ray and Faye Copeland, the Oldest Couple Ever Sentenced to Death in America* (Windsor Publishing Corporation, 1993). I should also mention Kathy Braidhill's, *To Die For: The Shocking True Story of Female Serial Killer Dana Sue Gray* (St. Martin's Press, 2000). Also valuable to the Gray chapter was Ramsland's series for *The Crime Library*, and *Crimeshots True Crime Forums*, "Female Serial Killer Dana Sue Gray," (May 17, 2004).

Introduction

This book is about serial murder but it takes a very different approach from the other works on this subject. The basic premise of this work is that a significant amount of serial murder is partly if not entirely motivated by money. There are most likely multiple motives behind multicide, as serial slayers seem to vary. Some kill for sex, others to wield power and still others want to communicate a message to the world. In many cases there may be multiple motives. I argue that profit-motivated serial slayings ought to be included in our definitions and understanding of serial murder.

Commercial motives have been noted in serial murder cases throughout history. This book provides a dozen cases of profit-motivated serial murder which are representative of hundreds of similar cases over the years. The problem is that some definitions and typologies of serial murder specifically exclude commercially-oriented repetitive killings as being included in this category. As a result there are distorted and inadequate understandings as to what can and cannot be considered as serial murder.

This Introduction addresses several main points to justify why a book such as this is necessary. Because of the plurality of definitions and the fact that some exclude consideration of commercial serial murder, it is argued that we should include profit-motivated repetitive homicides as serial murder.

SERIAL MURDER DEFINITIONAL DIVERSITY

There are a great many different definitions of the term *serial murder*. A recent partial search revealed more than fifty definitions from various sources. This definitional diversity is democratic but it has also distracted scholars from more important concerns and impeded scholarly progress. Constance McKenzie wrote in the *International Journal of Offender Therapy and Comparative Criminology*, "From the outset there has been much confusion concerning the definition of serial murder."[1] Keeney and Heide suggested in the *Journal of Interpersonal Violence*, "Definitions of serial murder reported in the literature have lacked uniformity."[2]

Definitional diversity is not a mere matter of semantics because there is great importance in how the term serial murder is interpreted. John Liebert, author of "Contributions of Psychiatric Consultation in the Investigation of Serial Murder," noted that "The problem of definition in serial murder is subject to interpretation of the crime scene for theories regarding the motivation for murder."[3] In other words, many definitions of serial murder require analysts to be able to discern the killer(s)' motivation to properly categorize the behavior as constituting serial murder or not. Hinch and Hepburn explained in "Researching Serial Murder: Methodological and Definitional Problems," that "The stereotype of a sexually sadistic killer has become paradigmatic in scholarly efforts to understand serial killers. Definitions, research methods and typologies reflect this paradigm. Serialists who do not match the stereotype are excluded on arbitrary grounds."[4] They added that "An expanded definition of serial killers" and "eradication of the lust killer stereotype" would prove beneficial and "contribute to an enriched understanding" of serial murder.[5]

DEFINITIONS EXCLUDE PROFIT-MOTIVATED SERIAL MURDER

Commercial serial murder is often excluded from consideration due to the motive. One common and quite lengthy definition begins this way, "One or more individuals (males, in most known cases) commits a second murder and/or subsequent murder, is relationshipless (no prior relationship between victim and attacker; is at a different time and has no connection to the initial murder); and is usually committed at a different geographic location. Further, the motive is not for material gain and is believed to be for the murderer's desire to have power over his victim."[6] Holmes and Holmes realized the tendency to exclude commercial serial murder:

> Even today, many deny that some serialists who kill for material gain are serial killers. The prosecutor in the Richard Kurlinski case stated emphatically that the convicted killer was not a serial killer because he did not kill for sex; he killed for money (Bruno, 1993). On the other end of the scale, Dorothea Puente is called a female serial killer even though she killed her victims for their disability and Social Security checks. In essence, there is little consistency in the definition of serial murder.[7]

Hinch and Hepburn generalized that "It has been common practice for analysts to exclude events in which the killer profits financially from the crime ... simply because the motivation for the killings is assumed to be different from the 'true' serial murderer."[8]

COMMERCIAL SERIAL MURDER EXISTS

Is this motive-based exclusion justified? Hickey found profit-motivated serial murder in one-quarter of his male offender sample, one-third of his serialist teams, and half of his female serial killer sample.[9] In my study about 15 percent of the 1,000 killers researched were motivated by profit. No wonder Hinch and Hepburn concluded, "The evidence clearly demonstrates that some serialists kill for profit. This means that excluding some serialists ... is unjustified and unjustifiable without more careful study. It could be argued that the exclusion of extrinsically motivated killers, especially those who kill for profit, amounts to an ideological conception of serial murder."[10]

The realization that serial murder may be motivated by monetary gain is not a recent one. As long ago as 1924, in the book *Murder and Its Motive*, F. T. Jesse hypothesized six categories of "natural motives" for murder and the initial type was "Gain."[11] Egger reported that 47 percent of female serial killers admitted to "some" monetary motivation, and "money only" was the motive for more than a quarter of female serial killers.[12] Similarly, one of the serial murder categories proposed by Holmes and Holmes is the "Comfort" killer, "The comfort killer has a different set of motives and anticipated gains from the other types of serial killers. First of all, the motive for killing rests with material gain," they observed. They added that despite monetary motives, a pathological personality nevertheless exists in these cases, "There was no great pathological reason for murder; the motive was rational; and conscious. The mindset of this killer certainly reflects a psychopathic personality in which a human being's life is measured in terms of its monetary worth."[13]

A MORE COMPREHENSIVE DEFINITION OF THE TERM IS DESIRABLE

If contemporary interpretations and definitions of serial murder exclude profit-motivated crime, that may well be a suboptimal situation. Serious scholarship on this subject assumes definitional validity or the whole enterprise may well be misdirected from the start. The "real world" significance of this reconceptualization of serial murder was suggested by Hinch and Hepburn, "Investing resources in scholarly study can contribute to law enforcement efforts to understand the lust killer stereotype, overcome linkage blindness, and facilitate a paradigm shift. These changes are essential if policy decisions and intervention strategies are to be informed by reliable empirical data."[14]

"Does it make a difference that the anticipated gain is material rather than psychological or sexual?" Holmes and Holmes asked. They answered their own question, "Probably not. Also, it would be a huge mistake to insist on some form of mental pathology or sexual aberration as a basic motivating factor for someone to be considered a serial killer."[15]

At the present time this definitional exclusion results in biased scholarship. Lester noted that "There seems to be a bias in the type of murderer who is labeled a serial murderer. The term is most commonly employed to persons who murder women and children and who also sexually assault the victims."[16] The consequences of arbitrary exclusive definitions may well include less accurate scholarship and the resultant reduction in the value of that research in efforts to combat serial murder. Schmid agreed with this analysis:

> Logically, the crime of serial murder should include any offender, male or female, regardless of motive, who kills over time, normally with some type of pattern to their killing, in terms of motive, victim selection, and/or type of weapon used (Hickey 8). But since 1983, the assumption that serial murder can be unproblematically equated solely with sexual homicide can be found in more or less explicit form in practically any discussion of serial murder, whether in the mass media, an

academic treatise, a public policy document, or a psychological study of an individual offender.[17]

To summarize, this Introduction has argued that there are too many inconsistent and exclusionary definitions of serial murder. One result of this definitional diversity is the exclusion of repetitive commercial slaying from inclusion as serial murder. This narrow interpretation of serial murder is unjustified and arbitrary, and results in an inaccurate interpretation of the motives behind serial murder. In fact, a substantial percentage of serial murderers have been partly or entirely motivated by money. Serial murderers are a diverse group and there are numerous motives, including sexual, psychological and sociological factors; revenge; anger; and retaliation. The purpose of this book is to add profit-motivated crimes to the category of serial murder.

Each chapter in this book follows a common pattern. The first section in each chapter describes the murderer or murderers, followed by a section that outlines the murderer's (or murderers') other crimes. The third section in each chapter discusses the murders themselves, and the commercial motive is explained in the final section.

CHAPTER 1

The Bloody Benders

Our initial example of commercial serial murder took place in the great agrarian heartland of America between 1870 and 1873. The case of the Bender family—John Sr., "Ma," John Jr. and Kate—represents the worst of greed and inhumanity. This scheming collection of biologically-related human beings killed at least eleven people and perhaps as many as twenty-one. They pretended to offer meals, lodging and entertainment to travelers on the southeastern Kansas plains, but instead they dished out death.

Who were the so-called "Bloody Benders?" Why did they descend on Labette County, Kansas, in 1870 and begin a two or three year murder spree? While certain answers to these questions remain unavailable, we can suggest some likely responses.

THE MURDERERS: JOHN SR., "MA," JOHN JR. AND KATE BENDER

Immigrants from Germany were referred to as "Dutchmen" by native Kansan farmers in the years immediately following the Civil War. The Benders immigrated from Germany to the U.S. in 1870 and settled soon after in Kansas. Some accounts allege that the Bender men came first followed by the women after a house was built.[1] It might be interesting to consider the reward poster issued by Kansas state officials, to introduce the Benders. W.H. Smallwood, Kansas

Secretary of State, issued the proclamation in 1873, and it was signed by Governor Thomas Osborn:

> Whereas, several atrocious murders have been recently committed in Labette County, Kansas, under circumstances which fasten, beyond doubt, the commissions of these crimes upon a family known as the "Bender family" consisting of:
>
> JOHN BENDER, about 60 years of age, five feet eight or nine inches in height, German, speaks but little English, dark complexion, no whiskers, and sparely built:
>
> MRS. BENDER, about 50 years of age, rather heavy set, blue eyes, brown hair, German, speaks broken English:
>
> JOHN BENDER JR., alias John Gebardt, five feet eight or nine inches in height, slightly built, gray eyes with brownish tint, brown hair, light moustache, no whiskers, about 27 years of age, speaks English with German accent:
>
> KATE BENDER, about 24 years of age, dark hair and eyes, good looking, well formed, rather bold in appearance, fluent talker, speaks good English with very little German accent.[2]

Descriptions of the family tend to be unflattering. According to Bolitho, "They were a family of northern primitives."[3] One account claimed that the entire Bender family practiced what was then called "Spiritualism," although only Kate was active in that behavior.[4] Bolitho concluded that the Benders were unpopular landlords and no one who lived anywhere nearby would have eaten a meal there or stayed at Benders' tavern. The courageous few who dared pass that way late at night told tales of frightening noises emanating from within.[5]

Allegations of incestuous relationships between Kate and both her brother and father have been published. It was alleged that Kate Bender was not John Jr.'s sister, but actually his girlfriend, Jones noted.[6]Some writers believe that John Jr. was in reality the offspring from his mother's first marriage. He and his half-sister, according to this notion, had been conducting an incestuous relationship.[7]Adleman added that Kate was having sexual relationships, perhaps at the same time, with both her father and her brother.[8]

John Bender Sr.

Sometimes referred to as "Pa" Bender or "Old Man" Bender, John Bender Sr. was the patriarch of his four-member family. One account described both John Sr. and his son as being "large, course-appearing men."[9] Bender was sixty years old at the time of the crimes according to Schechter, and Everitt agreed on that approximate age assessment.[10]

A portrait of John Bender Sr. depicts a stolid-looking person, unremarkable in any visible way while another reveals an unkempt-appearing miscreant.[11] Then-Governor of Kansas, Thomas Osborn, described the senior Bender as about 60 years, of medium height. He was a German by birth who spoke little English. He was dark, slender and beardless claimed another version.[12] Jones concluded that everyone agreed about two things, old man Bender was unpleasant and surly.[13]

Bender was "just covered with hair," according to another account, with "a bushy black beard."[14] The elder Bender could frequently be seen reading a Bible, a view discounted by others who considered the Bible a prop to dispel suspicion and allay fears.[15] Bender fell asleep at a school board meeting but awoke and vanished when the topic of conversation turned to the recent disappearances of travelers in the vicinity.[16]

"Ma" Bender

History has not been kind to "Ma" Bender. Not only has she been frequently characterized in decidedly unpleasant ways, but in the ultimate indignity her first name has been forgotten. She was described as "a masculine, savage creature who, although sixty years old, could still do the work of a horse."[17] Schechter was much kinder to "Ma" on the age issue, referring to her as "just forty-two years old but with the cold-eyed, wizened looks of a hag."[18] John Sr. was about sixty, and the slightly younger mother was referred to as "Ma" Bender.[19]

Kansas Governor Osborne described her as being about ten years younger than "Pa" Bender, "heavy in frame," with blue eyes and brown hair.[20] A contemporary description portrayed her as about fifty-five years old with a broad appearance due to her bone structure, not excess weight. Her hair was greasy-looking black with gray streaks, and her close-set eyes and "heavy mouth" gave her a sullen look. She also had a moustache.[21]

John Bender Jr.

The younger Bender man was not typically described in positive or flattering ways. In fact, he is almost made to be the stereotypical half-witted criminal, with a lack of brains and a loathsome appearance.

According to Schechter's description John Bender Jr. was a hulking, stupid-looking twenty-seven-year-old man.[22] Another analysis depicts John Jr. as being in his late twenties, someone who "gave the impression he was dimwitted."[23] Both Bender men were considered to be coarse-looking individuals.[24]

There was considerable diversity in descriptions of the younger Bender male. In fact, John Bender Jr. was described as a rather ordinary-looking man of about thirty; some thought that his face had the look of an angry hyena.[25] The Governor of Kansas declared, "There was nothing distinctive about John Bender Jr.," adding that the young man was twenty-seven, slightly built, with a light brown moustache, who spoke English well with a German accent.[26] John Jr. was six feet tall with red hair and fair skin. He frequently emitted a high-pitched giggle-like sound.[27] He was away from the Bender home frequently, "on business unexplained," as Jones put it.[28]

It was believed by some that John Jr. was not actually a Bender at all. Instead, he was John Gebhardt, "Ma" Bender's son from a previous marriage.[29] No documentation has been produced to support that claim.

Kate Bender

Kate Bender was the key to the Bender crimes but Kate might not be her true name. A Catholic Prayer Book was reportedly found in their cabin after the Benders disappeared, with an inscription noting the birth of Johanna Bender, who was about the age of the woman known as Kate.[30]

She was the most colorful and romanticized of the family, with a wide range of representations.[31] Kate Bender's appearance has been interpreted and reinterpreted by a host of writers over the years, whose collective misimpressions have ranged from a large, masculine-looking, red-faced unattractive woman to a relatively pretty red-haired woman who was a seductive siren of extraordinary allure.[32] A contemporary description read as follows, "About twenty-four years of age, dark hair and eyes, good looking, well formed, rather bold in appearance, fluent talker, speaks English with German accent."[33]

Two women were tried in Michigan, accused of being "Ma" and Kate Bender:

> Kate Bender, Jr., was between eighteen and twenty-four years of age. Her hair was a rich, dark auburn. She had deep, grayish-blue, or dark-grey eyes . . . rose complexion. She was good-looking, a remarkably handsome woman, rather bold and striking in appearance, with a tigerish grace and animal attraction, which but few men could resist. She was a fluent talker, gifted with fine conversational powers, but she did not display any educational advantages of a high order.[34]

Others perceived Kate as a beauty, as well. The *Internet Crime Archive* called her "a beautiful, voluptuous girl."[35] Another depiction referred to the seventeen-year-old beauty as being tall and willowy with silky dark hair marked by auburn and blonde highlights. She had deep hazel eyes, full red lips and high cheekbones.[36]

A less attractive Kate emerges from other descriptions. Bolitho depicts her in these terms, "Kate Bender was a rectangular, red-faced woman of twenty-four."[37] Schechter was even more critical, "Although Kate has gone down in legend as a red-haired temptress, she appears to have been a ruddy-faced, mannish-looking female."[38]

Kate's spiritualist activity is the one aspect of her life agreed upon by virtually all commentators. She believed in spiritualism, gave public lectures on the subject and was a medium at séances. "Adult daughter Katie was apparently a spiritualist who claimed to summon ghosts," Ramsland recalled. The *Internet Crime Archive* referred to her as "a self-proclaimed healer and spiritualist." Everitt added that she practiced faith healing and other spiritualist ventures in their lodgings in addition to lecturing on spiritualism in local towns. She used the name Professor Miss Kate Bender on a tour of Parsons, Oswego, Labette and Chetopa, Kansas.[39]

Kate was the leader of the pack, the brains behind the operation, "the leading spirit of her murderous family." Bolitho observed that "Miss Kate was the youngest, and the leader of the family." Kate was "the brains of the operation," Schechter asserted. According to Adleman, "There was never any question that Kate was the one with all the say in the Bender house."[40] Kate was the key to the crimes, as Everitt explained, calling her "a key element in the family's most lucrative enterprise: murder for profit."[41]

She was a very active young person. Kate was an avid horsewoman, danced well, and attended Sunday School. She also had worked for a few months as a waitress in the Cherryvale Hotel dining room.[42]

One final aspect of Kate's role in the murders deserves mention. She did not merely beguile and distract the victims in the moments before their death. She slit their throats to make certain they were dead.[43]

THE MURDERS

The commercial murders of the Bender family were relatively complex acts and deserve full consideration. To fully appreciate these crimes multiple topics will be investigated.

Number of Victims

No one knows precisely how many murders were committed by the Benders. There is not even agreement over the number of bodies discovered at their place of business. Despite this uncertainty we can attain a better understanding of the number of victims claimed by the Benders.

"When suspicions were finally aroused, in 1873, the Benders fled. A search of their property disclosed eleven bodies buried in the garden," suggested the *Internet Crime Archive* .[44] A Kansas Historical Monument erected near the Bender cabin asserts that eleven bodies were discovered as did separate studies by Adleman and Jones.[45]

Other estimates can be considered. On the low side, Schechter described the discovery of eight graves at the Bender place, while Ramsland wrote that "ten bodies were exhumed."[46] Some estimates, on the other hand, were higher, "By the time the posse finished digging up the orchard, they had uncovered the bodies of a dozen people."[47] Independent research by serial murder experts Michael Newton and Peter Vronsky arrived at an identical conclusion—about a dozen murders.[48]

In light of the diversity of estimates, no wonder Jones concluded that the number of murders varies in different reports. Some writers add alleged Bender victims to the list of eleven bodies found. But others instead suggest fewer murders, anywhere from seven to ten, resulting in Jones' estimate of ten to twelve victims.[49]

My best estimate suggests at least eleven victims and as many as twenty-one. In addition to the eleven corpses found at the Bender's cabin, the bodies of two unidentified men were found in that vicinity at that time, along with the bodies of William Jones and Joe Sowers, all killed in the same way as the Bender victims. In addition, at least a half-dozen letters were received inquiring about missing relatives who had traveled through the area then disappeared.[50]

Time Frame

There is less disagreement about the timing of the Bender crimes, although exact dates of several murders are unknown. Both the *Internet Crime Archive* and the State of Kansas give a time frame of 1871 to 1873.[51] A bit narrower estimate was provided by Newton, "The murderous Bender clan dispatched at least a dozen travelers in 1872-73," a conclusion concurred with by Vronsky.[52]

However, even greater specificity in estimating the time frame of the murders can be established. Jones referred to "whatever they did during the autumn and winter of 1872 to 1873."[53] Schechter and Everett noted local public concern, "In the spring of 1873, the citizens of Labette County, Kansas, were concerned about the alarming number of travelers who had vanished while passing through the region."[54]

Location

Where was the Bender cabin? It was in Labette County, Kansas, most authorities agree.[55] According to Bolitho, "They lived off the beaten track, eighteen miles from the boundary of Kansas State, in a ramshackle frame house, with a small half-acre orchard behind it."[56] They were situated in the southeastern part of the state.[57] More specifically the Benders resided within the township of Cherryvale, named after the railroad town.[58]

The Homestead Act Land Claim form offered further precise location. The Bender plot was in the northeast corner of section thirteen, in township thirty-one, on range seventeen, located six miles north and two miles east of Cherryvale and twelve miles west of Parsons. Their cabin was situated on the old Osage Trail, the main road that connected Ft. Scott and the Osage Mission with Independence.[59]

The Bender Cabin

By now you might be curious about the Bender cabin, the infamous lodging where the dastardly deeds were done. One cybersource described it this way, "a small house partitioned in two rooms by a canvas cloth. It had a table, stove and grocery shelves in front. In back were beds, a sledge hammer and a trap door above a pit-like cellar."[60] Bolitho noted, "In the front of the house was a room where meals were served to wayfarers."[61] A little more detail was added by Schechter; the building was nothing more than a rectangular box, measuring approximately sixteen by twenty feet in size. The inside had been bisected by a canvas curtain. On one side was the family's living quarters and the other was converted into an inn.[62]

"It was built in a small hollow at the end of a long vale in the prairie," according to Jones, who described the cabin itself as "a two-room unit, with a curtain dividing the halves. The front room had tinned goods and other items for sale, and somewhere or other in the house sleeping space was found for travelers who cared to stay all night."[63] Adleman provided additional detail, noting that the front room was about twice the size of the family's area and that the partition only extended two-thirds of the way across the width of the room. The front room had shelves and a long, low counter about which were scattered kegs, stools and a few tick mattresses. A stove was placed in between the two rooms and a bench and table sat against the partition.[64]

There is controversy surrounding the name of the Bender's commercial establishment. One source suggests that Bender's Tavern was the name while another recalls that the Bender Inn was the given moniker. The sign outside read, "Groceries."[65]

MO

The *modus operandi* (MO) of the Bender family was relatively consistent. They used the same basic scheme throughout the serial slaying spree, with the exception of a change in the disposal of bodies. In this section we will consider the general Bender MO, the head injuries and the throat slashing. The intrinsic horror of the Bender crimes will vividly emerge from these descriptions.

"As it turned out, the 'Bloody Benders' had been preying on unwary travelers for years, having turned their ramshackle farmhouse into a kind of hotel-from-hell," Schechter and Everitt recalled.[66] Ramsland added that "Adult daughter Katie . . . had sufficient charm to learn a traveler's financial status and persuade him to sit in a certain area for dinner. Behind him hung a canvas curtain, and behind that stood Old Man Bender with a sledgehammer. He would deliver the fatal blow, while Ma Bender, Katie and John Jr. removed the victim's money and dropped him down a trapdoor."[67] A similar portrayal was provided by the *Internet Crime Archive*, "Travelers stopping for a meal were seated on a bench backed tight against the canvas."[68] Another description was offered by Bolitho, "It was easy to see how the crimes had been committed . . . . In the middle of the floor was a trapdoor, and a great hole from which the smell came."[69]

Another extended explanation of the Bender MO was provided by Schechter:

> The Benders, it turned out, were really running a frontier murder-and-robbery operation. When a prosperous-looking traveler showed up, he would be ushered into the dining area and seated with his back to the canvas divider. While Kate beguiled him with some dinnertime conversation her father or brother would be lurking on the other side of the curtain with a sledgehammer at the ready. When the unsuspecting guest leaned his head back against the curtain, the hammer would come crashing down, shattering the back of the skull. The body would then be dragged into the bedroom, where it would be robbed, stripped and dumped through a trapdoor into the cellar. There, the throat would be cut for good measure.[70]

Other studies have arrived at similar conclusions. Everitt corroborated that "Katie" distracted and guided the victims, and that one of the men hit the victim in the head with a sledgehammer when "the traveler's head made a clear impression against the canvas."[71] A similar set of details was reported by Jones, "The diner sat on a bench or chair, with his back to the curtain which separated the two compartments," until the traveler "leaned back and showed the outline of his head."[72]

Additional details were provided by Adleman. "Pa" Bender was the lookout, and when he saw a likely victim approach Kate was sent to "freshen up," and change into her loveliest outfit. While she made an excuse to "hug" the visitor and ascertain the size of the money belt typically worn under his shirt, the men were outside assessing the traveler's horse and wagon. If the visitor was a young man Kate would lure him outside just after dark, but older men or those uninterested in Kate for any reason were killed indoors. The Bender men would kill the traveler and the entire family then robbed and stripped him before dumping the body through the trapdoor to the cellar, where the throat was slit, typically by Kate.[73]

One central aspect of the MO was the devastating injury to the back of the victims' skulls. One source referred to "skulls crushed by hammer blows through the canvas."[74] Schechter and Everitt concurred, describing "skulls crushed with a sledgehammer."[75] An identical conclusion was arrived at independently by Bolitho, Ramsland, Schechter, Everitt, Jones and Adleman.[76]

Another distinctive aspect of the Bender murders was the redundant murder method. Undoubtedly already dead or nearly so, the victims had their throats slit after the assault with the hammer. Everitt noted, "Then, one of them slit the victim's throat, just to make sure he was dead."[77] In agreement with this account were Bolitho, Schechter, Jones and Adleman.[78]

The Victims

Since we lack a precise death toll, it is similarly difficult to name each Bender family victim. Found at the Bender residence were the bodies of Dr. William H. York, Henry McKenzie (sometimes called McKigzie), George Brown, Benjamin M. Brown, Johnny Boyle, Bill McCrotty, John Greary, a Mr. Longcor, his daughter and two unidentified newlyweds.[79]

There were other likely victims. William Jones and Joe Sowers were probably killed by the Benders although their bodies were discovered elsewhere, as were two unidentified bodies. Each of these victims had their skulls bashed in and their throats slit.

The victimage of the Longcors was considered to be especially terrible judging by contemporary and subsequent accounts. Jones described the likely cause of the daughter's death, suffocation because she had been buried alive.[80] Schechter and Everitt referred to "a baby girl who had been buried alive with her father's corpse."[81] Ramsland's depiction noted that ten bodies were discovered, including a little girl who had been thrown into the grave alive and subsequently crushed underneath her father's body.[82] According to Bolitho, "The little girl bore no marks of violence, and appeared to have been thrown, living, into her father's grave."[83] Schechter emphasized that the Benders had thrown her into the hole with her father's corpse.[84] Everitt added that she was buried alive underneath her father's body.[85]

Post-Discovery Events

We conclude our discussion of the Bender family crimes with a look at the events that took place after the flight of the family and the discovery of bodies on their property.

When the Benders arrived in Labette County, their neighbor turned out to be a German immigrant, Rudolph Brockman. Because of their shared linguistic and cultural bonds and physical proximity Brockman and the Benders were associated in the public eye as fellow Dutchmen. This was unfortunate for Brockman when bodies were found.

Here is an account of what transpired next:

> The crowd back in Cherryvale was doing ugly things, in its frenzy. They had caught a Mr. Brockman, at one time a partner of Old Man Bender. As both were Germans, and at one time close friends, the crowd took him to the woods; there attempted to make him reveal the whereabouts of the horrible family. This he was unable to do. At any rate he was hanged and revived three times, and then allowed to go away.[86]

Additional detail of this incident was offered by Adleman. Few of the local residents liked Brockman so they immediately suspected him of complicity in the murders. Mrs. Hagstrom, wife of the feed store owner, reportedly exclaimed, "Let's make a cottonwood blossom out of him," a colloquial way of suggesting a lynching.[87]

There were arrests in the immediate aftermath of the grim finding at the Bender estate. In light of the number of arrests and the subsequent failure to prosecute any of those detained, it appears that the contemporary law enforcement effort was ineffective:

> The Roach family of Ladore, seven miles from the slaughter den, consisting of the old man and his wife, the son and wife and stepson John Haines and wife and Thomas Tyak, a wife and daughter, have been arrested. A.M. King, a traveling district preacher, has been arrested at Parsons, and a notorious murderer, once pardoned from the penitentiary, named Major Macford, and a woman with him, were arrested at Ft. Scott.[88]

A third noteworthy post-discovery event must be mentioned—the substantial national publicity and public interest. Virtually every major newspaper in the country covered the crime and the news coverage and public interest lasted a considerable amount of time. This might be attributable to the apparent fact that the Benders escaped.[89] "This story swept the nation, adding the 'Hell Benders' to the tales of Indians and outlaws who posed dire threats to families hoping to settle in Western lands," Ramsland recalled.[90] Everitt agreed, "The news shocked not only the region but the entire nation."[91]

Public fear was another consequence when bodies were located at the Bender's cabin. Church attendance reportedly increased during this time frame, women were discouraged from unaccompanied trips to town after dark, and travelers avoided the road between Independence and Ft. Scott if at all possible. Town meetings were held and vigilante groups formed but to no avail. It is safe to say that the local citizens were first terrorized by the disappearances and then horrified by the finding of the Bender murder victims.[92]

Did the Benders get away? That is the opinion of most experts and those who have expressed their opinions in public or been fortunate enough to have them published. We will consider these consensus views and then entertain a startling alternative version.

"When Dr. William York disappeared in 1873, his brother came looking for him. The Benders soon abandoned the place," Ramsland noted. In agreement was Newton, who described the Benders "fleeing the state one jump ahead of vigilante justice."[93] An Internet source observed, "The end of the Benders is not known. The earth seemed to have swallowed them up, just like their victims." A posse investigating the strange disappearances visited the Bender's cabin, with an unexpected result, "To their surprise, however, when they rode up to the door, there was no sign of life. The Benders seemed to be away, all the windows were shuttered."[94]

A decidedly different version of this story was documented in a letter from the Cherryvale Chief of Police. Written in 1910, the letter from J. Kramer read as follows:

> Dear Sirs,—Yours received. It so happened that my father-in-law's farm joins that of the Benders and he helped to locate the bodies of the victims. I often tried to find out from him what became of the Benders, but he only gave me a knowing look and said he guessed they would not bother anyone else. There was a vigilance committee organized to locate the Benders, and shortly afterwards Old Man Bender's waggon [*sic*] was found by the roadside riddled with bullets. You will have to guess the rest.—I am, respectfully yours, J. Kramer, Chief of Police.[95]

"The Benders denied all knowledge of the missing Dr. York. A few days later, however—fearing that they were under suspicion—they pulled up stakes and fled," Schechter recalled. He added that "To this day, no one can say for certain what became of the Benders." Although there were rumors about the Benders appearing in Michigan or Texas and another story claiming they were murdered in and never left Kansas, there is no proof substantiating any of the versions.[96]

Two brothers who lived near the Bender residence noticed that the Bender livestock appeared to be untended and neglected. When they checked the house to see if something was amiss they were greatly surprised. The house had been abandoned and the farm was in disarray as though a hasty departure had occurred.[97]

COMMERCIAL MOTIVE

By now it should already be apparent that the Bender crimes were profit-motivated. In this section we will attempt to quantify how much money they made through murder and consider related topics.

Bender Crime Revenue

There is no one complete and comprehensive accounting of the total Bender family take from their crimes, only anecdotes and estimates. For instance, Ramsland mentioned that a visitor's financial well-being determined his degree of danger as a guest at the Bender's.[98] Vronsky referred to the Bender crimes as "profit-motivated serial homicides."[99]

"Why did they kill? Sometimes, but not always for money, for one or two of the bodies were tramps with nothing to give for the trouble of their slaying," Bolitho concluded.[100] Everitt quantified the revenue, "The Benders' murder inn was in business for about a year and a half, in which time, it is estimated, they stole about ten thousand dollars from their victims."[101] He referred to the crimes as "murder for profit."[102] The Benders were carrying seven thousand dollars when they were apprehended one source stated.[103] At least three of the men had been carrying large sums of money—McCrotty, Ben Brown and McKenzie.[104] And it was common knowledge that Dr. York carried considerable cash when he traveled. Adleman's contemporary account of the Bender crimes noted, "To put it as bluntly as I know, the victims weren't people to the Benders, they was simply the way they made their living."[105]

Another quantification of the Bender murders was provided by *Kansas* magazine in 1936:

> Murder with Miss Bender was as strictly a commercial and dispassionate business as the operation of a sausage case factory or a rendering

plant. The gross receipts, and there was practically no overhead, were $4,000, six horses, two wagons, and bits of jewelry of the sort that every young girl holds dear. Considering that the murders were carried out in the period of a year and a half during the months preceding the great panic of '73, that was pretty good.[106]

Evidence of Commercial Intent

We can infer motive or intent from the deliberate acts undertaken by the Benders. For instance, they advertised Kate's spiritualism gifts in an attempt to elicit visitors. In addition their choice for the site of their lodging was indicative of their homicidal intent.

The Benders used a newspaper ad and a poster in an attempt to market their lethal lodging house. The newspaper ad copy read as follows, "Professor Miss Kate Bender can heal disease, cure blindness, fits and deafness. Residence, 14 miles east of Independence, on the road to Osage Mission." An identical version of the ad, which ran on June 18, 1982, was reported by Jones.[107]

The copy of the poster was the same but with extended directions for finding the place. It read, "Prof. Miss KATE BENDER can heal all sorts of Diseases: can cure Blindness, Fits, Deafness and all such diseases, also Deaf and Dumbness. Residence, 14 miles east of Independence, on the road from Independence to Osage Mission one and one half miles South East of Norahead Station. KATIE BENDER. June 18, 1872."[108]

The location of the Bender cabin also attests to their criminal intent. It was sited on the most heavily-traveled road in that vicinity. Adleman observed that:

> The Bender family came to the area with the express purpose of setting up their murderous operation. Because they located their inn at a logical resting place on the journey from Osage Mission to Fort Scott, because they put up the "grocery" sign even before the women had arrived, and because they built in the cellar and the trap door and set the table conveniently over it, it can be logically held that these were professional robbers and murderers, not lunatics.[109]

CONCLUSION

"Pa" Bender reportedly committed suicide in Michigan according to one tale.[110] Kate's fate has many speculated scenarios, including being a community leader in San Francisco, a prostitute in Montana and a nuisance in several locations.[111] The State of Michigan held two women in the belief that they were "Ma" and Kate Bender, but all charges were dismissed due to lack of evidence.[112] Popular stories placed the Benders in Texas and in Michigan.[113]

No matter whatever became of them, the deeds of the Bender family stand as mute but clear testimony on the nature of commercial serial murder. The murders were almost incidental to the motive which was personal enrichment through armed robbery and murder. The murders made the robberies possible and covered them up as well. The killings were not sex crimes nor the acts of lunatics or psychotics. The Bender family murders were almost certainly motivated by money.

CHAPTER 2

Dr. H. H. Holmes (Herman Mudgett)

Dr. H. H. Holmes (Herman Mudgett) was called "the most notable 19th century U.S. mass murderer," and "America's worst mass murderer."[1] He was the "best known American murderer," according to one expert, and "one of the most prolific U.S. serial killers," in the words of another.[2] At the time of his criminal career his notoriety was only exceeded by that of Jack the Ripper.[3] His real name was Herman Webster Mudgett but he is known to history as H. H. Holmes or Dr. H. H. Holmes.

The discovery of the contents of his murder castle and his murder of three children "sent shock waves throughout the country."[4] "When the atrocities of Dr. H. H. Holmes were uncovered . . . the American public couldn't get enough of them," Schechter observed.[5] This substantial public interest in Dr. Holmes and his crimes was described by Ramsland, "It wasn't long before true crime pulp paperbacks were published to slake the public's thirst and turn a profit."[6] *The Chicago Daily News* on July 29, 1885, noted the public interest:

> Cyclists, evidently away on a day's outing, dismounted and left their steeds in the alley back of the castle while they fought with the street gamins for advantageous loopholes in the wooden sidewalk, through which they could peep at the men digging in the soft mud of the cellar.

> By 9:00 fully 100 men, women and children were lying flat on the sidewalks above the cellar peering in through every conceivable crack or knothole.[7]

Holmes was a decidedly strange man with unusual thoughts and concerns. He was afraid that medical scientists or curiosity seekers would exhume his body after burial. So he requested that his body be interred in a casket full of cement and that the casket be buried under more cement, "At his request, his body was placed in a pine casket, embedded in cement and buried 10 feet under another two feet of cement. His wishes were to be safe from grave robbers and medical science."[8] No wonder one expert called him "one of the most prolific and inventive criminals."[9]

THE MURDERER: H. H. HOLMES

Mudgett was a man of many talents and facets. Nine main topics will be explored to enhance our understanding of this unique serial killer. Mudgett's birth name will be used in this section to refer to him but he will be called Holmes elsewhere because he was known by that name throughout his criminal life.

Family

Mudgett was born in May of 1860 at the beginning of the Civil War.[10] He was born in New Hampshire but there is controversy over whether he was born in Gilmanton, or Gilmanton Academy.[11] His father Levi was a postmaster and his mother Theodale a housewife.[12] While little is known about his early life it is believed that he was severely beaten by his father on a regular basis.[13]

Childhood

His childhood was not a happy one. According to Everitt he was considered a strange child, and Schechter added, "Among his schoolmates he was also known to be slightly odd."[14] He was frail, with blue eyes and brown hair.[15] Mudgett was a loner, "Throughout his childhood, Herman kept mostly to himself, shunning other children."[16]

As a boy Mudgett was unpopular and relatively friendless. And his solitary friendship was not long-lived.[17] A boy named Tom was

Mudgett's only friend. Until the day Tom and Herman explored an abandoned house together and Tom fell to his death from a window. Some observers think that Tom was Mudgett's initial victim.[18]

An incident in his childhood may have had lifelong implications. As a boy Mudgett was often bullied, "Partly because of his delicate stature and partly because of his peculiar personality, Herman was often persecuted by the village bullies." On one occasion, they dragged him into a doctor's office, and placed a skeleton's hand against his face, "then let Herman go and left him shrieking on the floor." The consequences of this event were traumatic and long-lasting, "Mudgett reportedly became fascinated with cadavers when his schoolmates, playing a prank, dragged him into a surgery room where there was a skeleton."[19] There were behavioral consequences, as well, "By the time he was eleven, he was already conducting secret medical experiments—first on frogs and salamanders, then on rabbits, kittens and stray dogs."[20]

Personality

"A charming swindler and ingenious criminal" is how one source described Mudgett's personality, adding that he was handsome and suave.[21] Morrison and Goldberg referred to him as "a mad scientist out of a B movie."[22] On a more serious note two independent analyses concluded that he was a sexual sadist.[23]

Education

Mudgett's early education has been obscured by the years but we do know something about his higher education. He began college at the University of Vermont before transferring to the University of Michigan.[24] Medicine seemed a natural discipline for him as he manifested a lifelong fascination with anatomy.[25] Lane and Gregg mentioned that Mudgett studied medicine at Michigan, while other sources acknowledge that he was a graduate of that institution with a medical degree.[26]

It was during his college years at Michigan that Mudgett's trouble began. An Internet source, *CrimeLife.com*, recalled, "His demented behavior first surfaced while he was a medical student at the University of Michigan." Despite contrary evidence, the same source claimed that Mudgett was expelled from the University of Michigan.[27]

Intellect

Mudgett was called "the brightest lad in town."[28] Seltzer noted that Mudgett was an "inventor, entrepreneur, medical practitioner and serial murderer," a combination of occupations requiring a diverse and considerable intellect.[29] He invented a machine he named the ABC Copier which was a forerunner of the mimeograph machine.[30]

Medical Practice

"He practiced legitimate medicine only briefly, however, opting instead for a variety of quasi-medical and entrepreneurial scams."[31] Lane and Gregg concurred, adding that Mudgett studied medicine at Michigan and practiced as a doctor in New York for a short time.[32] He fled to Chicago to avoid prosecution for a life insurance scam.

Marriages

Little detail is available about Mudgett's wives, of which he had at least three. It is reported that he was first married at age eighteen to Clara Lovering, and that she was from a wealthy family and put him through medical school.[33] After graduation he abandoned her and their daughter Lucy and moved to Chicago.[34] He married Myrta Belknap, a socialite from Wilmette (a Chicago suburb) but after some time she returned to her parents' home instead of living with him.[35] His final wife, Georgia Yoke, was reportedly the true love of his life.[36]

Nicknames

Serial killers seem to attract nicknames and Mudgett was no exception. Later in his criminal career he was called the "Chicago Bluebeard" because of his penchant for seducing and then killing women.[37] He was frequently referred to in the press as "Holmes the Arch-Fiend."[38] Another popular nickname was "the Torture Doctor."[39]

Mudgett's Claims

Mudgett was an exceptional person and he uttered some remarkable claims during his life. He told one policeman that he could mesmerize his victims and in that manner control them.[40] He also once said that the Devil was responsible for his crimes.[41]

OTHER CRIMES

Mudgett was a criminal with a wide variety of criminal interests and enterprises. He was a true scoundrel; a bigamist, swindler and killer, according to numerous studies.[42] This section will document eight other criminal activities.

Confidence Games

Mudgett was a master at conning people out of their money. Everitt referred to "his confidence game of choice." Another source called him "a confidence trickster."[43]

Medical School Patient Corpse Scam

While in medical school, Mudgett first conceived one of his most basic scams, insurance fraud. It was simple enough. He would take out an insurance policy on someone, locate a person who resembled the insured, and the look-alike person would be killed to defraud the insurance company. According to *CrimeLife.com*, he was caught "using corpses stolen from the school's medical lab."[44]

Forgery

Mudgett's second wife (whom he married bigamously) was from a socially prominent, relatively wealthy family. He took advantage of the opportunity this afforded him. "He soon married a girl from a wealthy family and tried forging the signature of a rich uncle," Wilson and Wilson recalled.[45] Another study agreed, noting that "He bigamously married a well-to-do socialite. He had a falling out with her family after he forged her uncle's signature on a document."[46]

Fraudulent Acts

There were numerous Mudgett frauds. He peddled a phony cure for alcoholism and patent medicines of no medical value whatever. "He rigged up a tankful of smelly liquid with wires, pulleys and hoses, one of which secretly tapped a city gas main. He claimed that this 'invention' turned water to gas and sold the contraption for $2,000." Seltzer added, "One of the patent medicines Holmes marketed was an 'Elixir of Life'."[47]

Chicago Insurance Scams

Murder was Mudgett's main business in Chicago. But he also conducted insurance scams to obtain extra income. Ramsland referred to "insurance scams in Chicago that had provided him with funds to build a three-story hotel."[48]

The Pitezel Insurance Scam

Mudgett took a partner named Benjamin Pitezel. In a variant of the substituted corpse scam Mudgett instead decided to actually kill Pitezel and three of his children. The discovery of this crime was what led to the arrest of the serial slayer.[49]

Real Estate Scams

Mudgett also found the time to engage in fraudulent real estate transactions. One study referred to the "mortgage fraud that landed Holmes in jail." Spindler recalled that "He also began to engage in a number of shady real estate and promotional deals."[50]

Horse Theft

In a criminal career as rich as Holmes,' it is fitting that he be charged with this most serious criminal offense from the Wild West era. When Mudgett was apprehended in Philadelphia he was initially told he was under arrest on this charge which could have led to his extradition to Ft. Worth, Texas. "The charge was horse theft."[51]

THE MURDERS

Number of Murders

The number of Holmes murders is unknown. Estimates vary widely, from twenty-seven to several hundred. One study referred to "an indeterminate number" of murders. The reason for the uncertainty is simple. In his hotel, Holmes used vats of acid, quick lime and a crematorium to destroy almost all traces of his victims.

There were twenty-seven Holmes murders according to Eggers. Vronsky noted "at least twenty-seven victims." Research by Odell and Gregg also quantified the total at twenty-seven, while Hickey recalled that "However, a report citing police investigations indicated a body count of 27 victims."[53]

Others offer an estimate of thirty, forty or fifty murders. The conclusion of the Chicago Public Library was that Holmes killed thirty people. Jenkins suggested that the death toll "was perhaps thirty people."[54] A study by Odell and Gregg concluded that "He admitted to twenty-seven murders but the real number was thought to be nearer forty."[55] Schechter suggested that an accurate count was probably close to fifty victims.[56]

There were approximately one hundred victims several sources have decided. Lester recalled, "Authorities said they suspected Mudgett of killing as many as one hundred people." Another study noted, "Police were able to find evidence of slaughter to a toll of 100 men, women and children."[57]

Several studies have doubled the estimate of 100 deaths. For instance, Morrison and Goldberg recalled that "some estimate that he killed as many as 200 people." Lane and Gregg concurred, as did Everitt. According to Hickey, "H. H. Holmes was reported to have killed at least 200 women." Ramsland noted that so many men and women who had stayed at the castle were missing that estimates of his victimage reached two hundred.[58]

Some believe that the death count actually exceeded 200 victims. That was the conclusion of the Chicago Public Library, "He had about thirty known victims and was suspecting of murdering hundreds of others using poison and gas." Another source added, "In the burnt hulk of his building, authorities found the remains of over two hundred people." Schechter admitted that the victimage could be "possibly several hundred."[59]

Victimology

Holmes' victims were not chosen at random but selected for certain reasons. There was a deadly logic behind his victimology patterns.

Specific Individuals

Holmes' victims were chosen carefully. For instance, he killed a woman named Holden when he moved to Chicago. She ran a drugstore and hired Holmes as a pharmacist. Lane and Gregg recalled that Holden "disappeared mysteriously" soon after hiring Holmes, "and he repaid her memory by taking over the company." Another study added that "Then he became the assistant of a Mrs. Holden, who ran a drugstore. Within three years she had vanished, and Holmes was the new owner." Odell and Gregg concurred, adding, "In 1888 he worked as a drug store chemist and took over the business when the owner mysteriously disappeared."[60]

Holmes targeted other specific individuals. He killed three children of a confederate in an insurance scam to facilitate his getaway.[61] He killed a janitor because he thought the man was going to talk a maid into leaving with him.[62]

Employees

When he opened his hotel Holmes placed ads in newspapers to obtain employees. Those responding to these ads were told to bring all their possessions to the interview. Then they were killed and robbed. According to Lester, "Mudgett placed advertisements in newspapers offering young women lucrative work at the hotel. Over a period of three years, many, many young women came to work there, and were never seen again. Mudgett would tell the women to bring everything they owned with them." Another study, by *CrimeLife.com*, arrived at an identical conclusion, "Many employees and their families perished at his hands."[63]

World's Fair Visitors

There is considerable evidence that Holmes' murder castle/hotel was constructed specifically to prey upon visitors to the Chicago World's Fair. Seltzer bluntly observed, "The Holmes Castle was constructed as a tourist trap." He added that "Hastily built in the early 1890's, it was strategically located to house, and to victimize, its share of the massive crowds from the nearby World's Columbian Exposition." Vronsky added, "Holmes built "a custom-built 'murder hotel' in Chicago during the World's Fair."[64]

"In the United States, a sadist by the name of Herman Mudgett built a custom-made 'murder castle' in Chicago to dispose of women during the 1893 World's Fair," Dolan suggested. Similarly, Ramsland observed that Holmes used the hotel to provide rooms to women visiting the fair. Another source added, "Holmes made a particularly huge killing literally, during the World's Fair in Chicago in the early 1890's."[65]

Other authorities have arrived at similar conclusions. Morrison and Goldberg recalled, "During the high times of the Chicago World's Fair of 1893, Dr. Holmes attacked and murdered many wide-eyed fairgoers who used his castle as a kind of rooming house." Spindler noted that Holmes' hotel was "ostensibly built as a hotel for visitors to the Chicago World's Fair of 1893." Another study referred to "construction of a mansion that he planned to use as a hotel for the 1893 Chicago World's Fair."[66]

Women

It has already been mentioned that women attending the World's Fair were typical Holmes targets. In the last section, studies by Jenkins, Dolan and Ramsland all mentioned that women fair-goers in particular were victimized. Beyond that, women in general were always fair game for the smooth-talking serial killer.

"A number of the women Holmes targeted—perhaps as many as fifty—worked in 'the new female occupation of stenographers'," Seltzer recalled. Lane and Gregg added that "particularly vulnerable were attractive young women, whom Holmes lured to his lair, seduced and after sexual intercourse drugged and dispatched to the cellar via a specially constructed chute." The castle existed "to dispose of female visitors."[67]

Schechter referred to the "women who fell victim to the dapper H. H. Holmes." Jenkins noted that Holmes "especially victimized women visiting the Chicago World Fair of 1893." According to Everitt, "His activities in the Windy City would continue to involve a succession of women."[68]

One study nicely described the victimage of women:

> Handsome and suave, the proprietor of the grand edifice placed newspaper advertisements offering women lucrative work or advantageous marriage in a large city. One after another, pretty applicants responded to the ads, and Mudgett persuaded each of them to bring him all she possessed, as he bargained or wooed her into captivity. Over the next three years, a steady procession of gullible young women took up residence in the castle.[69]

Hickey contended that "Holmes was reported to have killed at least 200 women." *CrimeLife.com* decided that "Holmes also began renting out rooms and spending much time luring and seducing women in order to kill them and swipe their money."[70]

The Victims

Most of Holmes' victims were never identified. However some of them were known. In a few cases we have a victim's occupation but no name, or a partial name. His first victim may have been his friend Tom as previously noted. Next he killed a former schoolmate and friend Dr. Robert Leacock, for his life insurance.[71] In his castle he killed Julia Connors, her daughter Robin and her niece Gertie.[72] Another castle tenant named Dr. Russell was killed by Holmes during an angry quarrel over rent.[73]

A Virginian and friend of Holmes named Rodgers was killed on a fishing trip so Holmes could steal his ample amount of cash.[74] As previously mentioned Holmes killed the owner of the pharmacy where he was employed.[75] He also murdered Emily Van Tassel, Emily Cigrand, and sisters Minnie and Nannie Williams.[76] In addition to the janitor's death Holmes murdered the maid with whom the janitor was consorting, a girl named Lizzie. He also killed Benjamin, Howard, Nellie and Alice Pitezel.[77]

Other names can be considered. In his specialized study of Holmes and his crimes Schechter identified another nine suspected Holmes victims; Harry Walker, Wilfred Cole, Mabel Barrett, Kate, Liz and Anna Gorky, Mary Cron, a Miss Wild and a bookkeeper known only by a last name, Kelly. And in his confession Holmes himself added still other names, including Charles Cole, Sara Cook, Mary Haracamp, Rosine Van Jossand, Robert Lattimer, Anna Betts and Baldwin Williams.[78]

MO

It is believed that most serial killers rely on a standard MO which they tend to stick with and refine over time. Not Holmes. He murdered his victims in about a half-dozen ways. Everitt noted that Holmes killed for a variety of reasons, including profit, convenience, pleasure and concealment of his crimes, and in a variety of ways both mundane and reminiscent of a gothic horror tale.[79]

Poisoning was a common method. Holmes poisoned the Pitezel children prior to dismembering and burning their bodies. Robin Connor was also poisoned.[80] Gassing victims was another method, as

Ashbury recalled, "Apparently one of his favorite methods of murder was to lock a victim in one of the rooms and then turn on the gas."[81] The Chicago Public Library noted rooms in the castle "equipped with gas chambers."[82]

Some victims were incinerated. Ramsland recalled, "Sometimes he'd ignite the gas and incinerate them."[83] The Chicago Public Library study referred to the use of "incinerators and other horrific devices."[84] Other victims were suffocated, or asphyxiated, in airtight, sealed rooms. A fiancée named Emiline Cigrand was suffocated. So was a maid in the castle named Lizzie.[85] And according to Boswell and Thompson, "Sitting comfortably in his office, Holmes, apparently, could asphyxiate at will any of his guests he had a mind to."[86]

He strangled Benjamin Pitezel. Holmes killed his fishing companion Rodgers by beating him with an oar.[87] And in perhaps the meanest technique of all, "He left one wife in a sealed chamber to hear her scream for days as she gradually died of starvation." Holmes locked a janitor in a soundproof room, and "relished the sight of the man's agonies as he slowly starved to death."[88]

Torture

He tortured some women to force them to sign over their property to him and others were tortured for his enjoyment. When police searched Holmes' Castle they found "instruments of torture." A similar account was rendered by Seltzer, "In the basement, investigators discovered also several other 'strange machines,' including an elaborate structure resembling a torture rack."[89]

"The building had secret passages, false floors, rooms with torture equipment, and a specially equipped area for surgery," Ramsland recalled. Another study determined the presence of "a torture room." According to the Chicago Public Library, Holmes "embarked on a career of swindling, torture and murder."[90] One study explained the commercial motive behind the torture, "Mudgett took some of the sufferers below-stairs while they were still alive, there to torture them if he felt they still had riches to reveal."[91]

Medical Experiments

Holmes was a medically-trained individual. He enjoyed experimenting on some of his victims. To this end his castle was equipped with an operating room and mortuary.

The girls were taken to Holmes' dissection room where he performed his "experimental surgery," Lane and Gregg recalled. Holmes maintained a working laboratory, complete with a medical dissection table, a full set of surgical instruments and an oven designed to burn a human body. At his trial a former employee "described helping his employer strip the flesh from human bodies."[92]

The horror of the experiments was documented by an Internet study, "In the basement of the castle he dismembered and skinned his prey and experimented with the corpses." Morrison and Goldberg reached a very similar conclusion. They asserted, "But what put Dr. Holmes deeds [*sic*] into the serial killer category is the way he ruthlessly experimented upon the persons whom he murdered. Dr. Holmes cut his victims, skinned them, removed chunks of flesh, burnt and prodded them, placing them in acid baths."[93]

The Murder Castle

Holmes' Castle is one of the most interesting aspects of a truly fascinating case. It has been rightfully described as a building built for murder. To appreciate the terrible significance of this edifice, the foundation for the crimes, eight topics will be discussed.

Location

Holmes built his castle across the street from the drug store where he worked upon arriving in Chicago. The location was 63rd Street and Wallace Avenue. That intersection is located in the Chicago suburb of Englewood.[94]

Date of Opening

There is disagreement over when Holmes' building opened. Morrison and Goldberg noted that "the building opened for business in May 1890." Lane and Gregg disagreed, citing an opening sometime in 1891. But both Seltzer and Time-Life Books stated that the hotel opened just before the 1983 fair began, perhaps in that same year.[95]

Holmes' Name for His Building

When he referred to the building Holmes proudly called it "The Castle." Lester recalled that "The Castle, as Holmes called his hotel, was a row of three-story buildings all joined together." A number of other studies confirm this fact.[96]

Nicknames

As is the case in many serial murders the media and law enforcement bestowed their own monikers on Holmes' castle. These nicknames included "the Murder Castle" and "Nightmare House."[97] The hotel was also called "Holmes' Castle."[98]

But there were other nicknames as well. For instance, the building was referred to as "the Torture Castle."[99] And, finally, some designated the edifice "the Horror Castle."[100]

Construction

Holmes' hotel differed from most conventional construction in one crucial respect. He continually hired and fired workers so no one besides himself knew all of the nuances and intricacies of the building. "Mudgett reportedly had the three-story house built in shifts, firing work crews every few weeks so no one would learn the mansion's secrets." Seltzer concurred, adding that "A series of separate building crews were abruptly hired and dismissed (generally swindled and unpaid) so that Holmes alone could set in place and control the master plan of the bizarre structure."[101]

The Number of Rooms

Common knowledge about the Holmes case would lead one to believe that there were exactly 100 rooms in the hotel. That is the consensus of opinion among authorities.[102] On the contrary, Seltzer suggested that there were thirty-five rooms on the second floor and an additional thirty-seven on the third floor for a total of seventy-two rooms. Schechter referred to thirty-five rooms on the second floor, with fifty-one doors.[103]

The Building's Purpose

Hotels are generally intended for the benefit of travelers, offering them respite and rest from their travels. There was a far different and most horrible alternative purpose behind Holmes' hotel—murder. Seltzer observed, "Holmes' smart home was designed as a machine for killing in: as a murder factory for the production of corpses." Odell and Gregg agreed, referring to the hotel as "a virtual murder factory." Also concurring was Vronsky, who termed the castle "a custom-designed 'murder hotel'."[104]

Descriptions

It is difficult to do justice to Holmes' Castle in one section of one chapter of a book. This intricate, multifaceted killing complex defies easy description. Collectively nearly a half-dozen descriptions of the hotel will shed some light on this building.

An initial description was provided by Lester:

> The ground floor was comprised of shops and the top floor housed Mudgett's own apartments and offices. In the middle, Mudgett had constructed a maze of 100 secret rooms without windows, stairways that went nowhere, hidden trap doors and chutes that ended in the basement which served as both torture room and mortuary. The rooms were soundproof and built so that his prisoners could not escape and doors were rigged with alarms in case they were opened. Mudgett also hooked up gas lines with which he could asphyxiate prisoners whenever the mood hit him.
>
> Mudgett could dispose of a body by opening the chute and sending it swiftly to the cellar. Once the bodies were in the cellar, Mudgett burned them in a huge furnace or he threw them into a lime pit that was beneath a metal door.[105]

Lane and Gregg offered a briefer but similar account of the "Gothic-style hotel." Some rooms were equipped with chutes down which victims slid to the basement. Other rooms were functional gas chambers and still others were completely sound-proofed and stocked with surgical instruments.[106]Morrison and Goldberg added this depiction, "He liked to inspect his place, opening and closing fifty-one creaky doors on the second floor, firing up a kiln with a cast-iron hatch, inspecting tubs of quicklime and acid, testing chutes that led to the basement. To sealed rooms he added gas jets, stairways that went up but ended at a wall, and trap doors. He also built an instrument like a modern-day rack that was said to be able to stretch a person into twice his height."[107]

"The ground floor of Holmes Castle, as it was dubbed, contained shops, offices, a hodge-podge of turrets and bay windows, and Holmes's living quarters," Spindler recalled. However, "It also held, police discovered, concealed staircases, false walls and ceilings, airtight and soundproof rooms, and chutes leading to the basement. And in the basement were two sheet-iron tanks containing human bones and a large furnace, believed to be a crematory."[108]

Possibly the most-respected account of Holmes' Castle was provided by Ashburyin 1940:

> Half a dozen rooms were fitted as ordinary sleeping chambers, and there were indications that they had been occupied by the various women who had worked for the monster, or to whom he had made love while awaiting an opportunity to kill them. Several of the rooms were without windows, and could be made air-tight by closing the doors. One was completely filled up with a huge safe . . . into which a gas-pipe had been introduced. Another was lined with sheet iron covered by asbestos, and showed traces of fire. Some had been soundproofed, while others had extremely low ceilings, and trapdoors in the floors from which ladders led to smaller rooms beneath. In all of the rooms on the second floor, as well as in the great safe, were gas-pipes with shut-off valves in plain sight. But these valves were fakes; the flow of gas was actually controlled by a series of cut-offs concealed in the closet of Holmes' bedroom . . . and the police believed that in the asbestos-lined chamber he had devised a means of introducing fire, so that the gas-pipe became a terrible blow-torch from which there was no escape.[109]

COMMERCIAL MOTIVE

Holmes was primarily motivated by money. He may have enjoyed the pre-murder sex with his female victims but the money was the bottom line. Six topics will be examined to demonstrate the commercial nature of the Holmes murders.

Profit Motive

Vronsky referred to "the late nineteenth century profit-motivated murders of Herman Mudgett in Chicago."[110] Similarly, Schechter suggested that although Holmes certainly enjoyed the sex, his murders were mainly motivated by greed. Egger concluded that profit motive is a primary motive in victim selection seven percent of the time, and added that Holmes "found ready sources of money by killing family members."[111]

Targeting Based on Money

Specific individuals were targeted because of the profit to be derived from their death. One study noted, "Several murders followed in sequence. First, a fishing companion was killed for the cash he was carrying. Next a business speculator was also eliminated for money." Morrison and Goldberg agreed, "Mudgett had a penchant for killing some of those with whom he had relationships and collecting their money—either their life savings or life insurance policies."[112]

Hotel Built for Murder

Holmes built the hotel to make money from murder victims. Odell and Gregg realized that the criminal endeavors in the castle were a mix of robbery, murder and the hotel industry. And Schechter added that Holmes' hotel was "a structure erected, among other reasons, to keep himself supplied with corpses."[113]

Corpses and Skeletons Sold

There was a brisk business in both skeletons and cadavers in the 1890s as medical education required large numbers of both. Holmes profited from this demand. One study recalled, "Wringing every last cent from his victims, Mudgett even managed to sell several bodies, as cadavers or cleaned skeletons, to a nearby medical school for anatomical classes." *Southcoast Today* reported that Holmes sold corpses for $25–45 apiece, beginning with the body of a tenant named Russell, and that he sold a skeleton for $200. Everitt added that Holmes sold corpses and skeletons to medical schools.[114]

Numerous authorities have documented the sale of skeletons to medical schools by Holmes. Morrison and Goldberg depicted Holmes as a man who "smirkingly sold the skeletons to local colleges for well over $250." Ramsland added that after killing his victims, "He would deflesh them and sell the bleached skeletons to medical schools."[115]

Killed for Life Insurance

Some of Holmes' victims were killed for the proceeds from life insurance policies. Robert Leacock was murdered for a $40,000 policy windfall and Benjamin Pitezel died for a mere $10,000.[116] According to another study, "He killed his first victim, a friend named Dr. Robert Leacock, for life insurance."[117] And Morrison and Goldberg mentioned that Holmes killed for life insurance revenue.[118]

CONCLUSION

Whether we call him Herman Mudgett or H. H. Holmes, he was an amazing criminal. And despite the diversity in his murderous schemes, there was one constant—profit-making through murder. This was truly a case of commercial serial murder.

Holmes may have enjoyed the ladies, so to speak, prior to their death. And he even may have received some twisted satisfaction from the murders themselves. But the preponderance of evidence examined in this study points to a profit motive behind the murders. The hotel was built to profit from visitors to the Chicago World's Fair in 1893. His life insurance scams also connect murder and money as motive.

CHAPTER 3

Belle Gunness

Belle Gunness was not born in the United States, but after she emigrated to America she made quite a name for herself. One study suggested that among the women profit-motivated serial killers Gunness was the most effective and most savage.[1] Another study called her "America's most notorious murderess."[2]

Gunness was one of America's most prolific and effective female serial murderers of all time Kelleher and Kelleher contended.[3] A 2008 report concluded that Gunness was "the most prolific female serial killer."[4] A second 2008 study added that Gunness was "one of the most prolific serial killers in American history" regardless of gender.[5]

Yet another Gunness can be easily perceived and described. She was a pious woman according to the *New York Times*, "Mrs. Gunness described as a religious fanatic who got into crime as a result of the sudden wealth she inherited on the death of her first husband, Max Sorenson." Jones added, "She was sincerely pious and taught in the local Sunday School amongst the children she adored."[6]

Who was Belle Gunness? Was she a misunderstood religious woman or a cold-blooded murderer?

THE MURDERESS: BELLE GUNNESS

The passage of time has contributed to the difficulty in arriving at an accurate understanding of Belle Gunness. The same is true of her crimes. We will attempt to expand our knowledge of Gunness by examining thirteen dimensions of this criminal.

Name and Birthplace

One Internet source realized that "Belle Gunness' origins, like much of her life story, are shrouded in a web of differing accounts and deliberate inventions. Most of her biographers state that she was born on November 22, 1859, near Lake Selbe, Trondheim, Norway, and christened Brynhild Paulsdatter Storset."[7] A survey of several sources confirms the diversity in information about Gunness' birth.

Bella Poulsdatter was born in 1859 in Trondhjeim, Norway.[8] According to another source, Brynhild Paulsdatter Storset was born on November 11, 1859 in Selbu, Norway.[9] Wilson and Wilson recalled that she was born as Brynhild Poulsdatter Pederson on November 11, 1859, in the fishing village of Innbygde.[10]

She was born in Trondhjem, Norway, about 1860, Jones noted.[11] She was "Born Bella Poulsdatter near Trondhjem, Norway, in 1849," Lane observed.[12] Ann Jones said that Belle (nee Bella) Paulson was born in Selbu.[13] The Biography Channel noted that Brynhild Paulsdatter Storseth was born in Selbu on November 22, 1859.[14]

Gunness "was born in Selbu, Norway, in 1858," declared the La Porte County Historical Society.[15] The *Serial Killer Database* noted that Brynhild Paulsdatter Storset was born in Selbu, Norway, on November 22, 1859.[16] The La Porte County Public Library arrived at the same conclusion.[17] Brynhild Paulsdatter Storset was born in the Norwegian West Coast village of Selbu on November 11, 1859, Newton concluded.[18]

Parents

There is similar disagreement about her parents in accounts of the life of Belle Gunness. Not about their names, though. We know that Paul Pederson Storset and Berit Oldsdatter were her parents.[19] But her father's occupation is unclear.

Gunness was "The daughter of a stonemason," according to The Biography Channel.[20] However, one study asserted that Gunness' father was a poor farmer. Newton called her the child of a failed merchant.[21] Her father's numerous business efforts failed.[22]

Childhood

She seems to have had a somewhat unhappy childhood. One source noted that her family lived in poverty. The La Porte County Public Library concurred, adding that the family's plight necessitated Belle's employment. The family was impoverished and an adolescent Brynhild was employed on local farms working as a dairy maid.[23]

The teenaged Gunness was unhappy because she was not considered to be attractive. However, she was also considered to be intelligent.[24] One study noted the tendency of some historians to embellish and 'colorize' Gunness' childhood.[25]

Emigration

We know that Gunness emigrated from Norway to the U.S. but the exact date remains elusive. One study suggested that "Following the example of a sister (Nellie Larson) who'd gone to the New World sometime earlier, she migrated to the United States.—the exact date is unknown, but the move occurred between 1881 and 1883."[26] Belle was twenty-one when she emigrated to the United States in 1881. A study by Newton agreed with the Kellehers.[27] Others suggested that at age twenty-three Gunness emigrated, in 1883.[28]

Name Change

"After her arrival, she Americanized her name to Bella Storset, and would often refer to herself as 'Belle' when speaking to her friends," one study concluded. The La Porte County Public Library added that Gunness legally changed her name to Belle.[29]

Move to Chicago

It is not known with certainty when Gunness moved to Chicago. The La Porte County Public Library claimed that sometime around 1881 Gunness migrated to the United States, staying with her sister Nellie Larson in Chicago.[30] However, other studies instead claim that Gunness was in the United States for three years before moving to Chicago.[31]

Life in Chicago was not easy. She worked as a servant in a wealthy home. One study concluded that Gunness worked as a domestic servant and possibly on a farm.[32]

Mads Sorenson

"It was in Chicago, in 1884, that Gunness met another Norwegian immigrant, Mads Sorenson, and fell in love," asserted Kelleher and Kelleher. Gunness was a 25-year-old in 1884 when she married Sorenson.[33] The La Porte County Historical Society instead suggested that this marriage took place in 1893.[34]

Sorenson worked as a department store detective, later moving to work at the Chicago and Northwestern railroad. Geringer offered this perspective, "She wasn't in Chicago long before she met Mads Sorenson, a hard-working conservative who was eager to start a family in the states." Her neighbors recalled that Belle was a good wife.[35]

Peter Gunness

Gunness was married to Sorenson until his death. She then moved to La Porte, Indiana, where she met Peter Gunness. They were married on April Fool's Day, 1902.[36] The marriage only lasted eight months, ending when Peter Gunness' life ended.[37]

Love for Children

One account noted that Gunness was not an evil person even though she was a serial murderess. Her sister recounted her great affection for children, "I have seen as many as ten or a dozen of them running around her house. She would play games with them and treat them with the utmost kindness. She loved to spend money on them and was simply adored by every child in the neighborhood." Her neighbors declared that Gunness seemed to love her own children and others as well.[38]

It is claimed that she was a good mother. "We may assume she felt attachment to the children that she had brought up in La Porte," Wilson and Wilson suggested, adding that "Maxson spoke of her love of playing games with the children—they were playing just before the last time he saw them—and everyone agreed that she seemed to be a good mother." Another study stated that "She was a most devoted mother." And Geringer recalled Gunness warning her children, "Ja, ya all eats the broosel sprouts or dere iss no tappey-oca poodings for da dessert."[39]

Additional evidence of her love for children can be found in her will. She left money for underprivileged children. Depending upon the source consulted, she gave money to the Norwegian Orphan's Home, a La Porte-area Norwegian orphanage, a Chicago orphanage for Norwegian children or a Norwegian-American orphan's home.[40]

Appearance

Belle Gunness is sometimes described as an attractive woman, but more often than not she is portrayed negatively. One study noted, "On those occasions, Belle was seen wearing a corset and her finest clothing, with her hair done in the latest styles of the women's magazines that came from Chicago and New York."[41]

An extended explanation of her attractiveness was provided by Geringer:

> By 1908, Belle's once hourglass figure had fattened, but her silken blonde hair, accompanied by a full Nordic smile of white teeth and a pair of flashing blue eyes, still turned heads. Weighing in at 280 pounds, she was nevertheless able to tighten her corset to emphasize a 48-inch bust and a pair of curving 54-inch hips when curves, no matter how expansive the girth, epitomized sex appeal.[42]

Gunness is not characterized as positively in most other accounts. She was "over 200 pounds." Montaldo reported that she weighed 280 pounds.[43] George Anderson replied to her matrimonial ad and was disappointed in her looks. "Belle (now in her mid-forties, portly and coarse-featured) was not the beauty he expected. He also realized that she had a severe manner." Sexton observed, "She was a heavy-set immigrant from Norway with masculine features and it would appear masculine temperament as well."[44]

Gunness was relatively unattractive. Ann Jones described Gunness as an angry 250-pound fifty year old. "She was a housewife turned psychopath."[45]

Nicknames

Virtually all serial killers are christened with nicknames, typically by members of the media covering the story. Gunness' nickname was "Lady Bluebeard." Kelleher and Kelleher added that Gunness was known as "Lady Bluebeard" due to her murders.[46]

Relationships with Men

Her relationships with men were problematic. They didn't seem to stay. Geringer recalled that while the farm succeeded Gunness' luck with men did not. Farmhand after farmhand left her high and dry after having seemed like a potential suitor.[47]

But Gunness had sexual needs that had to be met. As a result Belle employed a succession of hired hands, many becoming her lovers. The men who slept with her and survived the experience stated that Gunness possessed a "natural talent for sex that soon made them her slaves." A second account noted, "Belle's arrangements with that hired man and the others who followed him never seemed to work out well because Belle—who by all accounts was a sensuous woman—would sleep with the hired man who in turn would begin to think of himself as the master of the place."[48]

Did Gunness hate men? That was the conclusion of one study. After the death of Mads Sorenson, Gunness developed a hatred of men because she was not attractive.[49]

Last Acts in La Porte

Recency theory suggests that final acts are particularly noteworthy. Gunness' last acts prior to her flight from La Porte are therefore important. For one thing she paid off her mortgage, perhaps to lessen the likelihood of someone inspecting her property.[50]

Then she made out a will, assisted by her attorney, M.E. Leliter or Leliler. She reportedly told her attorney that she feared that a former handyman she had fired, Ray Lamphere, might burn down her house, "I'm afraid he's going to kill me and burn the house," she is supposed to have said.[51] In another version, Gunness says, "That man (Lamphere) is out to get me, and I fear that one of these nights he will burn my house to the ground."[52] Later that evening, Belle's prediction was fulfilled as her house burned to the ground. Before leaving town Belle removed most of her money from the bank.[53]

OTHER CRIMES

Gunness engaged in other criminal activity. Her other crimes involved insurance fraud. She burned a candy store and multiple houses for the insurance proceeds.

"Several of her insured establishments had burned down," Ramsland recalled. In 1896 her candy store burned to the ground, followed by the destruction of her home in Austin, Illinois, two years later. According to another study, "Not long after Gunness married Mads Albert Sorenson in 1894, their store and home mysteriously burned down. The couple claimed the insurance money for both."[54] Gunness attributed the candy store fire to a kerosene lantern but none was found in the wreckage. Newton noted that fire gutted their home in 1898 resulting in an insurance payment. But more bad fortune plagued them as a second house burned to the ground. They opened an unsuccessful

candy store and within a year it burned to the ground under mysterious circumstances.[55]

"A year after it opened, the shop was mysteriously destroyed by a fast-moving fire," Kelleher and Kelleher suggested, emphasizing "the suspicious circumstances surrounding the fire." Lane also described the suspicious nature of the fire, and noted "the insurance company's churlish suspicions and their abject refusal to do further business with such a high-risk client." A study by Richard Jones confirmed Lane, "This time the insurance company became suspicious." Though obligated to pay Gunness because they had no evidence of arson, they "refused to have any further dealings with her."[56]

Gunness may have run a boardinghouse in Chicago. According to Jones, Mads and Belle moved from Austin, Illinois, to Chicago, "and invested her savings in a boarding-house which was shortly afterward burned to the ground." Lane claimed that after Mads' death Belle opened her boarding-house in Chicago, "Belle returned to Chicago and invested in a lodging-house. Poor Belle; hardly had she got the sheets on the beds than disaster once again visited in the form of a fire which gutted the rooming-house, leaving the owner with no more than the huge insurance claim for comfort."[57]

Others offer different versions of the insurance fires. The candy store fire was the initial blaze followed by the Austin house fire, Ann Jones asserted. Other studies, by Kelleher and Kelleher, *Bedlam Asylum Crime Files*, and the La Porte County Public Library, reversed the order of the fires.[58] Geringer suggested that the Gunnesses moved three times after fire destroyed their home, in addition to the candy store fire.[59]

THE MURDERS

The commercial murders of Belle Gunness were calculated acts. She was determined to get what she wanted. To facilitate understanding of these crimes three main topics will be explored.

Number of Murders

We will never know how many died at her hands. Lyons noted, "No one really knows how many victims she really had." Lane agreed, "Nobody is quite sure how many gentlemen of 'wealth and cultured taste' came knocking on Belle's door, but whatever the number, none ever left." The final death total is the subject of ongoing debate.[60]

The lowest estimates range from twelve to fourteen victims. "Twelve bodies and several miscellaneous body parts were eventually discovered," the La Porte County Public Library recalled. The La Porte County Historical Society concurred.[61] But three other studies quantified the death total at fourteen.[62]

There were in fact sixteen or eighteen victims according to some sources. *The Guinness Book of World Records* credited Gunness with sixteen "known" murders and an additional twelve possible homicides. Another study added that "It was thought that sixteen individuals were certainly murdered and possibly as many as twelve more."[63] Eighteen bodies were found according to Publications International Ltd.[64]

Some authorities recall twenty-five murders. That was the conclusion of Wilson and Wilson. An Indianapolis newspaper recently suggested, "Over a span of about five years, she killed at least 25 people, though some say the real number was at least 40."[65]

Forty or forty-two murders was the actual total. "Indeed, many investigators now believe that the actual number of her victims was forty or more." The Biography Channel claimed that the bodies of at least forty men and children were found. The La Porte County Historical Society noted that "Some estimated that Belle had buried 40 men on the farm." An Internet study added, "There were the remains of more than forty men and children buried in shallow graves throughout Belle's property."[66] Some would increase that victim total by a couple, to forty-two. "Belle's victim count was 42," Sexton suggested. The *Serial Killer Database* agreed as did another Internet study.[67]

Numerous studies identify forty-nine Gunness murder victims. Lamphere, Belle's accomplice, stated flatly that there were forty-nine victims. Montaldo estimated that "Belle Gunness (1896–1908) was responsible for killing 49 people on her small farm in La Porte, Indiana." An Internet study added, "She killed 49 people (known number)."[68]

A final estimate might be considered. "Estimates of her murderous habits put her at fifty to a hundred hits."[69] A last estimate is a poem, "Now some say Belle killed only ten. And some say forty-two; It was hard to tell exactly, But there were quite a few."[70]

MO

The Gunness murders followed a relatively rigid formula and the murder method did not vary much. Initially a couple of general descriptions will be provided, followed by discussion of poisoning, bludgeoning, dismembering and packaging, and the use of an accomplice. One study explained her MO in this manner:

> When a victim arrived, Belle made him comfortable, charming him and cooking a large meal. She then drugged his coffee and while the man was in a stupor, she split his head with a meat chopper. Sometimes she would simply wait for the suitor to go to bed and then enter the room by candlelight and chloroform her sleeping victim. A powerful woman, Belle would then carry the body to the basement, place it on a table, and dissect it. She then bundled the remains and buried these in the hog pen and the grounds about the house.

Another description was offered by the La Porte County Public Library; Gunness poisoned her victims and brained them with a meat cleaver. Then the bodies were dismembered and saturated with lye to facilitate decomposition and disposal. Corpses were buried in the chicken enclosure or the hog pen.[71]

Poisoning was her main murder method. "Belle drugged them in their sleep." Lyons agreed, noting "Gunness poisoned her victims with strychnine and then butchered the bodies." The *New York Times* reported, "Police scientists discover that Mrs. Gunness poisoned the first of her ten victims with arsenic and strychnine." Another study added, "To save time she sometimes poisoned her victim's coffee with strychnine."[72]

It has already been mentioned that redundant murder methods were used, with bludgeoning following poisoning, just in case. *The Serial Killer Database* described her MO, "Arson, poisoning, suffocation, slashing, bludgeoning and dismemberment." Sexton added this description of the primary role of bludgeoning, "Others were not nearly as fortunate; Belle would sneak into their room and cleave their skulls in twain."[73]

The bodies were dismembered and packaged. Ann Jones noted, "It was impossible to identify the bodies" which were "cut up and packaged—a sack for each arm removed from its socket, a sack for each leg sawed off at mid-thigh, another sack for the head and another for the torso." Andrew Helgelien's "dismembered body was wrapped in oil cloth," and "There were thirteen others, all cut up and neatly parceled."[74]

A final MO issue—was there an accomplice? Lamphere confessed helping her dispose of bodies but denied being involved in any murders. This confession was important because it was known at the time that Indiana authorities reportedly could prove that Gunness had assistance.[75]

The Victims

Not all of her victims were identified. It is believed that she poisoned her first husband. Her second husband died when a large metal cutting machine bludgeoned him. Belle poisoned her daughter Caroline and son Axel, and Jennie Olson.

The rest of her victims were men lured to their death by her ads or personal contact. They included Andrew Helgelien, John Moo, Olaf Svenhervd, Peter Carslon or Colson, Ole Budsberg, Eric (or Henry) Gurholt and Olaf Lindblom (or Lindboe).

COMMERCIAL MOTIVE

Profit Motive

"Occasionally, as in the case of Belle Gunness of Indiana, who advertised in newspapers for suitors, then promptly killed them once she gained access to their money, women will kill their husbands, fiances and lovers in order to improve or maintain their lifestyle," Hickey recalled. Kelleher and Kelleher agreed, adding "Most of the victims were murdered for life insurance proceeds or to rob their assets." Richard Jones asserted that "Her apparent motive was, of course, money." Ann Jones nicely concluded this survey of the Gunness profit motive, "Her business was marriage and murder."[76]

Husband's Insurance

INDYSTAR.COM noted in 2008 that "She is believed to have killed her first husband, Mads Albert Sorenson, for his life insurance money. In 1902 she married a second time to Peter Gunness. Less than a year later, he was dead, also." The Biography Channel offered similar information, "Sorenson died of heart failure on the one day his two life insurance policies overlapped. Although her husband's family demanded an inquiry, no charges were filed .... Several more unexplained deaths followed, including the infant daughter of her new husband, Peter Gunness, followed by Peter Gunness himself." Another study added, "She applied for the insurance money the day after the funeral. The swiftness of this act fueled the suspicions of her in-laws. Sorenson's relatives claimed that Belle had poisoned her husband to collect on the insurance."[77]

Belle profited handsomely by Sorenson's untimely death. Especially since he was poorly paid, making about $15 a week. Most authorities on the case specify an $8,500 insurance payout, including Ramsland, Wilson and Wilson and the La Porte County Public Library. Lane instead quantified the sum as a mere $100.[78]

One factor seems to indicate that Sorenson was indeed murdered. He died on a most auspicious day. "The one and only day that his two life insurance policies with two different mutual benefit associations overlapped."[79]

Peter Gunness also seems to have been killed. A sausage grinder fell from a shelf and bludgeoned him to death, Belle claimed, although her daughter reportedly told schoolmates that "My momma killed my poppa. She hit him with a cleaver." The District Attorney who reviewed the case remarked, "This was murder."[80]

The insurance payout was $3,000. One source quoted it at $2,500 and another says that estimates range from $3,000 to $4,000. In any case it was a substantial sum.[81]

Children's Insurance

Belle and Mads had four children but two died in infancy. Their deaths were attributed to colitis, but strychnine causes the same symptoms. Wilson and Wilson recalled "insurance windfalls" resulting from "the deaths of two children from colic."[82]

Suitors Brought Money

Her advertisements informed potential suitors to bring earnest money with them, ostensibly as a sign of good faith and to deter financially unattractive men. Gunness meant to kill the men and keep the money. Numerous examples document this fact.

John Moo was a husky fifty-year-old man who journeyed from Elbow Lake, Wisconsin, to woo Belle. Moo "brought more than $1,000 with him to pay off Belle'smortgage . . . or so he told neighbors who were introduced to him by Belle as her cousin." Henry Gurholt took $400 when he left Scandinavia, Wisconsin, in May of 1905 to work for Belle. Similarly, Tonnes Peter Lien left Rushford, Minnesota, on April 2, 1907, bringing $1,000. And two sources report that in 1908 Andrew Helgelein "had sold his property, liquidated his assets and had come to La Porte with approximately $3,000."[83]

Suitors Obtained Money in La Porte

Some suitors disregarded her instructions to bring cash. These men often used a La Porte bank to conduct transactions, with Gunness at their side. John Moo, for instance, "drew $1,100 in cash from the La Porte bank on the day after Christmas, and was never seen again." Ole Budsburg, from Iolo, Wisconsin, "was last seen alive at the La Porte Savings bank on April 6th, 1907—when he mortgaged his Wisconsin land there, signing over a deed and obtaining several thousand dollars in cash." Another source suggested that Ole Budsburg withdrew $1,000 on April 26, 1907, using the bank in La Porte with Belle at his side. Andrew Helgelein obtained $2,900 from her bank, "There he had drawn out all his money from his local bank, with Mrs. Gunness at his elbow."[84]

Jennie Olson's Avoided Payment

Jennie was an adopted child of Belle's. When she turned eighteen she was due to receive a payment of $1,500. However, Jennie disappeared just weeks prior to that birthday, not to be seen again until her remains were found on the Gunness farm.[85]

Letters Emphasized Money

"Belle had written letters imploring him to sell everything and come to her, and after he visited, he disappeared," Ramsland recalled. Another study added that "Taken with her romantic literary style and her pleas to meet him, he set up a meeting. As an afterthought, she asked if he could bring $1,000 to help her pay her mortgage." Taylor agreed, noting that "Belle offered true love and a life of wedded bliss, but also mentioned a quick $1,000 that she needed to pay off a mortgage."[86]

Her letters portrayed herself as a proper Norwegian woman looking for a faithful husband and good provider for her family. As the written relationship progressed Gunness began to introduce monetary topics. When Helgelein decided to visit, Bellewrote back with some specific instructions:

> Do not send any cash money through the bank. Banks cannot be trusted nowadays. Change all the cash you have into paper bills, largest denominations you can get, and sew them real good and fast on the inside of your underwear. Be careful and sew it real good, and be sure do not tell anyone of it, not even to your nearest relative. Let this only be a secret between us two and no one else. Probably we will have many other secrets, do you not think?[87]

The Total Take

How much did Gunness make through her marital murder mayhem? We will consider a variety of estimates. Lamphere said that she made from $1,000 to $32,000 per victim. One study observed that Gunness "escaped with a bag full of money."[88]

The most conservative perspectives on her profit place the value at about $30,000. "Authorities later determined that Belle's victims died mostly of poison and collectively contributed $30,000 to Belle's checkbook," Montaldo recalled. According to another study, "Sheriff Smutzer estimated that Belle had made about $30,000 from her victims."

Wilson and Wilson referred to "a large sum of money—usually $30,000."[89]

Gunness made a cool $100,000 or more some authorities believe. Newton, for instance, recalled that she gained approximately $100,000 between 1903 and 1908. Lamphere claimed that Gunness had absconded with $100,000, claimed *Dead Silence: The Serial*

Killer Blog and Kelleher and Kelleher. Sexton noted, "It was estimated that this little dance of death netted her over $100,000 dollars."[90] She may have made as much as a quarter of a million dollars according to one source, "She had allegedly accumulated more than $250,000 through her lovelorn murder schemes over the years."[91]

The Advertisements

Two Kinds of Ads

She placed two different kinds of advertisements in newspapers; there were the relatively well-known ads in matrimonial columns and then there were help-wanted ads, "She also began to run advertisements in newspapers that catered especially to the local Norwegian population. Some of these advertisements offered employment at the Gunness farm, while others were designed to draw out prospective suitors for the lonely widow."[92]

"Lonely Hearts" Ads

"She started placing 'lonely hearts' ads in Norwegian-language newspapers throughout the Midwest," Newton recalled. The *Serial Killer Database* agreed, noting that Belle "often used 'lonely hearts' ads to lure her male victims." Recent research by Lyons confirmed these sources, suggesting that "lovelorn ads in a Norwegian newspaper" were an important part of the Gunness murder method. Another 2008 account reported that "Gunness began placing newspaper ads seeking male suitors, whom she separated from their money and property before poisoning them." Publications International Ltd. added, "She placed advertisements in the lonely-hearts column."[93]

"Personal—Comely widow who owns a large farm in one of the finest districts in La Porte County, Indiana, desires to make the acquaintance of a gentleman equally well provided, with view of joining fortunes. No replies by letter considered unless sender is willing to follow answer with personal visit. Triflers need not apply," ran an ad placed by Gunness in Chicago and other major Midwestern newspapers.[94] A different version of the same message was presented in another contemporary ad, emphasizing the need for a deposit, "Some little cash is required for which will be furnished first-class security."[95]

The Ads Were Effective

The ads seemed to work, judging by the amount of money gained, which may have been on the order of $30,000 to $250,000. Gunness had a steady stream of suitors, from Minnesota, Wisconsin and South Dakota. A La Porte-area group concluded, "A deadly gold digger, Belle lured wealthy Chicago men to her house with classified ads."[96]

"Seductive advertisement" is how Jones described her ads. Andrew Helgelein met Gunness through the mail-order brides column in *The Skandinavian*, a Norwegian-language newspaper.[97] We must conclude that her ads were very effective.

Ad Language

Were the ads written and published in English, Norwegian or both? None of the sources consulted in the research behind this book mentioned bilingual messages. But numerous studies specify ad placement in Norwegian-language newspapers.[98]

Belle's Letters

"Those passionate love letters" were described by Sexton.[99] "Sexually suggestive correspondence" was recalled by Lyons.[100] We might best understand these letters by reading one of them. Here is an example of her prose:

> Dear Friend: I have been overjoyed by your answer to my advertisement, because I feel sure you are the one man for me. I feel that you will make me and my dear babes happy, and that I can safely entrust you with all that I possess in the world. But I will be candid with you and tell you exactly how I stand.
>
> There must be no concealment on either side. Now as to the farm. There are seventy-five acres of land, and also all kinds of crops—apples, plums and currants. All this is pretty nearly paid. I lost my husband by an accident five years ago, and I am getting tired of this, and find it is too much to look after things and manage the children as well. Anyway, my idea is to take a partner to whom I can trust everything. As we have no acquaintances ourselves, I have decided that every applicant I have considered favorably must make a satisfactory deposit of cash or security. I think that is the best way to keep away grafters who are always looking for an opportunity. I am worth at least twenty thousand dollars, and if you could bring five hundred to show you are in earnest, we could talk things over.[101]

CONCLUSION

The case of Belle Gunness is somewhat shrouded in mystery because of the remaining unanswered questions. What happened to her? A headless corpse was found in the burned wreckage of her home and nearby were fragments of dental work identified as belonging to Belle. But the corpse was a foot smaller and one hundred pounds lighter than Belle and Ray Lamphere said that the burned body was not Gunness but instead a woman recruited to be killed and identified as Belle.

What is certain is that Gunness murdered many people for money. Some were insured family members, others were potential boyfriends and still others were her employees. The one thing all of her victims had in common was that their death would enrich Belle. She killed with poison and a hatchet and then dismembered her victims to facilitate disposal of their remains. Belle Gunness remains an enigma to us today.

CHAPTER 4

Fritz Haarmann

Fritz Haarmann was "one of the most ghastly twentieth century serial killers," and "one of the most gruesome serial killers of all time."[1] "One of the first serial killers at the beginning of the age of sexual killing, Haarmann lived a life fueled by an excessive need for murder." He was called a "werewolf, a vampire, and a sexual psychopath," and *Onpedia* referred to him as "a notorious serial killer."[2] The American serial murderer Albert Fish idolized Haarmann and carried a clipping about Haarmann in his pocket.[3]

Haarmann's crimes shocked the people of Hanover, Germany. "Panic erupted" after the press reported the discovery of Haarmann's victims and the disappearance of approximately 600 teenaged boys in a year's time. Gilbert reported for *The Crime Library* that "Hannover [*sic*] was at the point of public outcry. By late June of 1924 sheer terror had gripped the city. The quantity of skulls and corpses still being discovered was generating a national furor and a general lack of confidence in the German police."[4]

There was strong media and public pressure throughout the country to solve the case as quickly as possible. One study concluded, "The outrage from the Hanover townspeople was so strong that the judges ordered the beheading even though they doubted Haarmann was sane enough." *Monstropedia* concurred, adding that "Public opinion was heated and would not have approved of Haarmann just being locked away."[5]

Media reports both echoed and fueled public sentiment. Press coverage had substantial public impact. "After the publicity on this case, people developed *menschenfleischpsychose*, or the irrational fear of eating meat that might be human."[6]

Haarmann may have acted largely by himself or he may have had an accomplice named Hans Grans. We will consider both possibilities and examine the role of both men in these serial murders, but the main focus will center on Haarmann.

THE MURDERERS: FRITZ HAARMANN AND HANS GRANS

Fritz Haarmann

Birth

There is a virtual consensus on this fact. He was born as Friedrich Heinrich Karl Haarmann in Hanover, Germany, on Thursday, October 25, 1879. His parents were known as "Old Haarmann" or "Silky Olle," and Johanna Claudius.[7]

Family

Haarmann's father is not usually portrayed in a positive light. He was referred to as "a retired railway worker, cantankerous, miserly and inclined towards drunkenness." Morris added that the elder Haarmann was a locomotive stoker, "Little Fritz's father, known exclusively as 'Old Haarmann,' was almost certainly a manic-depressive. His were the blackest of moods, with Fritz often on the receiving end."[8]

Fritz definitely disliked his Dad. He loathed his father intensely, a lifelong hatred of the senior Haarmann, one study remarked. Gilbert agreed, adding that Haarmann had always hated his father and continued that feeling his entire life. An Internet study offered a similar perspective, "He loathed his father. They constantly threatened each other." Banks also observed this fact, recalling that Haarmann constantly argued with his father.[9]

He seemed to love his mother as much as he hated his father. She was seven years older than her husband and she brought with her a dowry that made the womanizing "Old Haarmann" a relatively wealthy man. Johanna was described as "a simple-minded, slightly stupid woman." According to another study, she was "a meek, unintelligent person." She was forty-one years of age when Fritz (the youngest of her six children) was born and his birth resulted in her remaining bed-ridden for much of her remaining life.[10]

Fritz consistently revealed great respect for and dedication to his mother. She was the only one he expressed fondness for, recalled one study. He was his mother's favorite, another source noted, adding that Haarmann often played with dolls and other girl toys:

> By the time Fritz was born, she was 41-years-old. His arrival left her permanently weakened and despite the fact that much of her time was spent in bed, the child was clearly her favourite [*sic*] and the recipient of whatever energies she had remaining. She doted on the boy, showering him with gifts and spoiling him at every opportunity. He was also treated more as one might expect a little girl to be, persuaded that playing with dolls was far more worthwhile than going out and involving himself in typical young male activities.[11]

Haarmann's siblings also reflected their dysfunctional upbringing. He had three sisters: Emma (with whom he played dolls and remained friendly), Frau Rudiger (a victim of the Great War, World War I), and Frau Erfurdt, his least favorite sibling. Each of his sisters suffered from obsessive-compulsive disorder and all three divorced their husbands shortly after their marriage. One brother, Alfred, became a factory foreman "with upright family and Philistine values." Another brother, Wilhelm, was convicted of child molesting while quite young and was killed in the First World War.[12]

Childhood

Early signs of trouble began to appear during his childhood. For instance, "As an adolescent he frequently dressed up in his sister's clothing as a favorite pass time" [*sic*]. In addition, Gilbert referred to "the notable feminine (possibly transvestite) tendencies that were exhibited throughout his school life." Lane recalled that Haarmann was "a lazy and rather weak-minded youth." Another study added that "He was remembered by school friends as being a 'mummy's boy,' pampered and spoilt, and one whose entire personality seemed governed by his mother."[13]

To be fair to Haarmann it should be noted that he was the victim of sexual abuse as a child. He was reportedly first abused when he was a seven-year-old. Then, at the age of sixteen, a "mannish-looking woman" lured him into her room, and soon after that Haarmann's own child molesting career began.[14]

On the other hand a positive and happy young Haarmann once existed. Morris noted that Haarmann was attentive to his studies and energetic during playtime, and "He made friends easily." Gilbert described him as being popular among children his age.[15]

Intellect

He was smart enough to murder for four years and avoid detection and arrest. Ramsland recalled, "He was a trained butcher with a low I.Q." A cybersource concurred, adding that Haarmann had a certain native intelligence despite his low I.Q.[16] Haarmann sought a career as a locksmith but he failed his apprenticeship.[17]

Military Experiences

Haarmann actually had two brief military experiences. Initially, he was sent in April, 1895 (when he was sixteen years old) to a military training school, Neu-Breisach, an academy for non-commissioned officers. He was thought to be a skilled gymnast and obedient officer, but after developing symptoms of epilepsy he checked himself out of sick bay and left the service in November 1895. Another study reported that Haarmann was a disciplined and undeniably competent gymnast and effective soldier.[18]

Five years later Haarmann tried the military life again, enlisting at the age of twenty-one. "For a while he was an excellent soldier," Wilson and Wilson recalled, until he was discharged from the army "after a diagnosis of mental deficiency." Haarmann later recalled this period of time as "the happiest of his life." "Haarmann alternated between theft and prison, with the years 1900 to 1903 spent serving with some distinction in a Jager regiment." Haarmann "quickly became a star soldier," Banks asserted, until "he was sent home due to mental instability."[19]

There is uncertainty over Haarmann's World War I service. Lester reported that Haarmann got epilepsy after receiving an injury in the First World War. But Lane and Gregg and Wilson and Wilson suggest that Haarmann was imprisoned during that war.[20]

Mental and Emotional Health

Soon after his brief experience at military school, "Haarmann was actually institutionalized at one point in the late 1800s, but he managed to escape." Lane agreed, recalling that "He was accused of indecently molesting small children and confined to an asylum from which he escaped." Ramsland referred to "a record of time spent in a mental institution." Haarmann was found to have "a congenital mental deficiency," and he was committed to Hildesheim, an asylum for the criminally insane.[21]

He was sent to Hildesheim because Haarmann was "incalculably demented."[22] He was "incurably feebleminded," in the words of another expert.[23] "One of the worst cases of clinical vampirism" was one diagnosis.[24] Wilson and Wilson noted, "He was in some ways mentally retarded."[25] Haarmann was both a narcissist and a psychopath, one study reported.[26] Cannibalism was a final mental problem manifested by Haarmann. According to Everitt, "Much of the boys' flesh was eaten by Haarmann himself."[27]

Sexuality

Haarmann was a diverse individual, sexually speaking. He had sex with men, women, boys and the dead. Perhaps his basic sexual orientation was homosexuality, as Morris noted that Haarmann was locally well-known as a predatory homosexual. Gilbert referred to Haarmann's "publicly homosexual status." In his early twenties he met a gay man named Adolf Meil and they began a relationship lasting until Meil's death.[28]

But Haarmann also successfully bedded at least one woman. Haarmann was engaged to a woman named Erna. Newton noted that in 1900 Haarmann was engaged to a local girl who became pregnant but he deserted her and the baby by joining the army, a conclusion also advanced by Schechter.[29] Other authorities claim Haarmann was married, "He seduced and married a large, pretty girl by the name of Erna Loewert," who became pregnant before he skipped out on her.[30]

Haarmann was a pedarist, or pedophile—a child molester, in other words. Lane referred to Haarmann's habit of "indecently molesting small children." The magnitude of Haarmann's sex crimes was documented by Gilbert—Sex crimes against children were virtually a daily occurrence.[31]

Haarmann achieved orgasm as he bit through the throats of his victims and tasted their blood. Schechter described how Haarmann "had orgasms while tearing open the throats of his victims with his teeth." "As he tasted their blood, he achieved orgasm."[32]

"Terminal sex" was a phrase Haarmann used in his confession to the police. It designated his habit of ending sex with the murder of his partner.[33] One final extreme act of Haarmann's sexuality might be mentioned—necrophelia.[34]

Relationship with Law Enforcement

Haarmann had a complicated relationship with the Hanover police. He was an informant for them and as a result they protected him. He reportedly ran a private detective firm named Lasso with a police official.[35]

"He even gravitated to the despised activity of police informer," Lane and Gregg recalled. In early 1921, "Haarmann elected to increase his income by becoming a paid-up police informant." Vronsky suggested that Haarmann "was a police agent and private investigator." An Internet source observed that he resided in Hanover's thieves' quarters, existing by stealing and snitching for the police.[36] "He was protected from more serious legal difficulties by his close relationship with the police, for whom he was a valuable informant," Jenkins recalled. Schechter called Haarmann's police activities being a "stool pigeon," noting that this status protected him from the police.[37]

He sometimes called himself, "Detective Haarmann." Another source noted, "In fact, some people knew him as Detective Haarmann." He even was given an official police badge.[38]

Health Issues

He suffered from meningitis as a child. His brain touched the inside of his skull at several places.[39] This may have resulted in his mental illnesses.

Haarmann sustained a concussion in a military school training mishap, Morris noted. Wilson and Wilson recalled that Haarmann was injured during exercise, suffering "a blow to the head." Gilbert noted that biological influences were present in Haarmann's repeated head injuries during adulthood.[40]

Haarmann also suffered from epilepsy, "He suffered from epileptic fits, and these may have accounted for his degenerate social behavior." The epilepsy was first noticed when Haarmann was at military school.[41]

Haarmann was afflicted with a medical malady, an STD. He had gonorrhea.[42]

Employment

He experienced a number of legal employment opportunities but he preferred illegal jobs. At one point he was a homeless vagrant.[43] Haarmann and his father frequently quarreled over the youth's refusal to take a job in his father's cigar factory.[44]

His father established him as operator of a fish-and-chips shop, Newton recalled.[45] He also worked in a paint store.[46] His best-known occupation—a butcher.[47]

Descriptions

Some very old black-and-white photographs of Haarmann reveal a charming, almost impish man.[48] One authority describes an obese middle-aged man looking a little like Hitler.[49] "Haarmann was certainly sympathetic in appearance, a simple man with a friendly, open expression and a courteous nature," Gilbert asserted. He added, "Of average height, broad and well built, he had a rough 'full-moon' face and neat, cheerful eyes. His features were generally small and as unprepossessing as the rest of his appearance, the only notability a well-groomed, light brown moustache."[50]

Haarmann was stocky yet effeminate-looking in appearance. He wore a moustache and was of average height, with a relatively small and pleasant face, Morris recalled. Another source added that Haarmann had feminine speech and mannerisms.[51]

Nicknames

Haarmann acquired nicknames. Some called him a German werewolf.[52] One nickname was "The Vampire of Hanover."[53] The other—"The Butcher of Hanover."[54]

Hans Grans

It is difficult to specify the precise role played by Grans in these murders. Five topics regarding Grans will be considered. Was he a killer or another victim?

Grans Was an Accomplice

"Once they had lured their victim to Haarmann's house in Neuestrasse, they killed them and sold their clothes," one study recalled. Other sources similarly indict Grans as being an active participant in the murders, "Grans would often help pin the boy down," one study noted. Another study claimed that Grans was charged with "instigating" two murders. Banks bluntly concluded that "While living in Hanover, Haarmann met and partnered with Hans Grans. They lived together and murdered together."[55]

Grans Was Not an Accomplice

Grans was not a murderer, some contend. Everitt noted that Grans helped lure victims but Haarmann alone carried out the murders. Schechter stated that Grans' role in the crimes is still controversial. According to one source, "His accomplice and live-in partner, Hans Grans, sold the clothing of his victims, and Haarmann claimed Grans urged him to kill handsome boys, but was otherwise not involved in the murders." Grans only sold the stolen items, others argued.[56]

Grans Lured the Victims

"Hans soon became aware of Haarmann's sexual peculiarities, and often procured young boys for him," Wilson and Wilson remarked. Sometimes Grans lured boys back to Haarmann's lair and sometimes the two acted together with the younger Grans able to set the young victims at ease. One study noted that Haarmann joined with a male prostitute named Hans Grans who could effectively attract the boys.[57]

Grans' Sentence

There is some disagreement over Grans' sentence. He was sentenced to twelve years of imprisonment. Hans received a life sentence, but was released after twelve years.[58] One study contended that Grans was executed along with Haarmann.[59]

His Eventual Fate

What happened to Grans? Several sources profess ignorance of his eventual fate, "Grans received a twelve-year sentence. What became of him after his release is not known." *Monstropedia* added, "What

exactly became of him is unknown, only that he continued living in Hanover until about 1980, when he presumably died." Banks was more definite, claiming that Grans "remained in Hanover until his death in 1980."[60]

The Haarmann/Grans Relationship

They met either in late 1918 or early 1919 soon after Haarmann's release from prison for child molesting.[61] Grans was the leader, according to some experts, "Grans was clearly the dominant partner in the relationship, treating Haarmann little better than he would a servant." Lane agreed, adding "The younger man quickly established a position of superiority within the relationship."[62]

Haarmann was actually the dominant partner other authorities have suggested. Wilson and Wilson recalled that "Haarmann was the teacher, Hans the pupil." A more complex relationship was suggested by Gilbert, "Inside the relationship between Grans and his mentor is certainly one of the more fascinating aspects of the case. Haarmann did love Grans and Grans took advantage of it. He was the cleverer of the two and thus continually toyed and jested with his companion."[63]

Their relationship was multifaceted. Newton noted that they combined business and pleasure as lovers and partners in crime. Gilbert added, "Remarkably, a friendship soon developed and Grans began living with the older man, where a bond of 'madness and spiritual parasitism developed.' The relationship was more than sexual and the insane ideas that surfaced in Haarmann's conscience always involved his young housemate."[64]

A final dimension of their relationship ought to be considered. After his arrest Haarmann implicated Grans in the murders. Some believe that Haarmann did this to retaliate against Grans and to mislead the police, whom he held in contempt.[65]

OTHER CRIMES

Fritz Haarmann

More is known about Haarmann than Grans and that is certainly true of criminal activity. Maybe Haarmann was more criminally active. Seven Haarmann crimes will be considered. It should be recalled that Haarmann also was a necrophile and a cannibal.

Confidence Games

"Numerous burglaries and confidence scams soon became a feature of Haarmann's life and, after 1904, he spent one-third of the following 20 years either in custody or in prison." Morris concurred, referring to Haarmann's quickly learning how the confidence trickster operates. Another study mentioned his "confidence scams."[66]

Pickpocketing

Pickpocketing was listed among more serious offenses on Haarmann's criminal rap sheet. Picking pockets was an initial Haarmann type of offense. Lane and Gregg recalled that Haarmann spent years apprenticing as a criminal by pickpocketing.[67]

Child Molesting

This was perhaps his 'basic' crime. He loved to molest young boys. In 1919 Haarmann was imprisoned for pederasty, one study observed. Another source agreed, noting that Haarmann was sent to prison in 1919 after being caught in bed with a young boy. Haarmann molested children for personal enjoyment.[68]

Robbery

Robbery is the taking of valuables from another usually by force or the threat of force. "Petty theft" was the term used by Lane and Gregg for Haarmann's robberies and Lester agreed. Jenkins referred to "a lengthy record of petty theft."[69]

Burglary

"He spent the First World War in prison for burglary," one source recalled. Morris noted that Haarmann burglarized many homes and businesses. Banks added that Haarmann's life was devoted to petty burglaries.[70]

Grave Robbing

This may have been his most revolting crime, along with cannibalism and necrophilia, which have already been discussed. Wilson and Wilson recalled that Haarmann "robbed graves, often digging up recently buried corpses." Schechter recalled that Haarmann's crimes ranged from burglarizing homes to grave robbery.[71]

Smuggling

Released from prison in 1918, he joined a gang of smugglers and prospered. Haarmann had acquired some useful contracts while in prison which he parlayed into a smuggling operation. The fact that Haarmann joined a Hanover smuggling ring after his release and prospered was also asserted by Newton.[72]

Hans Grans

Grans was only twenty-four when he hooked up with Haarmann. Nevertheless, he had already established a serious criminal record by that tender age. He was a small-scale thief, according to Morris. Another study concluded Grans "was a male prostitute." Grans was a homosexual pimp, Newton suggested.[73]

THE MURDERS

Haarmann's crimes were monstrous. He combined child molesting, necrophilia and cannibalism. In this section, six topics will be explored.

Number of Victims

There were two murders per week for eighteen months according to Lester and an Internet source. Another source suggested two victims per week during the entire crime spree. And some claim that there were two killings per week for sixteen months for a total of twenty-seven victims.[74]

The number of victims was in the twenties several sources suggest. There were ten to twenty victims Jenkins asserted. When the Leine Canal was emptied, bones of twenty-two, twenty-three or as many as twenty-seven victims were discovered, according to a number of studies. Haarmann was convicted of twenty-four murders but charged with and tried on twenty-seven counts of homicide.[75]

There were thirty or forty victims some have asserted. Several respected authorities, including Hickey, Newton and Wilson and Wilson, thought there were between thirty and forty victims. Haarmann confessed to having killed forty people.[76]

The highest estimate of Haarmann's victimage total is about fifty dead. There were between twenty-seven and fifty murders, according to Lane and Greg and an Internet study. Other studies found as many as fifty deaths. Wilson and Seaman's research, Everitt's analysis and that of Ramsland all suggested a total of fifty murders.[77]

The Victims

His initial victim was a boy whose first name was Friedl, Friedel or Fritz. His last name was Rothe or Roth.[78] Haarmann's other victims were Fritz Francke, Wilhelm Schulze, Hans Keimes, Roland Huch, Hans Sennefeld, Ernst Ehrenberg, Heinrich Strauss, Paul Bronischewski, Richard Graf, Wilhelm Erdner, Hermann Wolf, Heinz Brinkman, Adolf Hannappel, Adolf Hennies, Ernst Spiecker, Heinrich Koch, Willi Senger, Hermann Speichert, Alfred Hogrefe, Hermann Bock, Wilhelm Apel, Robert Witzel, Heinz Martin, Friedrich Abeling, Fritz Wittig, Friedrich Koch, and Erich de Vries.[79]

Victimology

Haarmann preyed upon a relatively defenseless group, homeless boys and war refugees. His victims were "rootless children and youths fleeing from homes broken by war and its aftermath." Everitt concurred, referring to the "young male refugees" that comprised Haarmann's target group. "His victims were young male vagrants."[80]

It is necessary to emphasize the maleness of Haarmann's victims. *Monstropedia* described Haarmann's targets as "young male vagrants and male prostitutes." All of the victims were male and between twelve and eighteen years of age, Lane recalled.[81]

MO

"His modus operandi rarely changed," Morris noted, adding that the most effective lure was free food or money, or posing as a police officer.[82] In fact, Haarmann had a dual MO, one for victim acquisition and another for the murder itself.

"He would seek wandering waifs in the train station and take them home," Ramsland recalled. "They'd take the boys to Haarmann's home, feed them and then Haarmann would force them to have sex," she added. Gilbert confirmed this victim acquisition MO, "The victim was met at the train station and offered accommodation or work, or apprehended on the pretence [*sic*] that his abductor was a police officer."[83]

The murders themselves were similarly systematized as this description of Haarmann's confession revealed. "As he talked, he called his victims 'game.' He described how he would grab the boys, sleepy from a large meal, and while sodomizing them he would chew through their throat until the head was practically severed from the body." Ramsland's account was substantiated by Gilbert, "Once in the Neuestrasse room the boy would be killed, according to Haarmann, by biting through his windpipe."[84]

Time Frame

There is disagreement over the time span of these serial murders. For instance, Lester reported that all of the murders occurred within a sixteen-month period.[85] Several studies (Lane and Gregg, *Onpedia*, and *Knowledgerush*) indicate that the time frame was between 1919 and 1924.[86] That may not be correct. In fact the initial murder was in September of 1918.[87] That would make the precise time frame 1918 to1924.[88]

Location

Where did the crimes occur? The city was Hanover, Germany (sometimes spelled Hannover), but the specific crime scene changed in time as did Haarmann's address. He resided "in the thieves' quarter of Hanover," Lester recalled. An Internet study concurred.[89]

Haarmann lived in the Kellerstrasse prior to moving with Grans to an apartment in the Neuestrasse. When police searched Haarmann's lodging at # 27 Kellerstrasse, which led to his imprisonment for indecent behavior with a child, his initial victim's head was wrapped in newspaper and wedged in a kitchen corner behind a cooker.[90]

One study concluded that Grans and Haarmann lived in the Old Quarter of Hanover.[91] Haarmann and Grans lived at # 8, Neuestrasse, according to separate studies by Morris and Gilbert. Wilson and Wilson agreed but called the street Neuerstrasse.[92] The murderous couple moved to an alley called Rothe Reihe, Lane recalled.[93]

COMMERCIAL MOTIVE

Profit Motive

"Haarmann murdered for profit, both sexual and financial," Gilbert asserted. Another study claimed that Haarmann considered merely disposing of his victims' remains as wasteful if he could profit. "Grans and Haarmann launched a wholesale scheme of homicide for fun and profit." The world was stunned by Haarmann's revelation that he "sold the flesh on the black market for human consumption."[94]

The financial incentive behind the murders was explored by Everitt, who noted that "The murders also had a sickening larcenous motive." An Internet source added, "In 1918 Haarmann did what most serial killers did in that era, he saw an opportunity for gain." Gilbert described the profit motive behind these crimes, "Always with a view to his commercial instincts, the body would then be dismembered and the clothes and meat sold through the usual channel for smuggled goods." Another Internet study noted, "Few killers have used these sadistic tendencies to earn a living. Fritz Haarmann presents a twisted tale where murdering not only provided food for himself, but also the impoverished town of Hanover." Haarmann had a stall in the marketplace across from the railway station and was known for undercutting the competition by charging less.[95]

Meat and Clothes Sold

Haarmann sold both the flesh and clothing of his victims. "Later joined by Hans Grans, Haarmann killed the boys and sold both their flesh (as meat) and their clothes," Lester recalled. The bodies were dismembered and the flesh sold as meat, Newton noted, adding that Grans kept some of the victims' clothes before selling the rest.[96]

Meat Sales

"Afterwards he sold their flesh to local butcher shops and restaurants, claiming it was pork," according to Vronsky. Everitt added that the meat sales were conducted in the marketplace near the train depot. "Haarmann and Grans would then peddle meat from the bodies of their victims as black market pork, turning numerous unwitting Germans, starving in the bleak depression crippling their country, into cannibals." A cyberstudy differed slightly, "After, Haarmann and his accomplice (Hans Grans) would butcher the victim. They would then sell the meat as black market beef."[97]

Monstropedia contended, "Rumours [*sic*] had it that Haarmann would then peddle meat from the bodies of his victims as black market pork, but there was no evidence." A similar tale was told by

Banks, "After he murdered them, his partner Grans would sell their clothing; he would (supposedly) sell the meat off their bones to local meat markets as black market pork." Haarmann removed the internal organs, sliced the flesh from the bodies, ate some, stored the remainder and sold it as pork or some other meat.[98]

A Consumer Complaint

On one occasion a woman took meat purchased from Haarmann to the police as she was suspicious. She was reportedly told by the police that she ought to be grateful for finding such fine pork. Everitt added that a woman found the meat to be "peculiar," and took it to the police. According to Newton, a suspicious customer had the meat tested by authorities, but the response was that the meat was pork. Lane added that a "police analyst" reassured the complaining woman that her meat was indeed pork. Morris noted that "a disgruntled customer" took meat to the 'police analyst,' who verified that it was pork and not human, as the buyer suspected. In a similar version, Gilbert recalled that "The police analyst unequivocally pronounced it pork!" One study said the meat in question was called beef, not pork, and the complaining customer was a male.[99]

Clothing Sales

"Once they had lured their victims to Haarmann's house in Neuestrasse, they killed them and sold their clothes," one study noted. Morris added that clothing and other personal items were placed in a sack that Haarmann or Grans later took to the black market. Several sources specify that Grans was the clothing salesman, "After he murdered them his partner Hans would sell their clothing." *Monstropedia* concurred.[100]

Sales Concealed the Murders

The sale of meat and clothes was intended to do more than produce a profit. It also served the function of eliminating evidence by removing it from the crime scene. Haarmann "disposed of the bodies by selling them as meat," Wilson and Seaman noted. Gilbert noted that selling the goods eliminated the evidence, "The clothing and meat of the victims had been distributed around Hanover and were practically untraceable."[101]

Clothes Incriminated Haarmann

When police searched Haarmann's abode after his arrest they found numerous stolen items. These goods awaiting distribution and sale thereby incriminated Haarmann. While in police custody, his home was searched and clothing and other possessions of some missing youth were discovered. During his interrogation, police confronted Haarmann with "a great deal of clothing that obviously belonged to young boys." The police found "piles of his victims' clothing awaiting sale." One source noted, "In Haarmann's rooms, they found piles of little boys [*sic*] clothes." Ramsland recalled that when police examined Haarmann's room, "They found clothing from missing boys."[102]

The magnitude of these incriminating items was indicated by Gilbert, "Several hundred items of clothing found in Haarmann's room or confiscated from his acquaintances were collected and identified as the property of the missing children." Morris described the evidence treasure trove from Haarmann's home, "They came up with a large array of clothing and bedding, some several hundred garments and various possessions. More items were later taken from Haarmann's acquaintances and identified by worried parents as belonging to their missing sons."[103]

CONCLUSION

Despite some clouds of confusion about some facts of the case, the perfect storm of serial murder that was Fritz Haarmann can be understood by realization of the commercial motivation behind the crimes. Haarmann enjoyed pre-murder sex with his victims, then doubled his pleasure by profiting from the murders through the sale of meat and clothes from the victims. These ghoulish murders were also profitable crimes.

CHAPTER 5

Marie Becker

Marie Becker died in a Belgian prison during World War II and little is known about the particulars of her demise. The Nazi occupation overshadowed less compelling events and circumstances. More recently, Belgium has warranted serious attention as a serial murder breeding ground, as a 2004 study by Peter Vronsky concluded, "But Belgium appears to be inexplicably emerging as Europe's newest serial slaughter hot zone."[1]

Marie Alexandrine Becker was born in the 1870s and she was quite unusual in some respects. For instance, "After each murder," *Women in World History* suggested, "she reportedly attended the funeral of her victim, dressed in black and making a dramatic show of her grief and sorrow."[2] In similar terms an Internet encyclopedia recalled that Becker made a dramatic scene at her victims' funerals.[3] Another Internet reference work noted, "Marie Becker was known to attend the funerals of her victims and to gesticulate wildly in her grief over their passing."[4] Crime expert Jay Robert Nash added this description, "Witnesses at Becker's trial told how they had seen the killer attend the funerals of her victims, kneeling at gravesides and weeping hysterically."[5] Becker dramatically acted as though she was deeply in grief at the funerals, another study concluded.[6]

One eerie aspect of this case was the series of exhumations conducted to discover evidence of Becker's past murders. After her arrest,

"Exhumations and medical examinations followed."[7] *Bedlam Asylum Crime Files* concluded that after Marie was arrested the bodies of her husband Charles, Lambert Beyer and some friends and customers were exhumed.[8]

The exhumations elicited evidence as one study noted, "The problem for her was that all the dead women that she had nursed, when exhumed, also contained fatal residues of the drug."[9] The exhumations obtained evidence of digitalin poisoning, Nash also claimed.[10] Bodies upon exhumation were found with lethal levels of poison, Seagrave asserted.[11]

Becker's intemperate comments enlivened the trial. *Women in World History* reported that "Becker was said to have gloated over her crimes."[12] Her trial "at times bordered on pantomime," Brian Lane and Wilfred Gregg suggested.[13] Becker testified at her trial that one victim, Mme. Lambert, "looked like an angel choked with sauerkraut."[14] Another victim, Mme. Castadot, was, in Becker's words, "dying beautifully, lying flat on her back."[15] "Beautifully, she lay flat out on her back," according to another rendition.[16]

THE MURDERESS: MARIE BECKER

It is difficult to learn much about individuals who lived a hundred years ago, particularly when they lived in a foreign land. Much about Becker is accordingly unknown. We can however inform ourselves about twelve dimensions of this intriguing female serial slayer.

Birth

She was born Marie Alexandrine Petitjean on July 14, 1879.[17] The place of her birth was Liege, Belgium.[18] She was "a native of Belgium," one study noted.[19] Another source recalled that she was born in 1877, a native of Liege, Belgium.[20] Becker was born somewhere around 1877, Seagrave observed.[21]

Childhood

As a girl, Becker "lived in the historic city of Liege."[22] *Serial Killers A-Z* added that she "was born and bred in Liege, Belgium."[23] Becker was born into a working-class existence.[24]

Marriage

Women in World History referred to her "cabinetmaker husband."[25] "Her dull and unexciting husband" was mentioned by one study.[26] Other authorities have confirmed Charles Becker's profession.[27] Seagrave noted that her husband Charles has usually been depicted as unexciting but there was no evidence of marital strife.[28] They were married for approximately twenty years.

Appearance

"The homely housewife" is how Nash depicted Becker.[29] But then she had an affair and everything changed. "She began to dress in gaudy clothes and extravagant make-up," one study noted.[30]

Employment

Her father-in-law owned a sawmill and she worked there as the bookkeeper.[31] After her husband's death to supplement her money supply Becker began making gowns and dresses.[32] Later, she opened her own business, "Becker had opened a dress shop some months earlier from the proceeds of her husband's insurance."[33] Another source says that she used money from an inheritance from her lover, Lambert Beyer, "to open a dress shop in Liege, Belgium. Her shop specialized in clothing for senior women."[34] Becker opened a fashionable little dress shop another study concluded.[35]

Virtuous Housewife until Beyer

Becker differs from most serial killers in the very late initiation of her serial murders. Married for twenty years, she seemed to be a proper and well-mannered housewife, but she was bored with her relatively docile husband.[36] Seagrave agreed, adding that Becker had led a quiet and law-abiding life for a half-century until greed and carnal desires overcame her common sense and self-control.[37]

"The 53-year-old Marie Becker of Liege, Belgium, was said to be a quiet, law-abiding housewife until she was captivated in 1932 by the advances of Lambert Beyer, a man she met while shopping," a reference book documented.[38] Lambert was forty-six years old and "a known womanizer."[39] The affair seems to have changed her life.

Personality

A former neighbor praised her demeanor, "A most pleasant person. Always ready to lend a helping hand and as kindly a soul as ever lived."[40] At the beginning of her trial, Becker seemed to be calm, cool and collected.[41] In many ways, Beck acted like a modern woman; she went out to clubs with friends a lot and liked to shop for expensive clothes.[42]

Late-Life Killer

She was in her mid-fifties when she began to kill. "Becker claimed her first victim when she was fifty-five years old," contended Kelleher and Kelleher, who added, "an unusually late start in life for most Black Widows."[43] Seagrave concluded, "A severe transition in her character took place in 1932 when Becker was a 55-year-old, white-haired matron."[44]

Loved to Dance

Much like contemporary women enamored of the club scene, Becker loved to dance. "She was known for her lively dancing," the *Crime Museum UK* asserted.[45] Going out to dance clubs was her passion, another source recalled.[46] "She took to dancing in clubs," an Internet reference work established.[47] Nash referred to Becker "haunting dance halls and nightclubs, wildly dancing with men half her age."[48]

Bored with Her Life

Perhaps it was her mid-life crisis. For whatever reason Becker decided her life was boring and needed drastic improvement. So, "Madame Becker was desperate for a change."[49] *Nationmaster.com* asserted that she was "seemingly bored and restrained in the marriage."[50]

One aspect of the new Marie Becker was "an insatiable sexual appetite."[51] According to *Serial Killers A-Z*, "She thought she had been playing the role of good housewife too long, but she didn't have much time left to change this. So she decided to get on with it and she started a passionate affair."[52] Becker "was a bored housewife," Nash bluntly realized.[53] Becker secretly was bored by the lifestyle shared with her husband another study contended.[54]

She Cut Loose

Because she was unhappy with her life she acted to change it. Her friends and neighbors were appalled at the extent to which she carried out her personal social liberation.[55] When she inherited money, "she spent it on her personal pleasures."[56]

"The once-proper Becker, much to the shock of neighbors, became a nightlife creature," Nash observed.[57] Becker's new lifestyle was costly, and "it also scandalized her neighbors," *Bedlam Asylum Crime Files* suggested.[58] "Not only did the widow recover from her grief with inordinate speed, but she lived a wild life, frequenting bars and nightclubs," Seagrave noted.[59]

Sought to Recapture Youth

Add it all up. A bored housewife longing for romance and excitement. You don't have to be Dr. Phil to realize that Becker was trying to regain her lost youth. "She hated the idea of growing old and felt that her dull and unexciting husband stood in the way of all the things she really wanted. The only way to recapture her lost youth, she decided, was to murder him and start afresh."[60]

After the death of her husband and her lover, "It almost seemed as though she had recaptured some of the lost years of her youth."[61] A similar account was reported by Nash, who believed that Becker was "convinced that the only way to recapture her youth was to murder her husband and go on with her girlish affairs."[62]

OTHER CRIMES

Murder was not Becker's only offense. In fact, she engaged in a quartet of other illegal activities. These were preliminary to and committed in conjunction with the murders.

The Affair

The affair with Beyer (some authorities prefer Bayer) was certainly a turning point for her.[63] One study contended that meeting Beyer was the watershed event in her life.[64] An Internet study explained the deadly implications of the affair for Becker's husband, "Her new experiences apparently gave her the impetus to dispatch with [*sic*] her staid, reliable husband."[65] Here is how Kelleher and Kelleher explained the affair's effect on Becker, "Becker fell in love with a local man."[66] "The passionate affair" would have dangerous and unexpected consequences.[67]

"A passionate affair with a certain Lambert Bayer [*sic*]" was recalled by *Serial Killers A-Z*.[68] The relationship was also described as "a deep love affair."[69] "The affair with him unlocked dark passions which Marie had probably concealed for a long time," one source declared.[70] The day they met, "The pair became lovers."[71]

Fraud

Many commercial serial killers commit fraud as part of their profit-motivated MO. Becker falls into the majority in this respect. Seagrave recalled, "In addition, Marie attempted to murder three others and committed various other crimes such as fraud and theft."[72]

Theft

Similarly, the majority of profit-seeking serial slayers swiped stuff from their victims. There were in fact acts of theft in this case as we just learned.[73] "Marie openly engaged in stealing from them."[74]

Forgery

Becker also engaged in forgery. This too is a common related crime in commercial murder cases. Seagrave recalled that Becker "on occasion attempted to forge a will."[75] Becker was tried on charges of murder, attempted murder and "fabricating false wills."[76]

THE MURDERS

Becker was a Black Widow who then branched out to kill friends, acquaintances and customers. Her crimes lacked drama and gore but her victims were nevertheless dead. We will examine five aspects of these murders.

Number of Victims

There is minor variance in the estimates of Becker's death toll. "Ten known homicides" were attributed to Becker.[77] "Becker is definitely known to have committed at least ten homicides," *Bedlam Asylum Crime Files* claimed.[78]

There were eleven Becker murders other authorities suggest. The *Crime Museum UK* declared that "Belgian poisoner Marie Becker . . . during the 1930s carried out a series of poisonings, killing eleven people in total."[79] A German Internet site devoted to serial murder quantified the total at eleven and possibly more.[80]

She confessed to a dozen murders.[81] Similarly, Ramsland suggested that "She had twelve victims before she was stopped and imprisoned."[82]Becker killed twelve people, Kelleher and Kelleher contended.[83] Seagrave's study also concluded that there were twelve victims.[84] And Vronsky, in *Female Serial Killers*, confirmed the death count of a dozen.[85]

But there may have been additional victims, perhaps several more. Nash admitted that while the official death count is ten, "there may have been twice that before Becker was arrested."[86] That same conclusion was advanced by *Bedlam Asylum Crime Files*.[87]

The Victims

Unlike many cases of serial murder, we know with some certainty the names of Becker's victims. Here they are, in order of death. Charles Becker, Lambert Beyer, Julia Bossy, Jeanne Perot, Aline-Louise Damorette, Maria Castadot, Madame Lambert, Madame Crulle, Anne Stevart, Mathilde Bulte, Madame Lange and Madame Weiss.[88] Mme. Doupagne was also reported as a Becker victim.

MO

There were several distinctive, idiosyncratic elements of Becker's MO. We will consider five such signature aspects of these crimes. Initially, the substance used was digitalis, according to the Society of Toxicology of Canada.[89] Ramsland also recalled the administration of digitalis.[90] The drug she used was "an extract from the foxglove plant."[91]

The exhumations ordered after her arrest confirmed her longtime use of the poison.[92] One study suggested that Becker actually administered "an overdose of digitalis."[93] She told a friend, Mme. Guichner, "I can supply you with a powder that will leave no trace."[94] She had killed her husband by sprinkling digitalis on his food.[95]

Her victims typically ingested the poison in tea, wine or a similar libation. One source described Becker, "dropping it in cups of tea in the back of her shop as they discussed the latest fashions."[96] She "administered it into cups of tea or glasses of wine," another source noted.[97] Nash recalled, "She began to poison her female patrons with digitalis, dropping this in a cup of tea in the back of her shop while discussing a new order with a customer."[98]

One key to her method was to ingratiate herself upon her victims. "By supplying attractive dresses and using flattery, Marie formed close associations with some of her customers, most of whom were elderly widows."[99] The flattery facilitated the pharmacological phenomenon.

Once the poison began to take effect Becker would accompany the victim home, assisting the woozy women in their personal care and domestic tasks. After robbing them in the dress shop, "while the customer was in a drugged condition, [Becker would] manage to get them home where they shortly died of 'unknown causes'."[100] "All her victims died after bouts of vomiting, some ailing for a few days, others dying in a matter of hours, all after spending time and drinking with Marie Becker."[101] After poisoning and robbing them, Becker "would then take the stricken women back to their own homes—where they'd die of 'unknown causes'."[102]

The victims who lingered longer than desired posed a challenge to Becker, who solved it by nursing those women in their final days until they died. When police investigated Becker's murders it quickly became apparent that "All had been nursed in their final days by Marie Becker."[103] For instance, Mme. Doupagne moved in with Becker after being told, "I shall be able to give you more attention and look after you better if I have you under my eye."[104] Similarly, "When Maria Castadot got sick in July 1935—she experienced some dizziness—Marie Becker offered to take care of her."[105] The official Canadian toxicological association concluded, "She murdered a series of elderly women whom she nursed."[106]

Victimology

Becker's choices of victims varied over time. She began with two men, a husband and a lover, then moved to elderly women. In time there would be additional shifts in victimology from friends to acquaintances to customers.

She killed two men and ten women, the two males being the initial victims.[107] Elderly women were always her favorite target; Seagrave noted victimization of "elderly women."[108] "A series of elderly women" was targeted one study concluded.[109] That same study specified that the victims were nursed by Becker.[110]

Friends and acquaintances were also favored victims. Becker only turned to killing customers after her friends and acquaintances were gone.[111] Becker's victims included "a number of others among the merry widow's friends and acquaintances."[112] "After that, most of her friends died, in a short period. Becker managed however to not once being suspected," *Serial Killers A-Z* claimed.[113]

Having already murdered her friends Becker then turned to killing acquaintances. "When money ran low she poisoned her acquaintances," Ramsland recalled.[114] An Internet site analysis confirmed Ramsland.[115]

Becker befriended strangers in restaurants and wound up killing them. The *Crime Museum* reported this assertion. "Her victims were mainly elderly ladies, whom she would befriend in coffee shops and whose trust she would rapidly gain."[116]

"She began to poison her female patrons," Nash recalled.[117] "Marie turned to poisoning her female customers," one study concluded.[118] A reference work on women in history observed, "Becker began poisoning elderly women patrons of her new dressmaking shop."[119] Becker's victims "patronized the dressmaking shop that she opened."[120] *Nationmaster.com* also noted the murder of elderly female store patrons.[121] Kelleher and Kelleher described the victimage of "ten elderly female customers of her dress shop."[122]

Time Frame

The precise time frame of Becker's murders is a matter of some disagreement. The variance is not tremendous in scope, but there is disagreement on the exact period of time covered by these murders. This disagreement is, of course, not atypical.

The murders began in 1932.[123] These crimes occurred "during the 1930s," claimed one study.[124] Ramsland estimated that the Becker murders occurred from 1933 to 1936.[125] A German serial murder site noted that Becker, "Als Serienkiller aktiv: 1932–36."[126] Kelleher and Kelleher agreed in English; they noted that her active period was 1932 to 1936, when she was fifty-five to fifty-nine years old.[127] The 1932 to 1936 time frame was also advocated by Lane and Gregg.[128] Another study also confirmed the 1932 to 1936 time frame.[129]

Other estimates vary, some being more restrictive and specific and some leaning towards vagueness. Seagrave mentioned that "The period from March 1935 to September 1936 was a murderous peak for Marie, who murdered nine women over that span of time."[130] And a final estimate referred to "a murdering spree that extended over several years."[131]

COMMERCIAL MOTIVE

Becker murdered for money to obtain men. It really was that simple. In this section we will consider ten dimensions of the commercial nature of these serial slayings.

Profit Motive

"Becker's motive was money," contended the *Crime Museum UK* in a blunt appraisal of her motive.[132] Kelleher and Kelleher concurred, adding that "Becker's victims were all murdered for profit."[133] An Internet source recalled her "lavishly spending the stolen money."[134]

Lust Motive

Not all authorities accept the notion that Becker's murders were motivated by monetary interests. For instance, Hale and Bolin instead argued, "Lust was a motive for Marie Becker, who killed to obtain the money that would make her attractive to younger men."[135] The serial murder Web site *SerienKiller* indicated that the "motiv" for Becker was "lust."[136]

These sources are partly correct. Becker certainly did lust after younger men but she did not kill them. Lust murderers generally murder the object of their lust but instead Becker killed others in a cold and calculated manner to obtain money. Perhaps it would be fair to assign dual motives in this case.

She Killed to Obtain Money for Men

The crimes were committed "to obtain money for subsequent romances with a series of gigolos."[137] Becker employed a succession of male prostitutes to satisfy her sexual needs, Ramsland recalled.[138] "Her temporary lotharios" were recognized by an Internet source.[139]

An electronic reference work mentioned Becker "paying them for various sexual services."[140]

Becker enjoyed a long succession of lovers half her age, "for whose 'services' Marie Becker was obliged to pay."[141] "She paid these gigolos to accompany her to her bed and was soon out of money."[142] *Bedlam Asylum Crime Files* observed succinctly that "She paid young gigolos (boytoys) for sex."[143] More specifically, as Seagrave sagely suggested, she lured young males by feigning wealth, "It appears that Marie attracted these men by pretending to be wealthy."[144]

Insurance

"On the death of her husband, Becker received a significant insurance settlement," one study noted.[145] Another added that "She gave him a lethal dose of Digitalis, and collected on his life insurance."[146] The relatively paltry profit pocketed by Becker after her husband's death was asserted by Seagrave, "She had got some money upon her husband's death, but it wasn't a great sum."[147]

Inheritances

Becker benefited financially from inheritances. When her lover Beyer died she was not forgotten, "He apparently left her money in his will—perhaps he signed his own death warrant via this bequest because Marie's funds were getting low."[148] "Because of the two inheritances, Marie Becker became a wealthy lady," one study concluded.[149]

Legacies

Life insurance. Inheritances. Wills. Each of these financial instruments was involved in the Becker case. In addition, she "received legacies from some of these women."[150]

She Changed a Will

"The delighted Mme. Doupagne moved into Becker's home in January of 1933. She then insisted on making out her will in favor of her new devoted friend," Seagrave recalled. That was a fatal mistake, because "Just two months later, in March, Becker dispatched her houseguest with a dose of digitalin."[151] Becker obtained a considerable sum from her inheritance of Doupagne's possessions and property. "The money from this murder kept Marie flush enough to finance her lovers for over a year."[152]

She Killed to Maintain a Lifestyle

Some authorities on the Becker case specify that her financial need resulted specifically from sex-related spending. Others have generalized her situation somewhat. For instance, the Society of Toxicology of Canada asserted that Becker murdered "in order to maintain her expensive lifestyle."[153]

Poverty Necessitated Action

She had to do something. Becker was broke. She was rapidly running out of assets, one study noted.[154] Another study observed that despite her dwindling resources she chose to murder Beyer rather than marry him.[155] As her finances progressively worsened she was in an increasingly precarious position.[156]

"But her fortune quickly shrunk. She had to find some income; otherwise, her future would be as gray as her past had been," a cybersource stated.[157] "Her new lifestyle was expensive," *Bedlam Asylum Crime Files* observed, adding that "The dress shop was popular, but the income it generated couldn't keep pace with her expenses."[158] "To hold her young men, Marie was forced to spend lavishly upon them. What resources she had diminished rapidly."[159]

Incriminating Items

A final dimension of Becker's commercial serial murder deserves mention—she was incriminated by the proceeds of her crimes. This is a virtually universal axiom of profit-motivated serial murder as it has proven true time after time. The Becker case was no different in this respect.

Inspection of her apartment revealed a large collection of women's clothing, jewelry and other personal items.[160] Another study offered a strikingly similar conclusion, "When Becker's house was searched, they found closets full of clothes that belonged to the victims, and a large amount of jewelry."[161] "A search of her house revealed jewelry, clothes and personal possessions belonging to the victims," one study noted.[162]

CONCLUSION

Marie Becker was a Black Widow who branched out into killing others. She killed her husband to be with her lover and she killed her lover to be free to cavort with anyone she wanted. Then she killed a series of people to be able to afford satisfaction of her sexual needs.

Her crimes were sensational at the time, just before the initiation of the Second World War. The indictment against her was so lengthy, approximately 12,000 words, that it took the court clerk three hours to read it aloud in court.[163] The courtroom was packed with spectators throughout the trial and media interest and representation was off the scale.[164]

Becker denied not only the murder charges but also proclaimed that she was innocent of having had affairs with numerous men.[165] The jury was not persuaded by her protestations of innocence and she was convicted. She was sentenced to death but her sentence was reduced to life imprisonment. She died in prison sometime during Nazi administration of the prison in the late 1930s or early 1940s.[166] The Becker murders were a profit-oriented venture designed to supplement her legal income with extra expendable income. She murdered to facilitate the thefts and conceal them. Her callous disregard for the lives of others as she purchased erotic entertainment was exceeded only by her voracious sexual appetite.

CHAPTER 6

Boysie Singh

Boysie Singh was a gangster, a fisherman, a gambler and a killer. Most of all, perhaps, he was a pirate. Boysie Singh's biographer Bickerton suggested that Singh was "one of the most remarkable characters in the recorded history of crime."[1] That he was, with a stylish Caribbean accent.

"The criminal career of Boysie Singh, gambler, womaniser [*sic*], thief, pirate, mass murderer" was recalled by Hilton, while Bickerton stated that he was a "mass-murderer."[2] Singh was "a multiple murderer," Lane and Gregg contended.[3] Singh's commercially-motivated serial murder is the focus of this chapter.

For a decade, "from 1947 until 1956, he and his gang terrorized the waters between Trinidad and Venezuela," *TripAtlas.com* observed.[4] Singh turned to piracy after a successful career as a gangster and as a result fear spread throughout the Caribbean.[5] A recent blog noted, "He then turned to murder and piracy and from 1947 to 1956 used to terrorize the waters that were between Venezuela and Trinidad."[6]

The Port-of-Spain waterfront was terrorized by the reemergence of piracy as a maritime peril. Photographs depict virtually the entire commercial fishing fleet confined to the relative safety of the harbor, the crews too frightened to put to sea.[7] Singh terrorized Trinidad from the 1930s through the 1950s, one study concluded.[8] "He was held in awe and dread by most of the population."[9] *Time* reported in May of 1950, "For a time this month smugglers and even honest fishermen feared to venture to sea. Word had run along the waterfront that once again pirates were operating in the Gulf of Paria."[10]

Singh aroused strong reactions. During the fourth day of his first trial a small gang of disorderly schoolboys attempted to attack the car containing Singh.[11] After his execution a mob accosted the hearse carrying Singh's body to the mortuary and a horde of spectators accompanied the body to burial at a pauper's field.[12]

Why did he cause such a commotion? Perhaps it was his intrinsic Trinidad-ness. Dr. Selwyn Cudjoe claimed, "His eyes were reddish with murder."[13] "In those days, Boysie was like a falcon," Cudjoe added.[14] He concluded, "Ah tell yo' Boysie Singh was a criminal but he was a true true Trini."[15]

Singh was a complicated character and we will accordingly devote extra effort to understanding this killer from the Third World.

THE MURDERER: BOYSIE SINGH

He was a very interesting person. Singh truly was a gangster involved in numerous diverse enterprises and he had careers besides being a gangster. Seventeen dimensions of this fascinating man will be explored, and at that much about him of potential interest and importance has been deleted.

Birth

He was named John Boysie Singh.[16] He was born on April 5, 1908.[17] The location of his birth was a house at Number 17, Luis Street, in Woodbrook.[18] Woodbrook is a northwestern suburb of Port-of-Spain.[19] He was born on an inclement, thunderstorm and lightning-laden evening.[20] His mother reportedly was unable to breastfeed him herself for three days, but a local woman who was nursing assisted.[21]

Parents

His ancestry was Indian as both of his parents were full-blooded Indians.[22] Singh's father, Bhagrang Singh, ironically was himself a fugitive on the run from the law. He came from the warrior caste in India and was forced to emigrate to Trinidad because he murdered a man of higher social rank.[23] The senior Singh was from Punjab, and a tribe called Chutri.[24] Singh's father may have killed an Indian

Prince after his service in a cavalry regiment of the Indian Army.[25] Singh reportedly showed no grief at his father's death in 1926, but was said to have been depressed for some time afterwards.[26]

Little is known about his mother.[27] It was Indian custom for mothers to punish children, so as Singh grew up and became increasingly rebellious his mother resorted to punishment with greater and almost constant frequency.[28] She died in March of 1932.[29]

Childhood

Singh grew up as the youngest of four children.[30] He had a brother twenty-eight years older, and eighteen and four-year-old sisters.[31] He was the youngest in the family and was spoiled by his parents and his siblings. His father refused to correct him because it is customary in Indian families to reserve the physical punishment of children to the mother.[32] Perhaps as a result of this non-parenting Singh's attitude towards his parents was apparently one of indifference.[33]

Gang violence was the main feature of his childhood. He formed his own gang as a young man rather than join someone else's organization several sources have noted.[34] Here is an indigenous description of his childhood gang fighting, "Boysie Singh didn't go to no UN to make no appeal. He beat de shit out of dem French Creole boys who feel dey could mess with he and get away wid it. Stay and fight; doah run and moan, like a sissy!"[35] Street brawls between the gang led by a man named David Leach and Boysie's boys resulted in public distress and numerous hospitalizations.[36]

School

A stellar student Singh was not, he himself would have admitted. He was perceptive but not cognitive, although details of his education are not abundant. There was no official record of his education, Hilton noted.[37] He attended two elementary schools, Ackal and Newtown, but limited information suggests that Singh was a weak student. At one trial he claimed that he was illiterate.[38] Bickerton theorized that Singh's independent spirit caused his suboptimal academic achievement.[39]

Strength and Toughness

The School of Hard Knocks was where Singh was on the faculty. He weighed about 180 pounds and was described as "burly."[40] He carried a stick made from poui wood which he called "Three Little Trees," and which had been "mounted" by a magician to give its blows extra force.[41]

He was a good swimmer. He could seemingly swim forever so great was his endurance. He was able to hold his breath underwater for well over a minute.[42]

When Singh was fourteen he fought and beat up a man named Harris Timson who was eight or nine years older than him, because Timson was the informal leader of the local gang.[43] Singh sought to gain a reputation because to acquire an appropriate reputation was the main goal of working-class Trinidad youths at the time.[44]

Singh was bigger and stronger than the other youth, Bickerton recalled.[45] He also described Singh as possessing the strength of two normal men. And he never seemed to succumb to fatigue.[46]

Two sisters named Zena and Rosie were "communal girlfriends of the San Juan mob," his bitter rivals. One afternoon Singh visited the sisters to socialize intimately with them. Angered by this affront approximately sixteen members of the San Juan gang surrounded the sisters' house and when Singh emerged he beat up many of them and fled from the rest.[47]

Mental Health

He was feared and respected but it is unlikely that many of his contemporaries thought that Singh was crazy. To the psychiatrist Singh might have seemed to be a dangerous psychotic or sociopath.[48] He presented a textbook case of megalomania, one study asserted.[49]

Clothes

His outfits have typically been mentioned by analysts, who may have failed to appreciate the changes over time in Singh's wardrobe. The standard description of his garb reads as follows: Singh was seen "strolling grandly about Port-of-Spain in the early 1950s wearing bright, stylish clothes."[50] "A sharp looking zoot suit" was depicted as being Singh attire.[51] Most descriptions recall the colorful threads.[52]

The symbolic significance of his clothes was discovered by Singh's biographer:

> Boysie had a strong consciousness, uncommon among criminals, of the periods into which his life had divided itself. In his prison diary he

> writes of his "Yankey [*sic*] days, Fishing days, Fighting days, Prison days"—and of course his piracy days, or "Paricey" as he preferred to spell it. Each period he marked deliberately by adopting a particular type of dress—the shorts and merino of the Fishing days, the Cab Calloway outfit of the Yankee days, and so on. Now he took to wearing the pirate's colour [*sic*], black; black shirt, black trousers, blackhat, black shoes.[53]

When tried for murder in 1950 he wore a different color suit each of the first nine days, with matching shirt, tie, socks, shoes and handkerchief.[54] In his late twenties Singh wore white shorts and a white merino, a Trinidad item like a thin vest.[55] He had worn this type of garb to an earlier trial—a worn cream shirt revealing his hairy chest and a pair of stylish flannel pants.[56] One source contended that he wore "a ten galleon [*sic*] hat."[57]

Personality

An extrovert by nature Singh was quite interpersonally adept. His personality was marked by his need to win and dominate others.[58] "During relatively good times he was generous and pleasant, but he also had a violent temper and was easily incited."[59]

From his youth Singh went his own direction, explained his biographer.[60] As a result he was headstrong and aggressive. The pleasant power of his personality was cited by one study; the single most outstanding factor possessed by Singh was a very charismatic personality.[61]

Employment

He made a living from an early age. In this section we will only examine his legal jobs, and the illegal ones will be considered in the section on other crimes. As a teenager, he caught land crabs in the swamps.[62] His next job was as a boat-jostler, where he loaded and unloaded the vessels, made them seaworthy and performed light maintenance.[63]

His main occupation for much of his career was nightclub owner. Several studies noted that "During World War II he, fittingly, owned a string of nightclubs."[64] These establishments were located on Duke and Henry streets.[65] He owned and operated the Sunrise Club, the Baltimore Club and the Dorset.[66] The closure of the Sunset and Baltimore reduced his income by $2,000 per week.[67]

His other main occupation was commercial fishing. In 1947 he decided to "go straight" and forsake his gangster days for the life of a fisherman.[68] Starting with his first boat, the Perseverence, he accumulated a fleet of thirty fishing vessels.[69]

Singh's net worth was considerable at times. By 1944 he had amassed a quarter of a million dollars and thirty-three properties in Trinidad.[70] Yet later in his life he found himself "broken as a bat," without assets and "hard put to find the price of a meal."[71]

Jewelry

His self-nickname was the Vagabond King and he accessorized for the part. A contemporary account noted that he wore "numerous rings."[72] He wore a $1,500 watch chain, a chain with a gold star around his neck, and two gold rings on each finger.[73]

Wives, Lovers and Children

An Indian girl named Rosie who lived in an orphanage was his first girlfriend, in 1926. His next romantic interest was Mana Lala, the mother of his son Anthony, called "Chuncie."[74] Chuncie was born in April of 1932, and he elicited from Singh a depth and quality of feeling radically unlike his normally callous and aggressive behavior.[75]

Singh cohabitated for many years with a former prostitute named Popo.[76] He began to beat Popo because he thought that she was mistreating Chuncie, and he tried to kill her by feeding her broken glass in some roti, a pancake-like food. She survived but left soon afterwards.[77]

He met his wife Doris in 1938 and she moved in as soon as Popo left. The period between 1938 and 1941 was the happiest time of his life he claimed. Doris was the only woman he ever loved it was said.[78]

Bogeyman

Singh was used in Trinidad as a parental means of child control. "Mothers and nannies would warn their charges, 'Behave yourself, mon, or Boysie goyn getchu, oui'."[79] Numerous studies have reported this Trinidadian tradition.[80]

Bad Boysie

Why would the specter of Singh be used to scare children into obedience? There was the claim, for instance, that he cut the hearts out of young women to rub on the hooves of his racehorses for good luck.[81] In Trinidad it is said that Singh once held the world record for the number of victims murdered.[82]

"Murderous and notorious" is how Shah recalled Singh.[83] "The cold-blooded Singh" was another description of Singh.[84] He ruled the West End of Port-of-Spain through intimidation and terrorism one study asserted.[85]

Punishment

A career criminal, he received a variety of punishments over the years. He received probation in 1926 for stealing a purse and then he was sentenced to six months at hard labor for picking a man's pocket of one dollar.[86] He twice received six lashes from a tamarind wand, once for gambling and another time for kite-flying.[87] His longest incarceration was four years at hard labor in the Carrera Prison for attempted robbery.[88]

Gambling

Gambling was his passion and lifelong pursuit. He began gambling with marbles as a small boy.[89] He then graduated to dice-based games of chance called "Sebby-Lebby."[90] He supported himself at times by playing a card game, "Whappy."[91] Like all successful gamblers, he had an edge—he marked his cards, by placing barely perceptible pin pricks through them.[92]

Health

Singh was a strong and vigorous man most of his life. His Alpha Male status was facilitated by generally good health. However, since his late youth Singh suffered from chronic gonorrhea. He probably contracted the illness from Popo but he refused to seek medical treatment preferring to treat it himself with Ferrol Compound. The disease left him impotent, and he believed that the gonorreah somehow changed into syphilis.[93]

Diabetes was his other health challenge. Immediately after his first murder trial he was diagnosed with an advanced diabetic condition.[94] Throughout 1956 and 1957 Singh was hospitalized repeatedly, oftentimes in a diabetic coma.[95] He was treated in the Port-of-Spain Hospital.[96]

Religion

Although he didn't show much interest in religion throughout most of his life he claimed to have an epiphany in prison. "Boysie Singh 'died like a Saint'," Hilton observed.[97] "In his last days he accepted Jesus and became a preacher man," Cudjoe recalled.[98] Lane and Gregg also observed Singh's jailhouse spiritual conversion.[99]

Released from prison around Christmas of 1951, Singh soon began an itinerant preaching career. His spiritual tools included a Bible, a table, a white cloth, two coconut shells, a large lantern and a candle.[100] He drove an autocycle to these services until the police stopped him for failing to register the vehicle. His response was to cease his preaching, "The Police arrest me for riding my Autocycle in 1954 late and that made me go back to ordinary life."[101]

OTHER CRIMES

Boysie Singh was not an entirely innocent man before his first killing. In fact it would be fair to depict his criminal record as an unusually long and diverse collection of relatively serious offenses. His biographer concluded, "Boysie himself seemed to have committed all the crimes there were except blackmail and simony."[102] At this point fourteen types of Singh's prior crimes will be described and documented.

Theft

He stole land crabs from other boys' traps; of course, they also purloined his crabs. He furnished his nightclubs with furniture stolen from unattended homes. "Innumerable petty thefts" were reported by Bickerton.[103]

Pickpocketing

Many serial killers have earned money by picking other people's pockets. But Singh was a clumsy pickpocket and was caught. His family had to sell a cow to make good his debt and prevent further legal consequences.[104]

Kite-Flying

Kite-flying in Trinidad in the 1930s was not a child's pastime but rather a complex sociological and gang-oriented activity. Kites were equipped with devices to allow them to "capture" other kites, and such incidents frequently led to gang warfare. When he was eleven years of age in 1919 he was arrested for kite-flying.[105]

Gangster

Like Al Capone or Lucky Luciano Singh was a big-time gangster. "John Boysie Singh who was also known as 'the Rajah,' was a successful gangster and gambler," one study noted.[106] "He had a long and successful career as a gangster and gambler before turning to piracy and murder," another study concluded.[107]

Armed Robbery

Singh robbed people when he wanted what they had. Because he was who he was, he felt he could take whatever he wanted. "Boysie Singh, robber," is how Cudjoe explained Singh's penchant for robbery.[108]

Fencing Stolen Property

Singh became a fence after his robbery career developed. He in fact frequently received stolen property. He was arrested repeatedly for receiving stolen property.[109]

Arson

Singh engaged in two different types of arson, arson of vehicles and building fires. He lit his first criminal fire in 1948. Singh was "an arsonist," Cudjoe noted.[110]

Gambling

He was an habitual gambler we have already learned. One study called him a life-long and successful gambler. Singh's love for money made him turn to gambling.[111]

Smuggling

There was a logic to his smuggling career. In light of his love of the sea and his criminal inclinations smuggling was a natural next step. "He reckoned there was good money to be made by smuggling goods across the Gulf from Cedros to Venezuela."[112]

Protection

Singh tried to extort "protection" money from businesspeople and any others with apparent assets. Arson was his typical enforcement mechanism for those who felt they didn't need protection. "Boysie graduated to the protections racket, with arson as his preferred method of "persuading" his clients to pay up, setting fires to cars and, when that failed to produce the cash, to buildings."[113]

Prostitution

He controlled the Port-of-Spain brothels and procured new girls from the country. His take was $1.50 of each $5 earned by the prostitutes.[114] "She is we and we is she," was the informal motto, referring to protection of the working girls.[115]

Human Immigrant Smuggling

Singh pretended to offer safe travel into Venezuela for those seeking illegal access to that country. Instead, once he lulled his passengers into a false sense of security, they were killed and tossed overboard, their valuables remaining behind. "From piracy he moved on to people smuggling," Hilton noted, adding "Stories told of his brutality are the stuff of legend."[116]

Narcotics

Relatively little has been documented concerning Singh's narcotics trade. A house at 55 Queen Street became the center of drug shipping and sales, taking advantage of the passage of sailors from every part of the world. Marijuana from Venezuela and opium from India were frequently available.[117]

Piracy

Last but not least he was a pirate. "Boysie would smuggle bandits into Venezuela without papers, making a laughingstock of the police.

They took all the cash they could carry—these outlaws—and jewels, too .... Then, when the sea was smooth and calm again, and rum had loosened tongues and chased away the fears of the dragon's teeth, he set upon his customers with a knife," one study recalled.[118]

In classic pirate tradition Singh would stop and board his victim. They'd kill the crew, steal the engine and everything else, then scuttle the craft.[119] In one widely-reported incident Singh and crew took on a Venezuelan Coast Guard boat, murdering all eleven members of the crew.[120] "In May, 1951, everyone had ceased use of the Gulf of Paria. Pirates had once again seized control," *Socialcritic.net* noted.[121]

"There was one pirate who made his presence felt in the 20th Century, John Boysie Singh," one source suggested.[122] Singh made his initial pirate cruise in March of 1950. His prey generally was Venezuelan smugglers.[123]

THE MURDERS

The diversity of his criminal activity and the vastness of his illegal empire defy easy description and understanding. That is equally true of the homicidal dimension of Singh's crimes. Four important aspects of the murders will be discussed in this section.

Number of Victims

There is a lack of consensus on the number of murder victims racked up by Singh. According to *Piracy in the Caribbean* Singh was responsible for "many deaths."[124] An equally vague but evocative estimate was provided by Shah, "And the body count of those he made 'walk the plank' in the Gulf remains a mystery to this day."[125] "Boatloads of people were robbed and killed," according to Joseph.[126]

The official tally is less impressive. He faced murder charges in three trials and was convicted of one murder, that of Thelma Haynes. He won two acquittals.[127]

Ian Gale, former Editor of the *Barbados Advocate*, estimated that there were forty to fifty Singh homicide victims.[128] Estimates of his victimage vary but typically predict double-figure murders. He killed and threw overboard as many as a hundred travelers.[129]

He may have killed seventy people, according to some; others place the death count at four hundred, Hilton observed.[130] "The number has sometimes been put as high as 400," *Magnoy Samsara* noted.[131] In any event the victimage was substantial.

The Victims

The names of most of Singh's murder victims are unknown to us and were most likely never known to him. We do know that he was convicted for the murder of Thelma Haynes. Interestingly there is reason to doubt that he was guilty as charged.[132] David Leach, a rival gang leader, was killed by Singh, as was Philbert Bumper Peyson, a former criminal associate. Fishermen Philbert Wilson and Sonny Cook were victims as was Leonard Olivari, another former associate. The final known victims were fishermen Hilary Tait and Reynold Mayers.[133]

MO

Singh used two different MOs for his two types of commercial murder. His initial scheme involved piracy, as his boat would overtake another vessel which was then boarded and plundered, with the occupants being murdered.[134] Later, when he launched into human smuggling, his MO differed according to the circumstances, "Singh's legend includes wooing boatloads of people into seeking better lives 'down the mainland' of South America and en route, relieving them of amassed cash and other valuables at gunpoint, before drowning the passengers."[135]

He also used multiple methods of body disposal. Methods included encasing the victims' feet in cement, dumping chum into the water to attract sharks and weighing the bodies down with heavy objects.[136] The corpses needed to be slit, Singh discovered, to allow for gas to ventilate from the body as it decomposed.[137]

Time Frame

There is some variance in the estimates of the time frame of Singh's lethal activity. Several sources such as Lane and Gregg place the murders between the 1930s and the 1950s.[138] This estimate rightly recognizes and includes Leach's murder.[139]

Several others situate the murders between 1947 and 1956.[140] According to Bickerton the homicides for the most part all occurred within a few weeks in the Spring of 1950.[141]

COMMERCIAL MOTIVE

The reason Singh committed his crimes, from gambling and brothels to piracy, was to make money. It was unimportant to him if some innocent people paid the price for his enrichment. Seven topics will be examined to facilitate our grasp of the profit motivation behind these murders.

Profit Motivation

Robbery was at the heart of many of Singh's crimes Lane and Gregg observed.[142] Hilton's analysis of Singh discerned commercial motives behind much of his criminal enterprise.[143] Inherent in the notion of piracy is the act of stealing something from someone, as *WordIQ* noted, "A pirate is one who robs or plunders at sea without a commission from a recognized sovereign nation."[144]

"None of Boysie's victims resisted, but they were killed anyway; moreover there are several facts, such as the placing of irons in the launch and the macabre jests on the outward journey, which indicates that the killing of victims was a preconceived and predetermined part of his criminal pattern," Bickerton observed. He concluded that Singh seemingly took a variety of crime—"mass murder, for profit"—which had previously been used only by lone-wolf types, and adapted it for the methods of contemporary organized crime.[145]

Profit was the bottom line behind the homicides. Victims were selected for one reason only, their potential profitability. Some victims, "clients for the chute," were criminals, but it was not for that reason that they died. They were killed because they possessed cash and had other valuable property on them and they could be murdered and disposed of without a trace.[146]

Contract Murder

Singh may have served as a hit man, in modern parlance. Boland Ramkissoon, a lifeguard and associate of Singh's, asked Singh to kill his wife Dorothy for $160.[147] Ironically, Dorothy Ramkissoon asked him to kill her husband's alleged lover, Thelma Haynes, for $500.[148]

Sold Engines

"Their technique was generally to board fishing boats, murder their crew, and steal the engine which they would later sell in nearby

Venezuela after sinking the boat,'' one study recalled.[149] Singh's pirates would "board the boat, murder the crew, steal the engine for sale in Venezuela and sink the boat.''[150] *Magnoy's Samsara* also documented the theft and sale of marine outboard engines.[151]

Why the fuss over motorboat engines? The marine engines which powered these boats were in scarce supply. Potential purchasers bid heatedly against each other for one of the motors in the paltry quota allowed to Trinidad. A nine-horsepower Johnson marine engine cost $600, twice the list price.[152]

Stolen Cargo Sold

When fishermen were the victim cargo was seldom a consideration, but occasionally Singh and his mates would encounter a cargo vessel. In these situations they stole whatever valuables they could find onboard. "If the cargo were valuable (liquor, tobacco, etc) that too would be stolen and sold wherever there was a market for the goods.''[153] *Time* reported the disappearance of a cargo ship carrying $3,000 in cloth; the craft "had never been seen again'' after journeying through the Gulf of Paria in May of 1950.[154]

Piracy Profit

There is very limited information available about the loot taken in each of Singh's pirate forays. It is known that on the very first pirate venture, $17,000 was found in one ship. Singh's share of the haul, as Captain, was one-third.[155] On another occasion, the plunder of a Venezuelan cargo ship yielded about 700 Bolivares ($360), and approximately $3,000 worth of cargo.[156]

Human Smuggling Murders

To this point we have discussed the profit arising from his piracy. In addition to that, however, were his crimes against the humans he ostensibly smuggled into Venezuela. In one incident two Chinese travelers were murdered and their $3,000 in cash taken by Singh.[157] *Sepia Mutiny* explained how the cash nature of the business gave Singh an inherent advantage since he knew his clientele would be carrying their valuables upon their persons.[158] Singh's legend was based upon his victimage of the humans he was supposedly smuggling into South America, Hilton observed.[159]

Stolen Items Were Incriminating

It is usually the case in crimes like these. The coveted items originally motivating the crimes wind up as incriminating evidence. *Time* reported, "The police raided the home of Singh's wife and son, and found silk and tweeds of the same patterns as those brought by the missing Venezuelans. They also found the outboard motor and fishing equipment of one of the first boats to disappear."[160]

Possession of the stolen goods resulted in his rearrest after release from prison. "Boysie's liberty was short-lived. No sooner had he been officially released than he was arrested on a charge of receiving a stolen outboard engine." The engine had belonged to two of Singh's victims, Wilson and Cook.[161]

CONCLUSION

It is an injustice to Singh to analyze him in anything less than a book. This multifaceted, reinventive and dynamic person both reflected and shaped the cultural milieu in which he struggled. In gang terms he was an "Invader," in a gang battle against "Tokyos" and "Casablancas."[162] He proudly earned the title, "Trinidad serial killer."[163]

Singh was the Michael Jordan of Trinidad. "Boysie was well-known to everyone in Trinidad," *Sepia Mutiny* reported.[164] His notoriety was partly due to his ability to escape the law, "He had successfully beaten two charges of murder."[165]

"You know who I is?"[166] With that question Singh overcame resistance and dominated situations. He was called the local "favourite" [*sic*] because he was the baddest of the bad boys, the Alpha Male.[167]

His relationship with the police bears deeper investigation than was possible in this chapter. Singh cited an incident when he was ten or eleven and was chased by the police for a couple of days as being formative in his criminal career.[168] Yet later as a top gangster it was widely rumored that he was a police informant.[169] But that status did not save him from the hangman's noose on August 20, 1957.[170]

Boysie Singh was a fascinating and important player in Trinidad in the period before, during and after World War II. He engaged in a vast criminal career, including more than a dozen different types of crime. It was the commercial murders of Boysie Singh the Pirate that led to his undoing.

CHAPTER 7

Raymond Fernandez and Martha Beck

Raymond Fernandez and Martha Beck were known as "The Lonely Heart Killers."[1] Together, they acted as a team whose goal was to fleece lonely women out of their money and other possessions, and if necessary their lives as well. They were an unlikely combination based on appearances, as he was relatively small and slender while she topped the scales between 200 and 300 pounds. Advertisements ran in the so-called "lonely-hearts" columns of newspapers and Fernandez then seduced those responding to the ads. After bilking the women out of as many of their assets as possible the pair fled or murdered the victims of Fernandez's gigolo-like confidence game.

Their crimes exploded across newspaper headlines from coast to coast in the sweltering summer of 1949. The heat inside the courtroom at the Bronx County Courthouse was the hottest, however, as Beck shared revelation after salacious revelation about the couple's constant sexual interactions and those involving their victims. "The day-to-day revelations about this bizarre couple had New York City's press working overtime to keep up with the story that seemed too sleazy even by tabloid standards. Martha's enormous size was the subject of never-ending speculation by the press who estimated her weight to be anywhere from 200 to over 300 pounds."[2] The trial served as bawdy and sensational entertainment for post-war America.

Most serial murderers tend to stay with familiar habits and tactics and seldom change their MO. In this case, however, there was a different MO for each crime. This diversity in murder method reveals that they were relatively unplanned and spontaneous events, with more attention given to obtaining the assets of the victims. Fernandez and Beck killed for one basic reason—financial gain.

THE MURDERERS: RAYMOND FERNANDEZ AND MARTHA BECK

The Lonely Hearts Killers murdered only a few of their victims. But included among the victims were a baby and two elderly women.

Raymond Fernandez

He was an interesting person in several respects. Fernandez was a ladies' man despite baldness and questionable looks. Eleven aspects of this man will be examined.

Birth

He was named Raymond Martinez Fernandez.[3] His birth occurred on December 17, 1914.[4] His place of birth was Hawai'i.[5] He later adopted an alias, Charles Martin.[6]

Parents

Little is known of Fernandez's parents. It is believed that they were from Spain.[7] The only other salient fact is that his parents reportedly did not particularly care for him. Gado recalled that "His parents were of Spanish descent and proud people who were disappointed in Raymond's frail and sickly appearance. His father especially was not fond of Raymond and wished for a stronger son."[8] Young Raymond was a small and puny child whose father rejected and despised him.[9]

Childhood

His childhood was not a very happy one. When your parents dislike you things are not going well in the first place and we should not underestimate the effect on Raymond of his parents' disapproval. Then when he was three they moved to Bridgeport, Connecticut.[10] He may have sought an escape through letting his mind wander, as one study suggested, "He spent his childhood wrapped in daydreams."[11]

Move to Spain

"The son of Spaniards, Fernandez grew up in Bridgeport, Connecticut, and moved to Spain in 1932 to live and work on his Uncle's farm. While there, he married a local woman named Encarnacion Robles," according to The Biography Channel.[12] He married at the age of twenty.[13] Lane and Gregg asserted that Fernandez fathered four children by Encarnacion and abandoned all of them.[14]

Did Fernandez really intend to abandon his initial family? Conventional thought indicts Fernandez for this act, as Mayo did in referring to Fernandez's "abandoning his wife and family."[15] One expert contends that Fernandez intended to bring Encarnacion and the children to the States before brain damage changed him and his plans.[16]

World War II

He joined the Spanish Merchant Marine when World War II began.[17] It is not clear how he wound up in British Intelligence but Lane and Gregg claim that he served with distinction in the British Intelligence Service.[18] The Defense Security Office in Gibraltar documented his performance, calling Fernandez a brave and loyal soldier in the Allied cause who carried out difficult and dangerous missions with great success.[19]

Head Injury

Neurological damage resulting from some sort of trauma to the head is often observed in serial murderers. A 1945 accident clearly affected Fernandez; Lane and Gregg contended that it "unhinged an already none too stable personality."[20] Another study noted, "He had suffered brain damage as a result of a shipboard accident."[21]

Fernandez became a criminal following a head injury that changed his personality completely, Wilson and Seaman asserted.[22] A more detailed explanation of the injury and its aftermath was provided by Mayo, "He suffered an unfortunate accident in 1945, when on board a freighter he was smashed on the head by a falling hatch. The heavy steel creased his skull so severely that it damaged his frontal lobe and put him in the hospital for months. After he was released, Ray was a different man."[23] A rather terse damage description might be considered; Gado mentioned that "Raymond was the victim of a life altering event."[24]

A final perspective on this incident and injury was injected by The Biography Channel. "A debilitating skull fracture" was suffered by Fernandez, and after a three-month stint in the hospital he "emerged a different man. The injury to the frontal lobe had caused a personality transformation."[25] One study noted major doubts about his sanity.[26]

Personality

Fernandez certainly seemed skilled at chatting people up. He was interpersonally effective, Mayo recalled, "By all accounts, Raymond had once been a normal, personable young man."[27] "He also exhibited an engaging personality."[28] When he was in Spain he was described in positive terms, "He had a calm and gentle manner and was well-liked in the village of Orgiva."[29]

But a far different Fernandez emerged during police interrogation. He suddenly manifested a boastful mean-spirited self. In jail he proclaimed that he made his living by fleecing elderly women.[30] "I'm no average killer," he bragged to the police while spilling his guts during a confession resulting in a seventy-three page document.[31]

Appearance

Fernandez was a chick magnet, a hunk, a ladies man. But there is some disagreement about his looks. He was a handsome, strong and clean man, one study asserted.[32] In court he was described as slender, well-dressed but balding.[33]

Not everyone was impressed with his looks. One report depicted Fernandez as wearing a hairpiece and gold teeth.[34] Publications International Ltd. stated that "Though not particularly handsome, Fernandez was clean-cut and a snappy dresser."[35] Another characterization of Fernandez suggested, "He was small and slight and swarthy with unsavory sideburns, and he was half bald."[36]

Much is made of his baldness. Mayo recalled that Fernandez charmed his way into the lives of lonely women with his romantic, albeit a bit oily, charm and Latin looks, including a mound of thick black hair that seemed unreal. As a matter of fact, it was—Fernandez pulled off his seductive scam wearing a wig over his bald head.[37]

When Delphine Downing first saw Fernandez without his toupee, she was shocked.[38]

Voodoo

Fernandez converted to Haitian voodoo while imprisoned.[39] The Biography Channel provided a similar account, "One of his cellmates, a Haitian man, introduced Fernandez to the practice of voodoo and the dark world of the occult."[40] He attributed his success with women to his voodoo powers.[41]

Power over Women

He made his living as a gigolo, seducing and then robbing wealthy women. Fernandez claimed to possess irresistible power over women.[42] Another study reported that he "came to believe that he possessed powers to compel others to conform to his wishes."[43] Fernandez believed that he had supernatural influence over women, Mayo observed.[44] "He had a way with lonely women which he freely exercized."[45] Fernandez told police that he had Voodoo power over women.[46]

Employment

His principal occupation was gigolo. But Fernandez had worked on a ranch as a young man. And he also was employed as a seaman and as a dock worker.[47]

Martha Beck

She was larger than life literally and figuratively. Her role in the Lonely Hearts Killings should not be dismissed. A dozen aspects of this killer will be explored.

Birth

Martha Jule Seabrook was born in 1919 in Milton, Florida.[48] Another study suggests that the birth occurred in 1920.[49] Other studies place her birth in Florida.[50]

Family

Little is reliably known about her family. It is believed that she was raped by her brother.[51] This violation happened around her thirteenth birthday.[52] She used a sexual abuse defense at her trial without success.[53]

She was the youngest of five children.[54] Perhaps for that reason her mother overprotected her—whenever she went anywhere her mother followed her. When boys demonstrated interest in Martha her mother chased them away with threats.[55]

Childhood

Given her family issues it is not surprising to find that Martha did not have an idyllic childhood. "She had an unhappy childhood full of humiliation because of her size," recalled Odell and Gregg.[56] She was teased incessantly by mean-spirited children, "Throughout her teenage years, Martha was the victim of cruel jokes and insults which drove her further into herself."[57] One study concluded that she became a recluse and withdrew from friends and family; she had virtually no friends her own age.[58]

Weight

Her weight was a substantial concern of Beck's and a major issue for us to understand. Ramsland called her "overweight," a term also used by Everitt.[59] "A prodigiously fat person," was how *CrimeLife.com* described her.[60] She weighed as much as 280 pounds according to Odell and Gregg.[61] Mayo recalled that she tipped the scales at about 250 pounds.[62] Jones attached a value judgment to his description of her weight, "She weighed 230 gross and quivering pounds."[63]

Sadly, her obesity began quite early, by her teenage years. Beck had become "prodigiously fat" by thirteen.[64] An Internet study suggested, "By the age of ten . . . she was already obese."[65]

Her excessive pounds did not result from diet or lifestyle but from a glandular condition. "Martha Beck had overactive glands," claimed Odell and Gregg, and as a result she gained enormous weight.[66] "As a small child, Martha developed a glandular condition that caused her to physically mature faster than most children," added Gado.[67]

Sexually Precocious

Her glands were also blamed for her problematic sexuality. She developed an interest in sex much earlier than was desired, "She had been an early bloomer, sexually mature at the age of ten."[68] A lurid recollection was offered by Wilson and Seaman, "Her introduction to sex and her subsequent sexual history in her teens are too sordid to be specified even in these uninhibited times."[69] Any mother's nightmare was recounted by Gado, "By the age of 10, she possessed a woman's body and the sex drive of an adult."[70]

Nurse Training

By all accounts Beck was an excellent nursing student and an effective nurse. It is well documented that she took nurse's training.[71] In fact, she became a Registered Nurse.[72] "Oddly enough, she was a good student. She became a trained nurse," Wilson and Seaman added.[73] Beck attended nursing school in Pensacola, Florida, and graduated first in her class.[74]

Employment

She had two very different types of jobs—as an undertaker's assistant and as a nurse. Beck was an undertaker's assistant, "because of her appearance, she was unable to gain employment in the nursing field. She was forced to take a job working for a mortician in a local funeral home preparing female bodies for burial."[75] Two studies contend that she was the superintendent of a home for crippled children in Pensacola.[76] Beck was the Head Nurse of that institution another source suggested.[77]

Failed Marriages

Beck was unlucky at love. Perhaps her weight was a factor and she certainly carried some emotional baggage from her past. She had three failed marriages.[78] Her marriage to Alfred Beck left her with two children.[79]

Sex Drive and Practices

We have already learned that Beck was sexually capable and active at an early age and that she was raped by her brother. In addition it seems that she "had an appetite for bizarre sex."[80] Beck was "obsessed with sex," in the words of Wilson and Seaman.[81]

Pregnancy and Fiance Story

Beck moved to California in 1942 and began picking up soldiers on leave in local bars. She became pregnant from one such erotic encounter but the father of this child attempted suicide in lieu of assuming parental duties. So Beck invented a marriage to a navy officer to somehow legitimize the pregnancy and then sent herself a fake telegram announcing her fiance's death.[82]

As Parent

She may not have been an especially good parent. She was declared an unfit parent and had her children taken away.[83] One source claims that Beck was fired, went to visit Fernandez in New York, and when Fernandez said he didn't want the children Beck took them to the Salvation Army and left them there.[84] This abandonment occurred on January 25, 1948.[85] Another version has Beck quitting her job and leaving her children with friends in Pensacola and then taking off with Fernandez.[86]

Hated Women

It is said that Beck hated other women. *CrimeLife.com* described "a hatred of other women."[87] The same sentiment was described in *Serial Killers A-Z.*[88]

The Relationship

There is reason to believe that there was a synergy or interaction effect from the combination of the two. Fernandez may not have killed before or without Beck. In any case, her encouragement seems to have been the catalyst to murder. Their relationship will be analyzed in several main ways in this section.

How They Met

There is some disagreement about the nature of their initial contact. Some suggest that they met at a club. The pair met "at a lonely hearts club."[89] The two got together "through her club membership," another study recalled.[90] A meeting at a club was also mentioned by Wilson and Seaman.[91]

A lonely hearts correspondence club sponsored the initial Beck/Fernandezencounter, according to Everitt.[92] Some friends of hers reportedly registered Beck's name with a lonely hearts club, and "The first Martha knew of it was when she received a letter from one Raymond Fernandez."[93] The Biography Channel remarked that "In 1947,

Fernandez began yet another letter-writing courtship, this time with Martha Beck."[94] The role of newspapers "lonely hearts columns" in their initial meeting was emphasized by Lane and Gregg.[95] Martha placed an ad in "Mother Dineen's Family Club for Lonely Hearts," which was answered by Fernandez, one study asserted.[96] A cybersource also specified that he answered her ad.[97]

He was scrawny and slight and she was obese, but love (or lust) is blind, and together they made magic. "Once in bed, they discovered that they were soul-mates, and their life became a non-stop sex orgy," one study concluded.[98] Everett added, "The first date for the seemingly mismatched Fernandez and Beck was sexually charged."[99]

Partners

Beck and Fernandez were more than mere animals together—they comprised a team, a partnership. "She became his partner," one study recalled. Jones added that they even selected their victims together.[100]

Beck's Issues

Beck faced two issues in their relationship—her jealousy and his independence. "Martha's fanatical demands on Raymond's fidelity" were recalled by Lane and Gregg.[101] "Beck was overwhelmed with jealousy," another source concluded.[102] And Fernandez was hard to control, exacerbating Beck's insecurity, "A born philanderer, Fernandez proved a difficult consort to control."[103]

Beck Dominated Fernandez

She controlled him and their relationship. "Before long she was no longer just an accomplice; she was the driving force behind their criminal enterprise."[104] A cyberstudy concurred, noting "with the more dominant Beck at the controls murder was soon an added result."[105] She wielded great influence over him, according to Jones, who added that Fernandez told police that Beck was the only woman he ever feared.[106]

Beck Caused the Murders

It is frequently alleged that Fernandez killed a woman named Jane Thompson and possibly her mother as well prior to meeting Beck. Nevertheless most authorities believe that Beck was responsible for the murderous dimension of their criminal repertoire. *Serial Killers A-Z* attributed the murders to her influence.[107]

"Martha egging him on" resulted in the death of Delphine Downing one study concluded.[108] In the same case another study recalled that Fernandez was "prodded by Beck."[109] Beck's arrival ushered in "one refinement; that they should murder the women after he had seduced and robbed them."[110]

OTHER CRIMES

Serial murder is seldom the initial crime on any given criminal's rap sheet. While Beck had no prior offenses Fernandez had been involved in several types of criminal activity. Four such sets of previous criminality will be considered.

Petty Theft

Fernandez was "a petty crook," one study decided.[111] "A petty theft landed him in prison," The Biography Channel recalled.[112] Three other boys were stealing chickens with him and their fathers interceded to prevent their imprisonment, but Fernandez's father let him go to prison.[113]

Bigamy

Fernandez married in Spain at the age of twenty and that marriage was never legally ended. That made any subsequent marriages grounds for a charge of bigamy. Everitt referred to Fernandez as a bigamist and gigolo.[114]

Romantic Swindles

"He preyed on women he met through lonely hearts clubs," Mayo recalled, adding that he used his Voodoo powers and plotted to rob them of their money and other valuables before he vanished. Most of the victims were too ashamed to do anything.[115] Fernandez's purpose and pleasure in life was seducing lonely women and swindling them out of their valuables.[116] Fernandez "specialized in seducing and swindling lonely middle-aged women," Seaman and Wilson recalled.[117] "He had 'married,' fleeced and deserted gullible females in a dozen countries," one study noted.[118] After Fernandez charmed a woman he would persuade her to sign over her valuables.[119]

We can quantify Fernandez's prowess as a Latin Lover. The Biography Channel noted that "Fernandez began writing dozens of letters to women in lonely hearts clubs."[120] There were more than one hundred victims according to a pair of studies.[121] A list of 125 women was found in Fernandez's room.[122]

Forgery

We might consider a fourth and final Fernandez faux pas, forgery. When he couldn't sweet-talk his victims into signing over property he forged documents after he killed them. Jane Lucilla Thompson was Fernandez's initial victim and her property was "legally" converted, "With the victim's forged will in hand."[123]

THE MURDERS

The crimes were brutal in some respects. Certainly the victims were shown no mercy. Three topics will be explored to facilitate our comprehension of these murders.

Number of Victims

How many people did they kill? There is not as much variance in the estimates of the Beck/Fernandez victimage as is common in these cases. We will consider four sets of death count.

There were three murder victims of Beck and Fernandez according to Ramsland and Wilson and Seaman.[124] Other research reached a slightly different conclusion. One study said there were two certain deaths and seventeen possible others while another recalled three deaths and seventeen suspected murders.[125]

Could Fernandez and Beck have murdered a dozen people? Respected researchers Ramsland and Everitt both mentioned that possibility.[126] But even greater victimage totals have been discussed.

Fernandez reportedly confessed to nineteen murders.[127] Both Holmes and Holmes and an online encyclopedia described twenty as an approximate number of murders while Publications International Ltd. said there were at least twenty suspected murders.[128]

The Victims

There is disagreement over some of the victims sometimes attributed to Beck and Fernandez. It is universally recognized that the pair murdered Downing, her daughter Rainelle and a sixty-six-year-old woman named Janet Fay. Beyond this trio of consensus victims there are other possible victims.

Jane Thompson and her mother were killed by Fernandez the year before he met Beck, a pair of Internet sources suggest.[129] "The game turned deadly when a whirlwind romance and marriage to Jane Lucilla Thompson ended with Thompson dead in her Spanish hotel room of unknown causes," The Biography Channel recalled.[130] Thompson died in La Linea, Spain, in October of 1947.[131]

Fernandez probably poisoned Jane Thompson in Spain during the year prior to his meeting Martha.[132] Thompson had traveled to Spain with Fernandez and her cause of death was not determined.[133] The case has never been solved.

There may have been another victim, Myrtle Young. After Beck and Fernandez hooked up she helped him manage and rob the victims. However, "When one of them, Myrtle Young, proved troublesome, they drugged her and managed to put her on a bus back to Arkansas where she died."[134] Fernandez had married Young on August 14, 1948, but that evening Young was surprised when Beck joined her and Fernandez in bed. Young was drugged with barbiturates and put on a bus to Little Rock, Arkansas, where she died in a hospital shortly after her arrival.[135]

MO

It is frequently said that most serial killers rely upon one standard MO in the commission of their crimes. That was definitely not the case in the Fernandez/Beck murders. "Approximately 20 women who answered these ads were strangled, battered, drowned, poisoned or shot to death," Holmes and Holmes noted.[136]

Delphine Downing was strangled and her daughter drowned, according to Ramsland.[137] Fay was hit on the head with a hammer Odell and Gregg recalled.[138] Another study asserted that Fay was bludgeoned and then strangled.[139]

Beck induced Downing to ingest a fistful of sleeping pills. While she was unconscious Fernandez shot her in the head.[140] Myrtle Young was intentionally overdosed on barbiturates.[141] Once the victim was dead the body was typically buried in the cellar or basement of a house.[142] Fernandez and Beck sent letters to relatives of some victims to make it appear that their loved ones were still alive. This backfired because Fay couldn't type, a fact her family shared with the police.[143] Beck posed as Fernandez's sister, a ploy to put the victims at ease and consequently less suspicious.[144]

COMMERCIAL MOTIVE

The case of the Lonely Hearts Killers is one of the clearest and most pronounced examples of commercial serial murder. The murders would have been completely unnecessary in the absence of the larceny. The murders were entirely motivated by the desire for financial gain and the need to conceal their deeds. Four main topics will allow us to better understand these events.

Profit Motive

The murders attributed to Beck and Fernandez shared an important trait. They were all intended to facilitate and conceal the theft of their victims' personal property. "They tricked dozens of women out of their money and possessions and murdered those who protested," Odell and Gregg recalled.[145] Fernandez confessed to police that he and Beck had scammed lonely women out of their valuables for two years. But, "Once in a while difficulties had arisen in the execution of this game. That was when murder had entered into the scheme."[146] The correspondence between Fernandez and his victims revealed the profit motive, "After engaging in increasingly affectionate letters to ascertain his marks' financial worth, he would arrange to meet them."[147]

Jane Thompson's Property

"Then he produced a will that gave him claim to Thompson's apartment, which was occupied by her mother," one study recalled. It added, "He moved in with her, and then had her evicted, making the apartment exclusively his."[148] Mayo noted that Fernandez murdered Jane in Spain in a manner still undetermined. He then returned to New York where he moved into her apartment.[149] After Thompson's death, "Fernandez took possession of her apartment and all her furnishings."[150]

Janet Fay's Property

Fernandez "plundered her savings via promises of marriage."[151] He "persuaded her to withdraw her entire savings and sell her house in Albany."[152] One source estimated that her savings amounted to $4,000.[153] Another put the value of Fay's savings at about $6,000.[154] Fay wrote a check for $2,000 (payable to herself) transferred $1,500 from her Albany bank to Fernandez's New York City account and withdrew $3,400 the next day, with all proceeds being turned over to Fernandez.[155]

Delphine Downing's Property

Downing reportedly agreed to buy a new car for Fernandez and open a joint checking account.[156] But another source claimed that she became suspicious and wanted nothing further to do with Fernandez and his "sister," which is why she was murdered.[157] "For the next two days they raided Delphine's checking account," Mayo recalled.[158] They "robbed her of what money and possessions they could."[159]

CONCLUSION

What are we to make of this tale of a Voodoo man and his super-sized serial slaying sweetheart? Was he a killer before they met or just a Latin Lothario intent on romancing and then robbing his victims? Did Beck's hatred of other women cause the murders or would they have happened anyway? These are important questions if we are to understand this deadly dyad and maybe prevent similar such cases.

Fernandez was primarily a non-violent ladies' man in my opinion. I suspect that Beck's presence actually did make murder more likely. If we are to accept the versions of Downing's death where Beck seemed to spur Fernandez to kill the victim then Beck's culpability cannot be denied. There did appear to be genuine affection between the two and a sense of shared purpose. Too bad that mutual mission was murder.

CHAPTER 8

Blanche Taylor Moore

Blanche Taylor Moore's father was a "primitive," or unordained informal country backwoods preacher in North Carolina, famous for his fire and brimstone sermons. But his wife had to subsidize his womanizing by kicking in half of her pay for his amorous adventures with younger women. Reverend Kiser lost often at cards and soon Blanche was reducing her daddy's gambling debts by servicing the sexual needs of the reverend's card buddies. One afternoon after a losing card game Kiser stopped the car at the side of the road. "I'm going to pull up over there under that tree. When I do, I want you to go fuck that man," Kiser told his adolescent daughter Blanche.[1]

Blanche Taylor Moore was born and never strayed far from her Tarheel roots. She was an archetypal Southern diva, supremely self-confident in her ability to seduce or persuade anyone of anything. Moore had "set up" a Kroger store manager in a bogus sexual harassment legal action and received a settlement of a quarter of a million dollars.

Her murder case was a dramatic and traumatic one, involving child prostitution, the poisoning of loved ones, seduction and exhumation, all behind a facade of Southern graciousness and style. She positioned herself as a Southern Belle, sincerely religious and governed by traditional Southern social rules and norms. Nevertheless, Moore poisoned a husband, a boyfriend, her father and a mother-in-law, and she did it under the guise of serving as the victim's caregiver.

The case raised the ire of the locals. Public opinion on the case indicated fear and frenzy noted Jim Schutze, author of a history of the Moore crimes.[2] He described substantial media and public interest both locally and throughout the country.[3]

"There were almost-daily stories in newspapers, and on radio and television," recalled a writer for a North Carolina paper.[4] During the first days of the Moore story the *Greensboro News & Record* uncovered a potential alibi letter and the rest of the media came running. Local and regional print and television media flooded into Graham and Winston-Salem and the national television networks and the national press called.[5]

THE MURDERESS: BLANCHE TAYLOR MOORE

Moore had a frightening childhood in certain respects. However, in many ways she had a normal upbringing and young adulthood until things began to unravel. Multiple topics will be explored to better understand this cold-blooded killer.

Birth

Blanche K. Moore was her official name according to the North Carolina Department of Correction.[6] She was born February 17, 1933, in Concord, North Carolina, and named Blanche Kiser.[7] She still resided on North Carolina's Death Row as of November 20, 2008, when she was seventy-five years old.[8]

Parents

Her parents were Parker (P.D.) and Flonnie Kiser.[9] Flonnie worked full-time in the local mills in addition to being a homemaker, bringing home approximately $40 per week.[10] Flonnie turned half of her weekly salary over to P.D., who spent the money on younger women, a fact known to his wife and family.[11]

P.D. was a strict father, not allowing the children to participate in any after-school activities or spend time with friends.[12] He was a "lay preacher," who occasionally took the pulpit at local churches or outdoor tent revival meetings—in his own words, he was a "primitive preacher."[13] And Reverend Kiser was also a gambler although not typically a successful one.[14] But most of all he was an alcoholic.

"Deep seeded [*sic*] hatred of her alcoholic father" was recalled by one study.[15] Another source described him as an alcoholic self-proclaimed "primitive" minister.[16] P.D. was an alcoholic from the Great Depression.[17] Kelleher and Kelleher called him "an alcoholic and self-righteous country minister."[18] Despite occasional efforts to abstain from alcohol he always relapsed.[19] P.D. and Flonnie divorced in 1959.[20]

Childhood

Moore probably did not have the best childhood, considering that her father forced her into prostitution and refused to let her socialize after school with friends. In fact, "Her childhood was utterly destroyed by her father," Kelleher and Kelleher suggested, referring to her "childhood prison of despair."[21] She was the fifth of seven children born to P.D. and Flonnie.[22]

First Marriage

Nineteen-year-old Blanche Kiser married James Taylor, her twenty-four-year-old beau, on May 29, 1952, at the home of a Baptist minister.[23] She was largely motivated by the desire to escape her home life, "She flew her small burgh of Tarheel by grabbing the first man who asked her to marry him," Geringer claimed. Another study added, "Young Blanche was left with one overwhelming wish for the future —to leave her perverse, sermonizing father and begin a new life that was far away from his abuse."[24]

The marriage seemed successful and produced a couple of daughters, Vanessa and Cindi. "The Taylor marriage appeared to be a happy one," one study recalled.[25] But by 1959 relations between the couple were strained and they had virtually no sex life at all.[26] There were several dramatic domestic altercations and a couple occurred in public. Blanche was dragged behind the car on one occasion and another time she was loudly confronted about an affair with customers at the Kroger supermarket where she worked.[27]

Taylor became an alcoholic much to Moore's horror. Memories of her alcoholic father were still fresh in Blanche's mind.[28] Taylor spent his time after work drinking at his favorite bar most nights.[29] According to another study, "James Taylor had proven to be a hard drinker who was also addicted to gambling."[30] He drank excessively in his youth and he gambled, frequently losing everything he had.[31]

Taylor was a furniture refinisher by trade, a respected local profession.[32] In the 1960s he reformed and became a religious person, giving up his old vices. He spent most of his time with his two girls or at church.[33]

Appearance

Blanche Taylor Moore was quite beautiful as a young woman. "Her face was sculpted in the high bird-boned features of the very prettiest Appalachian women," one study recalled, describing her body as, "Long, lithe, with generous breasts and a sleek round bottom perched on slender, perfectly shaped legs."[34] She had long black hair and eyes so dark that they looked black, too.

Personality

It is difficult to accurately characterize her personality because she changed it according to her needs. As a young lady she was outgoing and friendly, very energetic, and usually interested in something fun, Schutze recalled.[35] Others encountered a different Moore, "Blanche leaned towards the moody and grim," Ashley noted.[36] Another source depicted her as feeling frustrated about her dysfunctional domestic life.[37]

Health

Moore experienced a number of serious health issues during the course of her life. Initially, she suffered from asthma as a girl, and it continued through adulthood.[38] Moore also experienced insomnia quite frequently.[39] She complained about constant diarrhea.[40]

Breast cancer was her most severe medical challenge. She underwent a bilateral mastectomy in 1987. She lost her fingernails and toenails and much of her hair due to the side-effects of radiation and chemotherapy. Her feet were so numb from treatment-induced neuropathy that she had to use a walker.[41]

Religion

Many were convinced of her religious and spiritual sincerity while others considered her faith to be a tool or prop. Moore was a sincerely religious woman, a cyberstudy claimed.[42] She pestered her lover Raymond Reid to attend church with her.[43] She told a psychiatrist, "I have been quite religious all my life, or I was. I was very active in the First Disciples until the fire. After that, I just lost my interest in religion."[44]

"Her own deep religious convictions" were all that saved Moore from being permanently scarred by her dysfunctional upbringing.[45] Moore has granted several prison interviews. In one she admitted contemplating suicide, but "that would be against the Bible."[46]

Was her faith sincere or a façade? It is somewhat difficult to reconcile a truly pious Blanche with the woman who poisoned people she was pretending to be caring for. And she was a Southerner, as Schutze recalled and signified, "If there was any definite difference in the South, it was the length everyone went to, male and female, to maintain an outward appearance of Christian propriety."[47]

Employment

She worked at Kroger's in a job that meant a great deal to the course her life would take. When she was hired as a cashier at the Kroger's in Burlington, North Carolina, it "added to her growing happiness and self-esteem."[48] And in her case it wasn't just the pride of earning a paycheck. From her initial day at Kroger's Moore was always the featured attraction.[49] She enjoyed an unprecedented climb to Head Cashier, the top position open to Kroger's women employees at that time.[50] She was one of the very few Kroger's employees allowed to use a company car at home.[51] She also sold Tupperware at home parties, which she used as a cover for extramarital liaisons.[52]

Seductiveness

Self-confidence is a good thing but Moore had a fanatical belief in her ability to seduce or charm anyone in her path. Blanche Moore believed that she could seduce anyone, Schutze commented. He added that Moore had seduced her lawyers, the judge, the Kroger investigators and the mental health professionals. Later, during the time she was killing Raymond Reid, she seduced the doctors, the nurses, virtually everyone. She fed them, listened to their stories, and persuaded them into bending the rules for her.[53]

When a new assistant manager named Raymond Reid was hired at her store Moore wasted no time in trying to seduce him. He was happily married with a couple of young boys, but she persisted and after three years he finally relented, separated from his family and they became lovers.[54] "In 1962 Blanche focused her romantic attention on twenty-seven-year-old Raymond Reid, lately arrived as Kroger's new assistant manager in Burlington, but he was married, with two young children. It took three years of determined flirtation to land Raymond in bed."[55]

Deceptiveness

Simply put, she lied constantly. She lied for no reason and gratuitously. The prosecutor in her case remarked, "She lies so much. Everyone we talk to says Blanche would lie when there was no reason to lie."[56] Another source added, "Her outward personality was a construct that she maintained with difficulty. She lied all the time about little things because she thought she had to hide everything about herself."[57]

She lied to investigators about Raymond Reid suggesting that his death was a suicide.[58] She lied to Dwight Moore's daughter Debbie, telling her that her father was depressed and also suicidal.[59] She also misled Debbie on the phone in a classic Blanche act. When Debbie called to check on her hospitalized father Blanche said not to come to the hospital as he was only having tests done, when in fact he was quite near death. When she got off the phone Blanche told Dwight Moore that it was a pity his children had said they were too busy to come see him.[60] In the hospital she claimed that when she was a little girl she had diarrhea until her intestines fell out but she reinserted them herself.[61]

Inappropriate Comments

Moore said some strange things. Most were of a sexually inappropriate nature, and others were simply cruel and calculated to hurt someone. When she cooked a large meal for a family gathering attended by a friend of her son-in-law, she told the guest, "You know what you really need? You need a really good blow job." When the embarrassed boy backed away, she quickly added, "If I went down on you, it'd probably kill you. You probably couldn't handle it."[62] One day Raymond Reid's son Steve left the hospital room with a pretty young girl, and when he returned Blanche asked, "Well, did you fuck her?" He stammered a denial, and Blanche said, "Well, why not? Growing boy your age needs some pussy once in a while. What's the last time you had some good pussy?"[63] "That's all me in there, I swear," she would tell a roomful of relative strangers as she held her breasts in her hands and squeezed them together.[64]

Some of her comments were mean. When Dwight's sister Nola was crying in the car as they left the hospital, Blanche sang in a bird-like voice, "Nellie's bawlin'."[65] At a holiday gathering of Dwight's family, Moore said, "You see what you've missed, Dwight? By getting divorced from Lorene and losing your family like you have. You should be enjoying all these moments like this, but you can't because of what you did."[66]

Second Marriage

Dwight Moore was a minister in the North Carolina Church of Christ, who met Moore towards the end of Reid's unnaturally short life.[67] They were married on April 21, 1989, after having to postpone the wedding date because of her breast cancer treatment.[68] Blanche seemed very upset with Moore when he told her about the breakup of his first marriage due to a long-term affair he conducted with a church congregation member.[69] Moore suffered through two surgeries in an attempt to save his life before arsenic poisoning was diagnosed as the culprit.[70]

Sexual Activity

Moore had a relatively strong libido and manifested a healthy sex drive. She is believed to have enjoyed a series of lovers, both one-night stands and longer lasting liaisons. After her marriage soured Blanche retaliated with romantic affairs at the supermarket, *Serial Killer Central* recalled.[71] Geringer described her social prospects. She gave a lot of men the chance to strut their stuff with her. In fact, there followed a long line of men, anyone who paid attention to her and seduced her the way she preferred to be romanced.[72] Another study concluded, "Blanche began a series of romantic affairs with a number of male supervisors at the supermarket."[73]Moore was excessively flirtatious for Burlington, Schutze noted. When a handsome new delivery man entered the store, Blanche exclaimed, "Man, I'd like to see the dick on that guy."[74]

OTHER CRIMES

Murder was not her first criminal offense by any means. Nor was it her only violation of the law. In fact she had experimented with a half-dozen or so types of crime.

Prostitution

It wasn't her choice to hear her side of the story. "Speculators say Moore killed the men in her life because . . . of her alcoholic father that forced her into prostitution to help pay the family bills."[75] *Serial Killer Central* noted that Kiser convinced Blanche to work as a prostitute to satisfy gambling debts.[76] Her father "forced her into prostitution to pay family bills," Geringer concluded, and Kelleher and Kelleher added that the reverend "regularly enlisted his daughter as a prostitute."[77]

Arson

On January 23, 1985, her home was destroyed by fire in a blaze believed to have been deliberately set. Moore told a story about a suspicious-looking man who broke into her house in search of her underwear. One month later her replacement dwelling burned to the ground netting her a second insurance payout.[78]

"A mysterious fire broke out at her Burlington home. Blanche blamed a "pervert" for the blaze, and firemen confirmed arson as the cause," Schutze noted. He continued, "Blanche collected a 'little' fire insurance, investing the cash in a new mobile home. When fire razed the trailer a month later, she blamed 'that pervert' again and collected another insurance check."[79] When Reid asked her about her finances, she replied, "I have a little bit. I got paid for the fire."[80]

Embezzlement

Mary believed that Blanche Moore was embezzling. It seems that Mary Sharpe, a co-worker of Moore's at Kroger's, believed that Moore was stealing from the store by using other cashiers' registers and through other ploys. In 1979 a bag of cash disappeared under Moore's supervision and was never located. Kroger's regional managers never figured out why that store failed to generate profit.[81]

Fraud

There were a couple of fraudulent acts in Moore's past. She "set up" a Kroger's manager named Kevin Deaton on sexual harassment charges. In reality Moore had been leading Deaton on for more than a year, and Moore orchestrated an event where Deaton was left pantsless in a darkened room. She received a judgment of about a quarter of a million dollars before expenses for her thespian performance.[82]

After Reid died in the hospital Moore took his sons to his bank. Her purpose was to clean out Reid's safe deposit box. She misled the banker into believing that Reid was still alive after he had in fact passed away to facilitate her removal of the safe deposit box contents.[83]

Obstructing a Police Investigation

Moore intentionally interfered with the investigation into the poisoning of her husband Dwight as he lay in his hospital bed. Detectives investigating the case told Dwight and a nurse assigned to watch over him that Dwight should not get his hair cut until police lab technicians could collect hair samples to test for traces of poison. Blanche managed to have her brother trim Dwight's hair over the protests of the nursing staff.[84]

THE MURDERS

Moore's murders were monstrous. She took advantage of the trust placed in her and murdered under the guise of a caregiver. This section describes the number of victims, the victims and the MO.

Number of Victims

The range of estimates of Moore's murder count is a very narrow one. There were three victims, Montaldo suggested. When she was arrested on July 18, 1989, she was charged with three murders, although only one case went to court.[85]

Another Internet source claimed that there were, in fact, four deaths.[86] There were actually five fatalities according to Kelleher and Kelleher.[87] *Unsolved Mysteries* suggested that there were either five or six dead.[88]"The possible poisoning deaths of a half-dozen other people" might have been due to Moore, investigators suspected.[89]

The Victims

Moore was convicted of Raymond Reid's murder and charged with the death of James Taylor. There was insufficient evidence for charges in the Isla Taylor and P.D. Kiser cases, although strong circumstantial evidence seemed to incriminate Moore. Dwight Moore should have died—he had ingested twenty times the lethal dose for a man his size. Only his body's unique ability to break arsenic down saved his life.[90]

Besides these victims there may have been others. At one time exhumation orders were drawn up for five people who died suddenly after crossing Moore's path. They were Joe Mitchell, Mabel Parsons, Fred Vaughn, Ina P. Vinson and John W. Reiber.[91]

MO

The MO in this case was two-faceted. There was a typical murder method and a general means of application of the murder method. The method was arsenic poisoning and the means of application involved posing as a caregiver but instead murdering the victim in front of everyone present.

The Murder Method

Reverend Moore was being poisoned with arsenic, and Reid, Taylor and Kiser all died from arsenic poisoning.[92] She was convicted "of murdering her boyfriend by slipping arsenic into his food."[93] Another source added that "Blanche Taylor Moore killed 2 husbands, one or more lovers, a pastor, her father and mother-in-law in Burlington, North Carolina, by arsenic poisoning."[94] Dwight Moore ingested enough arsenic to kill a moose yet somehow survived.[95]

Means of Application

Blanche used caregiving as a pretext for murder. She pretended to be feeding her victims but she was actually poisoning them. She placed arsenic in the food and drink she was giving her "patients." The prosecution's closing argument referred to her victims:

> Three men, all of them in love with her, all of them intimate with her, all of them dependant upon her for care, for companionship, all of them loyal to her, all of them trusting in her, all of them fed by her when they were sick, all of them sick, two dead, all of them full of the same substance, all of them fed by her each and every time they became sick, all of them her victims, all full of arsenic.[96]

Moore feigned an attempted reconciliation with her father, instead poisoning him. Blanche pretended to forgive and make up with her father, until his health deteriorated soon after she arrived, *Serial Killer Central* noted. Moore stayed at her father's side all of the time until his final moments.[97] Another study concurred, noting that Kiser fell ill almost on the day when Blanche Moore appeared on his doorstep. She "remained at her father's side to nurse him back to health." He died within a week, chock-full of arsenic.[98]

Isla Taylor, her mother-in-law, was next to die. After the elderly Taylor became bed-ridden, "Blanche did her best to make the old woman comfortable."[99] Moore acted as nurse, "Taylor, who had never particularly cared for her mother-in-law, inexplicably rushed to the woman's bedside, allegedly to make her as comfortable as possible."[100]

Raymond Reid suffered mightily at Moore's hands. "On daily visits to the hospital, she brought him gifts of food including homemade pudding and milk shakes."[101] The poisoning lasted nearly a half-year, "Over the next six months, culminating with Reid's death on October 2, 1986, Blanche Taylor made daily visits to the hospital, always bearing . . . home cooked meals."[102] Her role in Reid's death was implicitly recognized and truly terrible. Reid died of poisoning and the fatal dose or doses were administered after he entered the hospital.[103]

Her former husband James Taylor also succumbed to his caregiver. The night he died he couldn't eat dinner. So she fixed him a bowl of ice cream with her special topping. Within an hour the fatal arsenic dose rendered him in agony en route to a painful death hours later.[104]

COMMERCIAL MOTIVE

Why did Moore murder? Maybe she had hard feelings towards her victims but was that reason to kill them? I contend that these were profit-motivated crimes. Several subjects will be considered to confirm my contention of commercial murder.

Profit Motive

"She indulged a taste for easy money that would land her on death row," asserted one study.[105] When Dwight Moore's test results in the hospital resulted in Blanche's arrest, this not only saved Reverend Moore's life but undoubtedly several other wealthy males Blanche might have seduced later.[106]

"Most of the murders were committed for the profit derived from life insurance proceeds or the victim's assets," Kelleher and Kelleher claimed.[107]The prosecutor in Moore's case said that, "Blanche is mean. Blanche is pure through-and-through Grade-A mean. She killed those men because she's mean, she's greedy, she's a criminal."[108]

The Taylor Case

"Taylor left a modest estate," *Serial Killer Central* noted.[109] The commercial motive behind both the deaths of Isla Taylor and her son James was explained:

> Taylor was designed to go (after eating one of Blanche's meals), but not before his invalid mother, for whom Blanche cleaned and cooked on a daily basis. Once Taylor had safely deposited the inheritance from his deceased mother into the family bank account, he inadvertently signed his own death warrant. Like Mr. Kiser and Widow Taylor, Jim Taylor's death was diagnosed as natural.[110]

Moore profited from Taylor's death. "James Taylor's death left his grieving widow with a small inheritance, which she quickly used to move to nearby Burlington, where Raymond Reid lived," noted Kelleher and Kelleher.[111]

There was a political variable in the Moore case; who would try her? Winston-Salem was where Raymond Reid was murdered, and it had better resources than Alamance County where James Taylor was killed.[112] "The Burlington Police and the Alamance County Sheriff's Department disagreed. They wanted to see Blanche brought to justice on their turf. They argued that the James Taylor murder clearly was a capital case—premeditated and carried out in order to achieve a pecuniary gain."[113]

The Reid Case

The jury form asked, "Had Blanche Moore murdered Raymond Reid for profit?" And the answer was, "Yes."[114] Moore received "nearly $46,000," according to one study.[115] She lost a fiancée but inherited fifty thousand dollars, Geringer recalled; Kelleher and Kelleher added, "The apparently bereaved Taylor mourned her longtime lover and quietly pocketed $50,000 from his estate."[116] Moore received $30,000 from Reid's estate and another $45,797 from his life insurance, one study concluded.[117]

Reid had other assets. For instance there was his safe deposit box in a local bank. Moore went to the bank unaccompanied and "emptied out the contents of Raymond's box." *Serial Killer Central* noted "untold contents looted from his safe deposit box."[118]

There was also a small personal safe in Reid's abode.[119] Reid's son Steven once looked inside the safe and was able to gauge the contents from that experience.[120] Later, when Moore showed the boys the contents of the safe, much had been removed.[121]

As Reid lay dying in the hospital Moore claimed that he spontaneously decided to amend his will, to leave one-third of his estate to "my friend, Blanche K. Taylor." So Moore asked Intensive Care Unit nurse Karla Ann Ruth to write out the new codicil.[122] Moore assisted him in drawing up a new will.[123] Moore then denied having anything to do with the new will despite testimony from numerous nurses.[124]

Moore benefited greatly from the new will. It gave her power-of-attorney to act on Reid's behalf in legal and financial transactions even while he was still alive.[125] She was given power after his death as the will named her executrix of Reid's estate.[126]

Moore reportedly tried to scam Reid's sons out of money to which she was not entitled. Reid's sons discovered from their father's attorney that they were not legally obligated to give Moore one-third of their father's assets.[127] She told investigators that she had returned all of their money to the Reid boys.[128]

When Reid died Moore took the boys with her to one bank. Withdrawing their father's money she claimed that they were going to start a family business together.[129] Instead her daughters Vanessa and Cindi acquired a tanning salon in Burlington.[130]

The Moore Case

While Raymond Reid was still alive Blanche accepted an engagement ring from Reverend Moore, purchased at the Van Scoy Diamond Mine. The ring had a large diamond in the middle with rubies set on two sides. She made him keep it a secret due to her sexual harassment lawsuit negotiations with the Kroger company.[131]

"Her name on both his will and bank account, Blanche proved expeditious in attempting to unload herself of the cleric," Geringer noted, adding that she began poisoning him on their honeymoon.[132] Reverend Moore was worth a quarter of a million dollars.[133] She knew all about her husband's finances; Dwight Moore had told her in a lengthy conversation about his savings, retirement plan, death benefit package, individual and group life insurance policies and the remainder of his temporal estate.[134]

Yet Blanche denied any such knowledge. When questioned by detectives during the investigation, "Blanche said she knew nothing about Dwight Moore's pension fund." That was a mistake on her part, because "Detective [David] McDougall had already interviewed a United Church of Christ official whom Blanche had approached about getting Dwight's pension papers changed to make her the principal beneficiary."[135]

CONCLUSION

"Blanche Taylor Moore poisoned her lover right under the noses of doctors in the hospital. Every time Reid was revived, Blanche would be there to poison him again," one study recalled.[136] Moore believed that she was smarter than everyone else and for a while she was correct. The horrible irony of Moore administering arsenic to Reid in the hospital characterizes her crimes as especially vicious.

Was she a religious woman or was she the mean-spirited person described by her prosecutor? Police obtained exemplars of her handwriting by making her write dictated sentences. When asked if she'd like to write anything, she wrote, "This sucks."[137]

Whether she was a saint or a sinner one thing is clear. She murdered for money. She may have sought revenge on her father and it should be noted that she did not profit financially from that murder. But except for that crime all of her killings were calculated to positively affect her personal financial situation. She killed for the cash.

CHAPTER 9

Richard Ramirez

Richard Ramirez is better known as the "Night Stalker" who terrorized Los Angeles throughout the summer of 1985. His murders actually began the year before in Los Angeles and ended with the murder of Peter Pan in San Francisco. In between was an exceedingly brutal string of serial murders, involving demeaning rapes, violent physical assaults, torture, mutilation and forcing victims to "swear to Satan." Richard Ramirez graduated from burglary to serial murder through a personal criminal evolutionary process.

Heavy metal music was his chosen genre and in particular he loved one band named AC/DC.[1] Their album, *Highway to Hell*, had personal relevance to Ramirez.[2] He was upset over losing his dark blue AC/DC hat at a crime scene not because it could incriminate him but because he loved the hat so much. Ramirez was a hard-core drug addict who graduated from beer and marijuana to narcotics such as cocaine.[3] This habit cost $1,500 weekly and motivated Ramirez's burglaries.[4]

Los Angeles, and later San Francisco, was thrown into a state of panic by these crimes. Ramirez "terrorised [*sic*] the middle-class homes of suburban Los Angeles."[5] To fully appreciate the magnitude of public reaction to the Ramirez crimes, it should be remembered that there were no less than five different serial killers or teams of killers at work in Los Angeles at this time.[6] But the reaction to the Night Stalker murders far surpassed the normal public response.

"A collective terror was born the likes of which had never been seen before in Southern California," noted Philip Carlo, a Ramirez biographer.[7] The attacks continued, throwing the city of Los Angeles into a state of panic."[8] The History Channel recalled, "Ramirez's reign of terror left the people of Los Angeles in a state of constant fear."[9]

THE MURDERER: RICHARD RAMIREZ

Ramirez was a complex human being sharing much in common with the rest of us. But there was a resident evil within him and it produced senseless carnage on about a dozen occasions. Dimensions of this serial killer will be explored to accomplish a detailed understanding of Ramirez the person as well as the criminal.

Birth

Richard Leyva Munoz Ramirez was born on February 29, 1960, in El Paso, Texas.[10] Montaldo suggested that "Richard Leyva a.k.a. Richard Ramirez was born on February 28, 1960."[11] *IMDb* reported that Richard Munoz Ramirez was born on February 29, while Time-Life Books noted that Richard Ramirez was born on the 28th.[12]

Parents

Julian Tapia Ramirez and Mercedes Ramirez were his parents.[13] His father was born in Camaraga, Mexico, the son of a strict disciplinarian.[14] Julian Ramirez reportedly had a fiery temper and used frequent and perhaps excessive corporal punishment techniques on his children.[15] He was a policeman in Mexico before moving to the U.S.[16] Mercedes Ramirez was from Rocky Ford, Colorado.[17] Her family moved from Colorado to Mexico in the early days of World War II because her mother did not want her sons to be drafted.[18] Mercedes was a devout Roman Catholic.[19]

Family

"He was the youngest brother in a devout Catholic Mexican family," Vronsky asserted.[20] Ramirez was "born into a poor Mexican-descended family in El Paso."[21] In many respects the Ramirez home was a happy and loving place.

There is disagreement over the number of siblings; there were seven Ramirez children, according to Time-Life Books.[22] There were five Ramirez siblings claimed the Bruno study for *The Crime Library*.[23] Ramirez biographer Carlo concurred with Bruno.[24]

Young Richard was especially close with his sister Ruth. He was her only little brother and she lavished time and affection upon him.[25] In other respects, however, the Ramirez home was dysfunctional because of Julian's temper. Richard often slept in a nearby cemetery. He feared incurring his father's wrath and paying the price at home.[26]

When Richard moved to Los Angeles he became somewhat estranged from his family. "Between 1978 and 1984 Ramirez became almost entirely estranged from his family," one study realized.[27] At one point Julian sent Ruth to Los Angeles to bring Richard back to El Paso but he rejected her pleas and refused to return to his hometown.[28] Ramirez's brother in Los Angeles, Ruben, accused Richard of making advances towards his wife Suzanne, and his brother Robert who lived in Tucson believed that Richard had "come on" to his wife Samantha.[29]

Childhood

Richard loved music as an infant and later as a child. He would sway and move in rhythm with whatever music would be playing on a radio.[30] He would play Cowboys and Indians, acting out both parts, to the consternation of his neighbors.[31]

He loved to get up early, drink a Coke, eat sugary breakfast cereals and watch his favorite cartoons. He especially loved scary cartoons, television programs and movies.[32] He was a loner, "Friends remember him as a loner, even when he was a boy."[33] "Richard was not a gregarious child," Carlo recalled, adding that "He preferred to be alone."[34]

School

Ramirez had academic potential but never applied himself according to some of his teachers. "He was a good student who paid attention and tried to do well, work hard and get along with others," Carlo suggested, while Schechter recalled that Ramirez was an average student until he encountered academic difficulties in high school. He had good grades until seventh grade.[35]

One of his teachers at Bowie Junior High School that year was a child molester who had molested two of Ramirez's older brothers and might have abused Richard.[36] Later, at the Lincoln School, Richard was the starting quarterback until his coach learned of his epilepsy and removed him from the team which reportedly devastated and demotivated the boy.[37] He occasionally attended Jefferson High School in El Paso.[38] He didn't last past his freshman year.[39]

Satanism

His belief in Satan was apparently a deeply ingrained core value. Ramirez talked like a Satanist and acted consistently with his rhetoric. Fox and Levin observed that "After being arrested for the string of murders, Ramirez claimed Satanic inspiration."[40] Lester added that Ramirez "proclaimed his ties to Satanism and had a pentagram tattooed on his left palm."[41] Hickey agreed, adding that Ramirez "ardently proclaimed his ties to Satanism."[42] He was "a known Satanist," Ramsland alleged.[43]

"When Richard Ramirez was arrested on August 25, 1985, a bizarre story involving Satanism and cult worship began to emerge," The History Channel noted.[44] Ramirez was "a serial killer who boasted of Satanic loyalties and displayed a pentagram symbol on his hand."[45] Ramirez read *The Satanic Bible* by Anton La Vey in the summer of 1978.[46] He believed that Satan protected him during his home invasions.[47] Bruno's comprehensive study of these crimes noted, "It would be hard to pinpoint exactly what influences sent Richard Ramirez in the direction of devil worship. He often drew the five-point pentagram, the symbol of the devil, on his own body, and at his trial he would shout, 'Hail, Satan,' in open court."[48]

His terrified victims would be forced to promise Ramirez that they had turned over all of their valuables to him, and he'd make them say, "I swear to Satan." "Swear upon Satan that you won't scream for help," he told one victim.[49] After killing one woman's husband, Ramirez "forced her to swear allegiance to Satan."[50] In one case Ramirez forced a woman to declare her love for Satan.[51] Ramirez forced at least four female victims to swear to Satan.[52]

Ramirez's Satanism was manifested visually at the crime scenes. He drew pentagrams and left Satanic graffiti. "In some cases, Satanic pentagrams had been inked on their bodies."[53] Fox and Levin added, "He inscribed Satanic messages on the walls and even drew Satanic pentagrams on the bodies of some of his victims."[54]

Ramirez drew pentagrams on Mabel Bell's body and on her bedroom walls.[55] Another study concurred, adding that "Ramirez violently beat them and then scratched Satanic symbols over them, and their house."[56] According to The History Channel, "But one similarity in many of his killings was scrawling black magic symbols such as pentagrams at the crime scenes."[57] The *Serial Killer Database* noted that Ramirez "drew Satanic pentagrams in lipstick on walls and on a victim."[58]

Drugs

He had sniffed glue and smoked marijuana before the eighth grade.[59] He "was heavily into drugs by the age of 12."[60] "By the age of 18, Richard was a habitual drug user," Montaldo claimed.[61] Ramirez was a cocaine addict and habitual marijuana smoker, who had dabbled with other drugs such as LSD, mushrooms and PCP or Angel Dust.[62] Ramirez was "usually high on coke or speed," Schechter asserted.[63] "A longtime drug abuser," when Ramirez was transported to San Quentin to serve his prison sentence police found a needle and syringe in a metal canister inserted in his rectum.[64]

A comprehensive analysis of Ramirez's drug history was provided by Carlo. Ramirez began smoking steadily with his brothers and sister as a ten year old. He tried magic mushrooms, LSD, PCP and peyote. But cocaine was his main addiction.[65]

Sexuality

His sexuality changed over the course of his life. His first girlfriend was a neighbor girl named Nancy Avila who recalled him as a gentle, considerate and caring sexual partner.[66] But by 1978, "He thought more and more about sadism as a way of getting off sexually. He was no longer interested in conventional sexual relationships."[67] He frequented L.A. porno theatres.[68] He even masturbated while viewing movies.[69]

His sexual appeal continued after his arrest and incarceration. Fox and Levin asked, "Why would hundreds of women attempt to visit Los Angeles Night Stalker Richard Ramirez?"[70] The History Channel noted that Ramirez received a massive amount of fan mail from young girls and women.[71] During his trial, "Hordes of groupies flocked to the proceedings, showering him with fan letters and love notes."[72] He married Doreen Lioy on October 3, 1996, in San Quentin prison.[73]

Health

Ramirez was in relatively good health for most of his life. He suffered from tooth decay, attributed to a fast food-dominated diet heavy on sugar.[74] As a result he suffered from extreme halitosis, or bad breath.[75] His dental health was so poor that surviving victims unanimously mentioned it, "Wide spaced rotting teeth," was one such witness description, while another witness referred to his "bad teeth."[76]

Epilepsy was his greatest health-related challenge. "He also had epileptic seizures," Vronsky recalled.[77] Ramirez suffered one to two dozen petit mal attacks each month until his teenaged years when they tapered off and eventually ceased.[78]

He suffered possible neurological damage as a child from head trauma incidents. "When Richard was two he was nearly killed by a dresser that fell on top of him."[79] Later he was knocked unconscious when struck in the head by a playground swing.[80]

Mental Health

Ramirez appeared to be and acted mentally unstable. Famed attorney Melvin Belli tried to convince Ramirez to use an insanity defense but he refused and was found competent to stand trial.[81] Vronsky referred to him as "a mentally unstable drifter."[82]

Personality

Ramirez was not born a satanic serial killer he developed into one over time. In his youth he was a nice kid, "Richard is remembered as shy and sweet."[83] Vronsky observed that "Girls at his school remember Richard as being 'nice'."[84] Family, friends and schoolmates remember Richard as being a bit of a class clown and a nice person.[85]

It is difficult to reconcile that Ramirez with the adult version. He would kiss his bullets as he loaded his 22. calibre pistol before setting out to victimize someone.[86] And while in a victim's home he would steal and rape, take a meal break then resume his frightening and lethal rampage.[87]

Appearance

He was scary-looking. "His general poor appearance" was described by Montaldo.[88] He habitually dressed entirely in black.[89]

His eyes were perhaps his most noteworthy physical feature. Victim Carol Kyle stated, "The look in his eyes was absolutely demonic. Never before had I seen eyes like his on a human being."[90] Fellow Ramirez survivor Sophie Dickman mentioned "ink-black eyes filled with a hatred that seemed inhuman, it was so intense."[91] "His eyes were like an animal's," recalled Somkid Khovananth.[92]

Inspiration

Although he was a Satanist he derived inspiration from a trio of sources. Initially, he was a heavy metal music fan. Ramirez "blamed his murder spree on the Satanic lyrics in the record, *Highway to Hell*, by the heavy metal band AC/DC."[93] Ramirez "listened incessantly to the AC/DC *Highway to Hell* album."[94] He "would play AC/DC's song 'Night Prowler' on his stereo for hours on end."[95]

Jack the Ripper also inspired Ramirez. Carlo noted that "When he was a boy he had read the story of Jack the Ripper, and it both fascinated him and had a profound effect on him."[96] Ramirez reportedly wanted to eclipse the notoriety of Jack the Ripper.[97]

A final source of inspiration for Ramirez—his cousin Mike. A Vietnam war veteran, Mike showed Richard graphic photographs of rape and murder from his war days and his young cousin was thrilled. One cybersource recalled, "Ramirez was influenced by stories told by his Uncle Mike who bragged to the ten-year-old with tales of torturing and mutilating Vietnamese women and showed him grotesque Polaroid pictures of his victims. Ramirez was also present when the cousin murdered his wife in cold blood."[98] Ramirez witnessed Mike murder his wife Jessie on May 4, 1974, by shooting her in the face at point-blank range because he was tired of her nagging him.[99] After Jessie's murder Ramirez reportedly lost interest in school and devoted himself to burglaries to support his growing drug habit.[100]

Employment

"Ramirez worked as a car mechanic and did odd jobs while in Los Angeles," one study observed.[101] In high school he briefly held a job at a Holiday Inn until he tried to rape a woman guest in her room.[102]

However, throughout his life his main trade would remain burglary. He was called 'dedos,' or 'fingers,' by his friends and family.[103]

OTHER CRIMES

Serial murder was not Ramirez's first criminal offense. There were at least seven additional crimes on his police record. Ramirez was inclined towards crime.

Night Stalker Charges

Ramirez was charged with thirteen murders and an additional thirty felonies, "ranging from rape to robbery."[104] Another source referred to "50 other felonies— including rape, sodomy, oral copulation, burglary and attempted murder."[105] Ramirez faced a total of sixty-eight felony charges, including fourteen counts of homicide.[106]

Child Molesting

In February of 1985 Ramirez twice molested young girls.[107] "Children (of both sexes, some as young as six) were either sexually assaulted in their homes or abducted, to be raped or sodomized before being turned loose on the streets," Wilson and Seaman recalled.[108] Ramirez sometimes combined home invasions with child molestation.

Kidnapping

"Ramirez was a known child-abductor," according to *Serial Killers A-Z.*[109] Another study added that "in between his murders sometimes he would just abduct young girls, sexually molest them and let them go."[110] He did not kill these young victims.

Traffic Offenses

Ramirez was a traffic outlaw. He had been arrested numerous times for violations of traffic laws, Newton noted. There were several Ramirez driving violations.[111]

Drug Offenses

"His habitual pot-smoking led to several arrests for possession," Bruno noted.[112] Ramirez was a lifelong drug addict so a record of drug offenses is not a surprise. One study referred to his "criminal record including drug and gambling offenses."[113]

"Peeping Tom"

Ramirez's sister Ruth married Robert Avila. Because of the domestic disturbances at the Ramirez abode Richard would hang out at Robert and Ruth's house. But late at night Robert and Richard would sojourn out on voyeurism expeditions, looking in bedroom windows and spying on attractive women.[114]

Theft

Ramirez was arrested on a misdemeanor theft charge as a youth. He was later arrested twice for auto theft, in 1981 in Pasadena and in Los Angeles in 1984.[115] By the age of eighteen Ramirez was "already arrested on numerous drug and theft charges."[116]

Rape

His first recorded rape attempt was at the Holiday Inn where he worked in high school. *Serial Killers A-Z* suggested that "The Texas native was eventually convicted of . . . a few dozen lesser crimes, including rape and burglary."[117] Carlo described each Ramirez rape during the Night Stalker crimes.[118]

THE MURDERS

Ramirez's murders were particularly cruel and vicious. He seemed to derive enjoyment from the pain he inflicted upon others. Six main topics will allow us a glimpse into the nature of these crimes.

Number of Murders

There is a lack of consensus on the number of Ramirez murders. He was convicted of twelve murders according to *Serial Killers A-Z*.[119] He was charged with thirteen murders, Lester recalled.[120] Time-Life Books claimed that he was convicted of thirteen murders but actually committed three more.[121] Odell and Gregg also documented conviction on thirteen counts of murder.[122] Ramirez was sentenced to death for thirteen murders according to Wilson and Seaman.[123] There were thirteen murders and five more attempted murders.[124] According to *bela.black* Ramirez murdered thirteen people.[125]

There were at least fourteen Ramirez murders, Publications International Ltd. observed.[126] He was credited with fourteen homicides another study contended.[127] Ramirez was charged with fourteen murders, an Internet source stated.[128] He was credited with sixteen murders according to one source.[129] Independent analyses by Caputi and Newton confirmed a total of sixteen Ramirez murders.[130] There were sixteen Ramirez murders and possibly more noted *Serial Killer Database.*[131]

Other authorities assert even higher Ramirez murder counts. There were in fact nineteen Ramirez murder victims Vronsky asserted.[132] And Ramirez himself told investigators, "I've killed twenty people, man I love all that blood."[133]

The Victims

There were sixteen Ramirez murder victims. In order of date of death, the victims included Jennie Vincow, Dayle Okazaki, Tsia-Lian Yu, Vincent and Maxine Zazzara, William Doi, Mabel Bell, Florence Lang, Patty Higgins, Mary Cannon, Joyce Nelson, Max and Lela Kneiding, Chainarong Khovanath, Elyas Abowath and Peter Pan. In addition to the deceased, of course, were the survivors of the vicious Ramirez assaults.

MO

Ramirez's MO was singular in that there were generic elements but also wide variations in crime scene conduct. Caputi described the MO this way; Ramirez "broke into homes late at night, indiscriminately assaulting those within."[134] The MO similarity was also perceived by Wilson and Seaman, "His *modus operandi* was to break into homes late at night at random, taking whatever opportunity offered by way of sex, robbery and murder."[135] "His modus operandi was to break into his victim's house late at night through an unlocked window."[136]

But there were MO dissimilarities, too. "The absence of a discernable pattern in his modus operandi and choice of victims confused police investigators," Fox and Levin recalled.[137] The only thing the crimes had in common was the death of an innocent victim, Time-Life Books claimed.[138] Ramirez differed from most serial killers, The History Channel contended, "He was hard to categorise [*sic*] because many of his crimes were so different in nature and he varied his methods many times."[139]

One additional aspect of his MO might be mentioned. Ramirez would first kill any men present. Then he would rape and terrorize his women victims.[140]

Mutilation

On one occasion Ramirez mutilated the body of a victim, Maxine Zazzara. Perhaps it was because she nearly killed him—she pointed her husband's shotgun at Ramirez and pulled the trigger only to discover that it was unloaded. "Her eyes had been gouged out, the bloody sockets empty. The mutilation was done post-mortem."[141] A source added, "Ramirez proceeded to carve out her eyes and take them with him."[142]

Viciousness

"Maxson had been butchered so badly his head was barely attached to his body," Bruno recalled.[143] The same quasi-decapitation was noted in the initial Ramirez murder of Jennie Vincow, "Her throat was slashed so savagely she was nearly decapitated."[144] Vincow's son discovered her body and immediately noticed the nearly decapitated head.[145] Ramirez had actually planned a decapitation, "He was going to remove the heads of his next victims and leave them on the front lawn for the police to find."[146]

Decapitation was one manifestation of Ramirez's viciousness. Extreme brutality was another as Wilson and Seaman recalled, "All Ramirez' murders were marked by extreme cruelty."[147] "It was obvious the Kneidings had been brutally murdered," Carlo remarked, adding that "There were blood splatters all over the walls and ceiling."[148] The History Channel observed, "He raped, mutilated and tortured more than 25 victims in one of the most vicious sprees in US [*sic*] criminal history."[149] Whitney Bennett, who miraculously survived her attack, needed 487 stitches to piece her scalp back together in a surgical procedure requiring four feet of suture wire.[150]

COMMERCIAL MOTIVE

Ramirez was an aberrant soul, a self-proclaimed Satanist with a sweet tooth and a decided proclivity for violence. It is impossible to precisely ascertain his motives but they undoubtedly included profit. Ten main sections will explore the commercial motive.

Ramirez Was a Burglar

"By trade he was a burglar, and he was good at his chosen profession," Ramirez's biographer concluded.[151] He was taught burglary techniques by an older brother.[152] He was convicted of fourteen burglaries in the Night Stalker case.[153] At the height of his burglary career Ramirez invaded two or three homes daily.[154]

Robbery Part of MO

When Ramirez set out at night to do his thing burglary was on his mind. It was his "basic" offense, if you will. Murder began to occur during these nocturnal forays. "His sole livelihood during 1982 and 1983 came from car theft and burglaries," Time-Life Books declared.[155] Ramirez's basic MO involved burglary followed by murder.[156]

"Simple theft led him to breaking and entering," Bruno suggested. He added, "Initially he probably stole whatever valuables he could find, then quickly left before he was caught. But as he grew more proficient he also grew bolder, staying longer in the homes he burglarized."[157] His MO included "Burglary, sodomy, rape, slashing, stabbing, bludgeoning, shooting, murder," according to the *Serial Killer Database*.[158] The same source suggested that valuables were his "trophies" frequently sought by serial killers.[159]

Killing Began after Failed Burglary

Ramirez may have decided to initiate homicidal acts after being disappointed by a burglary. He might already have been thinking of murder and this incident sent him over the edge into serial murder. "He became angry after not finding anything of value to steal, and began stabbing the sleeping Vincow, eventually slitting her throat."[160]

Valuables Were Sought

Ramirez chose homes to burglarize based on their financial potential. His primary interest was in acquiring valuables to turn into cash for the purchase of drugs. Bruno noted that in one case, "He rummaged through the house, looking for valuables."[161]

Individual Cases

The best way to ascertain the commercial motive behind the Ramirez murders is to examine his behavior at the crime scenes. In the initial attack on Jennie Vincow, Ramirez "ransacked her apartment and helped himself to her valuables," meager as they were.[162] The take from the crime? A small portable radio.[163] Vincent and Maxine Zazzara were his next victims. "Shut up, bitch, and don't look at me," Ramirez told Maxine, asking "Where's the money? Where's the jewelry?"[164] His ill-gotten gains included a video camera, a VCR, jewelry, watches and a shotgun.[165]

William Doi was next to die at the hands of the Night Stalker. His terrified wife Lillian complied with Ramirez's demands for valuables. The loot included both wedding bands, an Omega Constellation watch, a Masonic ring, a jade ring and a pocketwatch.[166]

Mabel Bell and her sister Florence 'Nettie' Lang also were victimized by Ramirez. The sisters were relatively poor. All they had to surrender were some pieces of costume jewelry, a cassette tape player and a couple of watches.[167]

The next victim was Mary Cannon. She was also quite poor and Ramirez felt cheated, taking it out on Nelson's body. Ramirez "ransacked Mary's house, taking anything of value he could find," Carlo recalled.[168]

Joyce Nelson apparently defied him. Her friends and neighbors thought she was feisty enough. Ramirez stole a VCR, a radio, watches and jewelry from her home.[169]

Max and Lela Kneiding were one of the few couples killed by Ramirez, who often let the wife survive his lethal assault. Both were brutally slain. The commercial gain in this case included a camera, a VCR, watches, jewelry and a radio.[170]

Ramirez next murdered Chainarong Khavananth and brutalized his wife Somkid in his most lucrative home invasion. The take included rubies, diamonds, a diamond bracelet, valuable rings, fifteen dollars and "a fortune" in gold Kruuggerand coins.[171]

Elyas Abowath was killed after Khovananth. His wife Sakina endured Ramirez's savagery. Ramirez stole some gold bars, gold bracelets and some rings.[172]

The last Ramirez murder victim was San Francisco resident Peter Pan. Barbara Pan survived the assault and gave Ramirez the couple's valuables. They included a VCR, the couple's wedding bands, watches and Peter's cufflinks.[173]

Stolen Automobiles

There were at least three Ramirez automobile theft arrests. But he was not caught each time of course. On August 25, 1985, Ramirez fled a crime scene in a car stolen from his victims.[174] Police were able to obtain a few fingerprints from the vehicle.[175] In a sense, the theft of the orange Toyota station wagon led to Ramirez's arrest.[176]

Stolen Items Sold to Fence

He met his main fence at the Los Angeles Bus Terminal, the near vicinity of which was a criminal clearinghouse and connection system. After each theft Ramirez took the stolen goods to the fence's home.[177] Felipe Solano was his name.[178]

Stolen Items Incriminated Him

Stolen items incriminated this profit-motivated murderer. When police learned the identity of Ramirez's fence they pressured him to assist them in the investigation. As a result, "He agreed to let the detectives into his house, where they discovered a bonanza of evidence—almost everything that had been taken in the Stalker robberies."[179]

Ramirez was essentially betrayed by his fellow criminals. Vronsky referred to "several street informants who dealt in stolen goods," who helped in finding Ramirez.[180] A fence in the El Sobrante section of San Francisco also was persuaded to cooperate with the investigation.[181]

Snuff Films Considered

Ramirez himself combined profit-making and murder. In a scheme that never came to fruition he had considered making a "snuff film," recording and selling depictions of his murders. "He also had visions of filming his conquests and maybe even selling the films; he knew there was a market for such things," Carlo noted.[182]

Significant Profit

Ramirez profited financially from his slayings. Newton estimated that he made at least $30,000 in cash and jewelry from the Khovananth burglary.[183] *AllSerialKillers.com* provided an identical estimate.[184] Bruno added that this crime involved his taking $30,000 in cash and jewelry.[185]

CONCLUSION

Ramirez was a loner and a loser. He was a hopeless drug addict and he paid for his recreation by breaking into people's houses and stealing their valuables. At a point in time, however, he began to kill as well as steal.

What caused the transformation of a shy, sweet little Chicano into a ruthless, completely cold-blooded killer? Was it his witnessing of his cousin Mike's shooting his wife Jessie in the face? Did his father Julian's alleged patriarchal rampages somehow change him? Or was it his dismissal from the high school football team because of his epilepsy? Perhaps one or more of these led to his obsession with satanic lyrics and his immersion in the drug culture.

Ramirez killed for reasons which are his own. He may have felt he was serving Satan but he did not contribute his evil earnings to the Devil, instead injecting them into his arm. Ramirez was a burglar who crossed over into murder and the motive was money.

CHAPTER 10

Bettie Lou Beets

Bettie Lou Beets was born a poor girl and she struggled to attain financial security throughout her life. She had to take on a housewife's tasks when she was twelve after her mother suffered a "nervous breakdown" and then her alcoholic father began to beat her. She married early to escape her home life only to discover that her alcoholic husband would beat her, too. She wed five times and repeatedly suffered from marital discord.

Marital discord is a mild way of putting it. She divorced her second husband, Bill Lane, but continued seeing him until he broke her nose and she shot him twice in the back. She then remarried him for a month.[1] Her next husband, Richard Threlkeld, claimed that she intentionally tried to run him over.[2] Then Doyle Barker and Jimmy Don Beets, her next two husbands, vanished without a trace.

Needless to say, such goings-on attracted substantial public and media attention. When police searched Beets' property in search of Jimmy Don's body, helicopters carrying Dallas Channel Eight television reporters, members of the media from Channel Seven in Tyler and the *Tyler Morning Telegraph* covered the event, as did ground teams from the *Athens Daily Review*, the *Cedar Creek Pilot* and the *Dallas Morning News*. Newspapers statewide cancelled their planned front-page stories, replacing them with photographs and stories about police digging up bodies, and television bulletins interrupted regularly scheduled programs to convey the salacious facts.[3]

"The case generated significant media interest on both a local and national level," wrote the court in *Beets v. Collins*.[4] The *National Enquirer* ran an inch-high headline, "SELF-MADE WIDOW." During both the trial and execution, major newspapers and the national television network reporters covered the story, and streets near the courthouse were gridlocked and jammed with media vans.[5]

Police found two derringers hidden in her vehicle when she was arrested.[6] To add to her troubles she may not have received effective counsel during the trial. Popular broadcaster Greta Van Susteren noted the ineffective counsel problem, "She had a lawyer who hid this information; this knowledge that she learned after the fact two years later. The reason the lawyer didn't withdraw and let the court know that she didn't know about the money at the time of the murder is because in his contract with her he had the media rights. He wanted to make more money from it." She concluded, "This lawyer later went on to become the D.A. in the county. He then himself was arrested by the FBI for soliciting a $300,000 bribe ... He went to prison himself. He was disbarred."[7]

The European Coalition to Abolish the Death Penalty also expressed concerns. "Because she couldn't hear, she didn't know what was going on during her trial. There were no speakers, nobody told her what was happening, and her attorney has [*sic*] later been charged for co-operation with the prosecution."[8] U.S. District Judge Robert Parker criticized E. Ray Andrews, Beets' attorney, for not testifying on her behalf.[9] Andrews pled guilty to violating the Hobbs act and received a twenty-two month prison sentence.[10]

THE MURDERESS: BETTIE LOU BEETS

Birth

She was born in Roxboro, North Carolina, in tobacco country. The date was March 12, 1937.[11] She was named Bettie Lou Dunevant, although eventually her legal name was Bettie Dunevant Branson Lane Threlkeld Barker Beets.[12]

Parents

James and Louise Dunevant were her parents.[13] Beets blogged, "My mother and dad were tobacco sharecroppers and lived in a shack without windowpanes, water or electricity."[14] But her parents had their share of personal problems as well.

Her father became an alcoholic during Bettie's adolescence.[15] Worried about his wife's mental health he was depressed and frustrated and he took it out on Bettie, beating her frequently.[16] At twelve Bettie was cooking and cleaning, doing laundry and running a household.

Her mother worked as a domestic in addition to sharecropper duties.[17] She and her husband also worked in cotton mills when possible. In 1949 she suffered "a psychotic break with reality" and was hospitalized for a week. Later she spent three months at Eastern State Hospital. There she received deep insulin coma therapy on seventeen occasions as well as repeated electroshock treatment.[18]

Childhood

She had a typical Depression-era childhood marked by poverty and deprivation. We have already heard the description of her birth into poverty. She lost eighty pounds as a thirteen-year-old, due to the pressures of cooking, cleaning and caring for her siblings on top of school.[19] "I was born into a poor family in North Carolina," Beets declared.[20]

School

Beets did not perform well academically. She was asked to repeat the fourth grade which caused her tremendous embarrassment.[21] She claimed that learning became more difficult and she felt isolated from others after a series of ear infections.[22]

"She suffers from severe learning disabilities and a hearing impairment she has had since early childhood," *Business Wire* reported.[23] The European Coalition to Abolish the Death Penalty also perceived Beets' learning disability.[24] The majority decision in *Beets v. Collins* noted, "Beets presented the district court with evidence that she was raised in abject poverty, experienced a debilitating hearing loss, [and] was afflicted with learning disabilities."[25] It should be mentioned that Beets successfully earned a GED degree while incarcerated.[26] She left school after the ninth grade to become a bride.

Personality

Her personality varied over time it seems. One constant trait, however, was manipulativeness. Jamie Beets, other family members and acquaintances had repeatedly observed just how manipulative Bettie tended to be.[27] There was an apparent variable in whether or not people liked Bettie—if she somehow stood to gain from them they usually liked her, but if she had no use for them that impression was also somehow clearly conveyed.[28]

"But when my wife makes up her mind, there's no changing it," Jimmy Don declared regarding Bettie's stubbornness. He also remarked, "Whatever Betty [*sic*] wants, Betty [*sic*] gets."[29] It wasn't just her husband's perspective—she was stubborn.

One disturbing aspect of her personality emerged after the disappearance of her husband. It didn't seem to observers that she felt any grief at all, and this judgment was leveled by those accustomed to dealing with grief-stricken people. In addition she planned a memorial service two days after he vanished.[30]

Bettie's personality began changing after she started taking over-the-counter diet drugs such as Dexatrim to control her weight. Her children noticed that she became two different people. Instantaneously she morphed from their gentle mother into a woman who employed profanity and obscene language and screamed at them.[31]

Appearance

Beets was considered very attractive. She was adept at selecting outfits that accentuated her buxom figure. She had a narrow waistline emphasizing her ample cleavage and she dressed in a provocative manner.[32] Males paid her close attention, Pence added.[33] She bleached her hair blond. *The Evil Divas* employed alliterative style in referring to her as "Bleached blonde barmaid Betty [*sic*] Lou Beets."[34]

Beets gave birth to six children and her figure had changed to reflect the strain on her body. To compensate and help her lose post-partum weight she began taking Dexatrim in amounts exceeding the recommending dosage. She began gulping down the Dexatrim one study noted.[35]

Her eyes were noteworthy on several occasions. "Betty's [*sic*] blue eyes flew open, [then] turned black, at O'Brien," after the detective hit a nerve during her interrogation.[36] When she was seducing Jimmy Don she leaned over in front of him and gave him "an opportunity to look deeply into her blue eyes."[37] An acquaintance mentioned that he had once said something Beets didn't like and "her eyes turned to slits."[38]

Health

"The heat escaped through the broken windows, leaving colds and influenza as Betty's [*sic*] constant companions."[39] Little Bettie got the measles when she was five and she was quite ill with a sore throat, hacking cough and fever of 105 degrees.[40] Then, "Ear infections further complicated her convalescence, and left her with a hearing loss."[41] A federal court referred to her "debilitating hearing loss," and the European Coalition to Abolish the Death Penalty noted "hearing-empairment" [*sic*].[42]

Beets may have suffered neurological damage, a common phenomenon among serial murderers. An Appellate Court noted that she "had received head injuries as a child."[43] A neurological examination revealed signs that Betty had suffered brain damage and substantial hearing loss during her episode with the measles.[44] Beets also claimed to suffer from migraine headaches.[45]

Mental Health

When she was forced to replace her mother as homemaker at the age of twelve one consequence was depression.[46] She later tried to commit suicide by ingesting two bottles of aspirin at sixteen or seventeen years of age.[47] She was depressed often.

Beets' claims of chronic abuse led to suspicions that she had Post-Traumatic Stress Disorder (PTSD). Bree Buchanan, of the Texas Council on Family Violence, commented that "Her long history of abuse, beginning as a child and continuing throughout adulthood, it certainly sounds like she suffered from battered women's syndrome and post-traumatic stress disorder."[48] The psychiatrists who examined her to determine her competence to stand trial concluded that she likely did suffer from PTSD.[49]

"Betty [*sic*] acknowledged having visual hallucinations and hearing a choir singing when nobody was around," one study reported.[50] In January of 1991 Beets was subjected to a complete mental health evaluation including administration of the Minnesota Multiphasic Personality Inventory and Wechser Adult Intelligence Scale.[51] Beets was found fit for trial and able to assist with her defense.

She Suffered Abuse

Her father beat her we are told, but first husband Richard Branson provoked no such accusations. However, Bill York Lane was her second husband, and "Bill began slapping her around just days following the wedding."[52] He liked to hit her in the face because she was so vain about her appearance and on one occasion he hit her in the face and broke her nose.[53] In her blog Beets described her abuse in detail.[54]

"At age five years old is the first I recall of rape," Beets blogged.[55] "To be sure, her life has been difficult beginning with a rape at age five," *About.com* declared.[56] The European Coalition to Abolish the Death Penalty concluded, "Bettie was abused all her life in one way or another, ever since she was three, since her earliest memories. She was physically, mentally and emotionally abused."[57]

The defense did not mention the abuse. Beets and her lawyers insisted that she "was the victim of years of abuse and should be allowed to live," the Associated Press (A.P.) noted.[58] *WIRED* observed, "Two United Nations experts on human rights had appealed to Governor Bush in a letter Thursday to spare her from execution, saying that the domestic 'abuse and extreme violence' she suffered was not made known to the jury that sentenced her to die."[59] *Business Wire* recalled the strange fact that "During her trial, Ms. Beets' defense attorney failed to present the jury with any information about her lifetime of abuse."[60] The Texas Execution Information Center stated, "On death row, Beets' supporters claimed that she was abused as a child and by all of her husbands, and that the jury was not told about this."[61]

Not everyone accepts the abuse alibi for her actions. Here is what the court asserted in *Beets v. Collins*:

> Andrews knew Beets personally and had represented her on a number of different matters previously. At no time during their acquaintance or while Andrews represented Beets on the capitol murder charge did she give Andrews any hint that she had been abused by previous husbands or boyfriends. Neither Beets nor any members of her family ever conveyed to Andrews any information giving him reason to believe that she had a history of being physically abused.[62]

Employment

She married at fifteen and was pregnant within a year. That left little time for an education or skills development. When she and Branson broke up, "I worked jobs waiting in tables and in a bar and along with these other jobs where you pay your own taxes, the so-called pat on the back jobs for respect. With being hearing impaired, I learned to work in degrading places I didn't like, learned to smile and keep going to make a living," she declared.[63] "I worked two or three jobs because one didn't pay enough to raise my children," she concluded.[64]

Most of her jobs were as cocktail waitress or barmaid. After a visit to a strip club in Dallas she decided that she could be a topless dancer, only to be arrested by a Dallas Police Department vice cop.[65] She told psychiatrists interviewing her that she was ashamed of the type of jobs she had held.[66]

Marriages and Family

Beets was a mother of six with nine grandchildren and six great-grandchildren.[67] "I married at fifteen years old to a man I loved dearly," Beets claimed.[68] She married Robert Franklin Branson on July 18, 1952, a month after she finished her first year of high school.[69] She had six children with Branson: Faye, Connie, Shirley, Phyllis, Robert and then Bobby.[70] After Branson, she was married to Lane, Threlkeld, Barker and Beets.

Numerous misconceptions surround her family life. For instance, one source noted this about her husbands, "Out of the five, four disappeared without a trace."[71] She had seven husbands another source reported incorrectly.[72]

The dissolution of her marriage to Branson threw their lives into chaos. She kept an eight-by-ten-inch photograph of him in her living room and repeatedly told the children that she still loved their Daddy. Bettie's dirty dancing with patrons at the Silver Slipper Saloon had alienated Branson who then found comfort in the arms of a younger woman. After that, the Branson children recalled, there was no more celebration of Christmas, Easter or other holidays, and the family split up. Faye married at fifteen, Connie moved out with her, and Phyllis and Robby were sent to live with their father.[73]

Beets' relationships were volatile and unstable. She and Lane continued to see each other after their marriage until he broke her nose. She shot him twice in the back, then he refused to testify against her, after which they remarried for one month.[74] Two of her children (Robby and Shirley) testified against her, and the other four supported her.[75]

Alcohol

"Her drug and alcohol abuse was her attempt to self-medicate and reduce the intrusive thoughts and feelings of traumatic events," her examining psychiatrist concluded.[76] Here is how Beets explained the initiation of her drinking, "After a while I started to drink and I had never drank before. At first I would go out to hide this from the kids," Beets contended. She added, "I would drink myself to sleep. I did this a lot. Even though I knew it would not change anything, it did take me away for awhile."[77] The European Coalition to Abolish the Death Penalty recalled, "She turned to alcoholism and went from one abusive relationship to another."[78]

Poverty

We have already learned about her poverty-stricken childhood. "Abject poverty" was the term used by a court in describing her family's gloomy financial prospects.[79] They lived in a pine cabin with no windows, electricity or running water. Meat, milk and fresh vegetables were rare.[80]

Her divorce from Branson revived childhood memories of poverty. After her divorce her perceived sense of vulnerability skyrocketed and she worried for hours about how she would pay the bills.[81] He never paid more than fifty dollars a month in child support despite a court order to provide $250.[82] "Sometimes he went a whole year without paying that," Bettie claimed.[83]

Good Bettie

Four of her children stuck by their mother, saying nothing but good things about her. Sheriff Charlie Fields, who ran the Henderson County lock-up, said, "She's a cute lady."[84] The manager of the Cedar Club (her employer) commented that "She was great. Brought in a good crowd, and everybody loved her. She knew everybody in town and everybody knew her."[85] "She was super-nice," declared Jackie Barker, brother of Wayne Barker.[86] Her mother testified that Bettie was a loving child who never caused trouble.[87]

Bad Bettie

On the other hand Beets involved two of her children in murders. She told Shirley in advance of her plans to kill Barker and Shirley helped dispose of the body. She told Robby that she was going to kill Beets and her son helped with that body. Then she blamed them in court for the murders.[88]

She was contradictory, former spouse Threlkeld recalled. One moment she was saying that her children took advantage of her and that she wanted relief from them—followed by a longing to visit them.[89]Her mood alterations were obvious; her son Bobby told a friend, "One moment we got along fine, and the next thing she's a different person. It was like she got hateful all of a sudden, and I mean all of a sudden."[90]

There was a darker side. Angry at Threlkeld she slashed all of his tires; on another occasion, she went after him with a car jack.[91] She took to cussing, and "now would say, 'fuck'!"[92] Beets bought several large Doberman Pinschers to keep Jamie Beets away from his father's cabin.[93] Her neighbors expressed relief at her arrest because she and her children frightened them with nighttime shooting, loud parties and reckless behavior at all times of the day and night.[94]

OTHER CRIMES

Murder was not her initial criminal offense. Prior to her serial murder career she had broken other laws. Five other types of previous criminality will be discussed.

Public Lewdness

Bettie decided that at the age of forty-two she could be a successful topless dancer. She told this to the manager of the Charley's Angels Bar in Dallas who informed her that she had to audition.[95] She auditioned on August 27, 1979, as "Sexy Tiger," but there was a mishap when a "pastie" (part of her clothing) fell off and she let a man named Archie Phillips help her replace it.[96] She paid a $250 fine and was sentenced to thirty days in jail and a year's probation.[97]

Attempted Murder

"Beets also admitted under cross-examination that she had been convicted of another misdemeanor offense that resulted when she shot her former husband, Bill Lane, in the side of the stomach," claimed a media advisory issued by the State of Texas.[98] *CNN.com* noted, "She had also been convicted of shooting and wounding her second husband."[99] *About.com* suggested, "In 1972, she shot her second husband in the back of the head (he survived), and was allowed to plead guilty to misdemeanor assault."[100] Bettie convinced Lane to claim that the shooting was his fault and they remarried for a month after her trial, then separated again.

Arson

Bettie experimented with arson as have many other serial murderers. The court held in *Beets v. State* that after Beets was unable to sell a house, "The house mysteriously burned."[101] A different court concluded a year after Jimmy Don Beets' death, "A trailer home that was Jimmy Don's separate property before his death was destroyed by fire," but the insurance company refused to pay on the claim because of the suspicious nature of the blaze.[102]

Jimmy Don's lake house burned in 1982 and responding firemen found that the water had been shut off. That same house caught fire two years later and a neighbor named J.R. Burton saw Bettie in that building shortly before the fire broke out. Again, Southern Casualty Insurance company declined to compensate Beets for her loss.[103] A fire at Beets' mobile home shortly before her arrest was also considered suspicious.[104]

Forgery

When Beets tried to insure Jimmy Don's life with an additional policy she forged his name on the application form.[105] A year after Jimmy Don vanished she forged his name on a power-of-attorney form as well as on sales documents as she sold his boat.[106] George Chaney, a former Documents Examiner with the Secret Service, testified in court that Bettie was a forger.[107] Bettie admitted in court that she forged the signatures, claiming that Jimmy Don wanted her to do that.[108]

Vehicular Homicide

Perhaps she had anger management issues. She shot and killed two husbands, and shot and almost murdered a third. Prior to that she almost ran over and killed her third husband Threlkeld.[109]

THE MURDERS

The murders committed by Bettie Beets were rather ordinary in certain respects. There was no mutilation, sexual activity or other crime scene carnage. We will consider four aspects of these crimes.

Number of Victims

Unlike most of the cases in this book there is no doubt about the number of Beets' murder victims. She was executed for the murder of Beets and was the only suspect in Barker's death.[110] The only suspicion of additional murders was voiced by *The Evil Divas*, who claimed four of Bettie's husbands had disappeared.[111]

The Victims

There were two murder victims, Beets and Barker. But there were also two survivors, one shot in the back (Lane) and the other almost run over by a car (Threlkeld).

MO

The basic Beets MO was simple. She shot her husbands at close range while they slept then hid their bodies in a wishing well or under a storage shed.[112] According to the lobbying organization *ProDeathPenalty.com*, Bettie Beets shot and killed Beets and Barker and buried their bodies in her yard.[113] Details of the MO in the Beets and Barker murder cases differed only slightly one court concluded.[114] Another court found, "Beets allegedly disposed of her fourth husband, Doyle Wayne Barker, in a similar fashion."[115] Although Beets' body was found in the well and Barker's buried under a shed several sources reported that both men were buried in the wishing well.[116]

Two more aspects of the MO might be mentioned as they characterized both crimes. Each man was shot "execution-style" according to authorities.[117] And both men were wrapped inside sleeping bags.[118]

Time Frame

We might conceive of two sets of time frames and maybe a third overlapping and all-encompassing one. Both murders took place in the 1980s, Barker in 1981 and Beets in 1983. The two attempted murders both took place in the 1970s; the Lane shooting was in 1972, and the Threlkeld incident in 1979.

COMMERCIAL MOTIVE

Bettie Beets killed her husband Jimmy Don for the money. However, previous husband and murder victim Barker had no insurance or pension that we know about. Nevertheless, thirteen factors lead to the conclusion that Beets was motivated by profit.

Profit Motive

"Although Beets insisted she was innocent, a jury convicted her of killing Jimmy Don Beets, a Dallas Fire Department Captain, to collect his life insurance and pension," the A.P. reported.[119] A *Pittsburgh Post-Gazette* story suggested that Bettie was "convicted of shooting and killing her fifth husband to collect insurance and pension benefits."[120] She "collected $100,000 in insurance and pension benefits," the Texas Execution Information Center recalled.[121]

An Internet source observed that Beets "Shot her fifth husband for his $100,000 insurance policy and dumped the body down a wishing well."[122] *The Evil Divas* noted, "The insurance payout which she claimed almost as soon as he disappeared also helped her to come to terms with her loss."[123] One study claimed that Beets was killed in his home near Gun Barrel City, Texas, in "a scheme to collect over $100,000 in life insurance benefits and a $1200 per month pension."[124]

The prosecution hammered at the murder-for-money message during the trial. "Prosecutors claimed that she killed him for a $100,000 life insurance policy," claimed *About.com*[125] "She did in fact shoot him for remuneration: his insurance policies, his estate, and his retirement benefits," prosecutor Bill Bandy contended during his closing argument.[126]

Convicted of Remuneration Offense

Beets was charged with murder for money, "Beets was indicted for the capital offense of the murder of Jimmy Don Beets for remuneration and the promise of remuneration," asserted a media advisory from the Attorney General of Texas.[127] The court held in *Beets v. Collins*, "Beets was convicted of murder for remuneration and the promise of remuneration on the theory that she killed her husband in order to obtain his insurance and pension benefits."[128] Justice of the Peace O.D. Baggett read Beets the indictment against her, which claims that she "unlawfully, intentionally and knowingly caused the death of an individual, Jimmy Don Beets, by shooting him with a firearm for remuneration and the promise of remuneration, to wit: an insurance policy from employment with the City of Dallas by the same Jimmy Don Beets in which the said defendant is the beneficiary."[129] *Beets v. State* noted that Beets was motivated by "money from the proceeds of retirement benefits . . . insurance policies . . . and the estate of Jimmy Don Beets."[130]

At her bail hearing the prosecutor successfully invoked the remuneration aspect of the case to convince the judge to deny Beets bail.[131] *ABCNews.com* referred to "the jury that sentenced her to die in 1985 for killing Jimmy Don Beets for insurance money."[132]

Her trial included evidence that Beets was motivated by money. "Various other witnesses testified at trial concerning Beets' attempts to collect life insurance and pension benefits after Jimmy Don's death," a Texas state government source noted.[133] Her son Robby testified that she told him in advance that she was going to kill Beets because "For one thing, he's got a bunch of insurance."[134]

Barker Death Profit

Did Bettie benefit financially from Barker's murder? Some sources deny that she did; in *Beets v. State*, the court noted, "There is also no evidence whatsoever in the record that might reflect or indicate that appellant financially benefited from Barker's death." Bettie did show up to receive Barker's last paycheck.[135]

Jimmy Don Beets' Net Worth

Jimmy Don was worth a bundle. During her trial prosecutors alleged that Bettie knew about $86,000 in life insurance, a second insurance policy for $24,000, $15,000 in back pay and $792 in monthly retirement benefits.[136] *Beets v. Collins* noted "approximately $110,000 in insurance, and $1,200 each month from [Jimmy Don's] pension benefits."[137] He left "$153,000 in insurance and the pension."[138] Finally, Jimmy Don also had an insurance policy worth $23,428 with Republic National Life Group Insurance Company.[139]

Bettie Did Not Know

"On appeal, Beets claimed that she did not even know of the insurance policy on Jimmy Don Beets until a year and a half after she killed him, when her lawyer told her," the Texas Execution Information Center recalled.[140] *CNN* correspondent Van Susteren commented, "She was indicted for murder for money. That's what made her eligible for the death penalty. But what is so alarming to lawyers is that it wasn't until two years after she committed this murder that she learned there was money, that there was a pension. She didn't know it at the time she committed the murder."[141] Bettie testified, "I didn't know a thing about any insurance until his family told me I was the beneficiary."[142]

A Federal District Court overruled Beets' murder conviction on May 9, 1991, "because, the court found, Beets's defense counsel at trial was a material witness who should have resigned to testify rather than represent her." And another attorney, Bruce Roberts, also perceived that Bettie was ignorant of any death benefits, "Bruce Roberts's testimony was intended to bolster that position. He indicated that Beets seemed interested in no other insurance claims than that pertaining to the damaged trailer."[143]

Bettie Knew

Bettie knew. Denny Burris, a City of Dallas Fire Department Chaplain, "met with Beets several times during the first few weeks after Jimmy Don was reported missing . . . Burris testified that Beets made inquiry of him whether she was covered by any insurance policies . . . as well as inquiring whether she would be entitled to receive any pension benefits."[144] That was the judgment rendered by the court in *Beets v. State*. Burris' testimony was clear and directly contradicted Beets' previous trial testimony.[145]

Burris initially visited Beets to console and assist her but she was too busy entertaining friends to see him. On his second attempt to see her, "Almost immediately she asked, 'If they don't find Jimmy Don, what kind of benefits will I be eligible for'?"[146] Her demeanor was devoid of grief or sadness and completely out of character, the chaplain recalled.

Bettie Did Not Care about the Money

"What were you going to do with the money?" Bettie was asked on re-cross examination by the prosecution. She replied, "I didn't expect it to be approved," to which Bandy asked, "Then why bother?" Beets answered, "Because I didn't have Jimmy Don."[147] Bettie's attorney from the fire insurance cases (Bruce Roberts) testified that Bettie was not interested in any other insurance possibilities. Andrews claimed that Beets displayed no apparent interest in life insurance or pensions she might be due.[148]

Bettie Applied for the Money

Whether she cared about the money or not she went to the trouble of applying for it. Jerry Hast, Benefits Supervisor with Personnel for the City of Dallas, "testified concerning an application for benefits that had been filed by an attorney for appellant." The Pension Board voted to finalize the Beets payment on June 10, 1985, they awarded Bettie $125,852 in a lump sum plus a payment of $790.42 monthly.[149]

Extra Beets Insurance Policy

Bettie tried to insure Jimmy Don with an additional policy, unbeknownst to him, by forging his signature. The only reason that this policy came to light, since "it had been filled out without Beets' knowledge," was that a niece of Jimmy Don's named Jackie Collins worked at the JC Penney Life Insurance Company office where the insurance was sought.[150] The address given for account correspondence was not Beets' address but the home of one of Bettie's daughters. Jimmy Don canceled the policy on May 19, 1983. The cancellation followed Collins' trip to her uncle's fire station.[151]

Beets Boat Sold

Jimmy Don loved his outboard motorboat but Bettie didn't need it after he vanished. A media advisory issued by the Office of the Attorney General of the State of Texas noted "her successful sale of Jimmy Don's boat almost a year after his death."[152] The sale occurred on July 24, 1984, with Bettie forging Jimmy Don's signature.[153] Beets faked a power-of-attorney form and advertised the boat in the *Cedar*

Creek Pilot for $3,250. The nineteen-foot long Glastron boat sold to Martha and Michael Miller.[154]

Administrator of Beets' Estate

Beets took the trouble to be declared Administrator of Estate over Jimmy Don's possessions. This involved securing a Determination of Death and obtaining a Death Certificate, which happened in February of 1985. Jimmy Don Beets was declared legally dead as of August 6, 1983. Beets was then named Administrator of Estate. Beets now legally had "full power over all of Jimmy Don's possessions." Bettie denied under oath knowing anything about being the estate administrator.[155]

Last Beets' Paycheck

It is clear that Bettie was interested in collecting Jimmy Don's insurance and pension money. We also know that she collected Barker's last paycheck. It should not be surprising therefore to learn that she also picked up Jimmy Don's last paycheck.[156]

Bettie Fought Jamie Beets over Money

Jamie was an heir to Jimmy Don and therefore a potential source of conflict with Bettie. Jimmy Don's disappearance led to strained relations between Bettie and Jamie, especially over Jimmy Don's Royal Oaks home. When Jamie stopped by he found all of his possessions piled in the backyard and the locks had been changed. Jamie was forced to take out an order for protective custody of his father's possessions.[157]

CONCLUSION

The murders of Bettie Beets were a simple matter of greed. Perhaps that is why the jury only deliberated for barely six hours to convict her of murder. The agonizing decision to sentence her to death required only forty-five minutes.[158]

Bettie Beets killed for money. She nearly killed two of her husbands who escaped with their lives but two others were not so fortunate. They perished because Beets thought she could benefit financially from their deaths. In the end she made nothing from her arson insurance and money for murder schemes.

CHAPTER 11

Ray and Faye Copeland

"I'm a tramp, not a bum," clarified Jack McCormick, the main witness against Ray and Faye Copeland as the elderly couple stood accused of murder.[1] She was sixty-eight and he was seventy-five when they were arrested and they were the oldest couple ever sentenced to death.[2] This case is considered to be an anomaly in that these geriatric serial killers were qualified for Social Security, worked as a team and killed for profit, none of which fits the typical profile of a serial murderer.

"The Copelands, who were in their late 60s, tilled the soil and raised cattle on their farm," recalled serial murder experts Ronald and Stephen Holmes.[3] The Copelands purchased a forty-acre plot of land for $6,000, near Mooresville, Missouri, in 1967.[4] Their dwelling was "a small run-down home" and there was a small pond on the property. They made a $500 down payment and paid $40 monthly.[5]

This case struck a nerve with the public and stakeholders all over the world. Amnesty International got involved, citing Article 4(5) of the American Convention on Human Rights. It declares, "Capital punishment shall not be imposed upon persons who, at the time the crime was committed, were . . . over seventy years of age."[6]

It also became enmeshed in politics. The death penalty debate was raging at the time and both proponents and opponents of the death penalty tried to adopt it for their purposes. Stranger still the Copeland trial became a matter of state politics in Missouri as state officials jostled to derive tactical advantage from the prosecution of the couple.[7]

The Copeland's children were harassed after the arrest of their parents. Wayne Copeland repeatedly received calls where the caller played the country song, "Diggin' Up Bones." The Copeland grandchildren were teased and taunted at school about their grandparents' notoriety and the families of Wayne and Al Copeland were ostracized.[8]

Local public interest was extreme and potentially violent. When police searched the Copeland farm intense local public and media interest was generated, recalled Tom Miller, author of a specialized study of the Copeland case. In fact, a pseudo-lynching attitude developed in the generally quiet farming community.[9]

Why would normal American farmers in Missouri in 1990 string up a seventy-five-year-old man, and possibly his wife as well?

THE MURDERERS: RAY AND FAYE COPELAND

To better understand the Copeland crimes, we will examine Ray Copeland, Faye Copeland, and their relationship. The clarity of his culpability and the ambiguity of her criminal status will become apparent.

Ray Copeland

History has not been kind to Ray Copeland. Most authorities portray him as a most unsavory character. That impression may well be fostered through eleven topics.

Birth

His birth name was Raymond Copeland.[10] He was born in Oklahoma in 1914 just as World War I was breaking out in Europe.[11] His Oklahoma birth in 1914 was confirmed by Miller.[12]

Family

His parents were Jess and Laney Copeland.[13] He was raised near Harrison, Arkansas, in the Ozark Mountains.[14] The Copelands moved frequently and eventually wound up in Ozark Hill, Arkansas.[15]

School

Ray Copeland was not destined to be a scholar. He had very little interest in and ability at school and dropped out during the fourth grade.[16] The cessation of Ray's education may have been a family necessity. During the Great Depression survival required that everyone contribute to the family's workload. Copeland dropped out during the fourth grade to work on the family farm.[17]

Personality

"Ray was an unpleasant man, despised by all of his neighbors for his poor demeanor and abusive treatment of his wife and children," recalled one Internet source.[18] We know little about Copeland's early life, his childhood and adolescence, but friends and acquaintances of the family recalled him in negative ways. He was stubborn, unfriendly, mean-spirited, dishonest and often insubordinate.[19] He was described as "gruff and crude" by Miller.[20] "Hardnosed and spoiled," Copeland was not generally perceived positively.[21] He also hated bankers.[22]

Appearance

He looked like many others of his age and background. As a young man he was a "Tall, strapping young hillbilly."[23] It has been noted that he seldom smiled.[24] As he aged he acquired a stooped or slightly bent-over posture and a "deeply lined face."[25] He habitually dressed in bib overalls.[26]

He Was Disliked

Ray Copeland was not a particularly popular person. Many of the Copeland's neighbors loathed him. He was a stingy, mean old man and several thought that he beat his wife and children.[27] No one was surprised by Ray's crimes. His brother John, like several others who remembered Ray Copeland, expressed no shock or surprise whatsoever at the revelation of Copeland's murders.[28]

Dishonesty

Copeland was a con man and schemer who was cunning enough to create schemes capable of earning a little money.[29] Ray Copeland's prevarication potential was explained by his older brother John.

"He could look you right in the eye and lie to you, even then," he reminisced.[30]

He Abused His Family

Copeland apparently abused his wife and children. The neighbors didn't care much for him for that reason.[31] "There was little doubt that Faye had indeed been a battered wife," Montaldo asserted.[32] A study by *The Crime Library* found that the Copeland's neighbors disliked Ray because of his treatment of his family.[33] Ray wouldn't let his sons Wayne and Al wear their "school shoes" while doing their chores. As a result they had to stand in "cow patties" to warm their feet when they milked the cattle during the winter.[34]

Health

Ray had his share of health issues especially towards the end of his life. Diabetes was his most severe health problem.[35] He also suffered from chronic back pain.[36] He had some minor hearing loss, not uncommon in someone his age.[37] Dr. James Merikangas diagnosed him with shrinkage of the brain, probably as a result of several small strokes.[38] Ray also developed high blood pressure and borderline hypertension.[39]

Prison

"During the course of their marriage, Ray was continuously in and out of prison for livestock theft and passing bad checks," one study asserted.[40] He died on Death Row awaiting execution.[41] His death in prison occurred in 1993.[42] Earlier in his criminal career he was forced to move back in with his parents after his release from prison.[43]

Employment

Copeland was a farmer. However he sometimes hired himself out as a day laborer. Copeland took part-time jobs, such as painting farm buildings, filling in and capping abandoned wells, clearing fence rows and burning solid organic waste.[44]

Faye Copeland

She is one of the enigmas of this case. Was she an active accomplice to serial murder, an unwilling assistant or completely innocent?

Those questions are included among the following nine topics intended to enlighten us about Faye Copeland.

Birth

She was born as Faye Della Wilson.[45] Her birthday was August 4, 1921 and she was born in Red Star, Arkansas.[46] She was born into a dirt-floor home in the crossroads community of Red Star.[47]

Childhood

Her parents were Rufus and Gladys Wilson.[48] Lohr described her early life; Faye Copeland's parents had no money but they raised seven children in their dirt-floored cabin.[49] Economic necessity curtailed her education—Faye Copeland's education lasted until the eighth grade when she dropped out so she could earn money for family expenses. By her tenth birthday she was employed out of the house, working for others doing domestic chores like laundry, housecleaning and baby-sitting.[50]

Personality

"She was just as mean as he was," declared Bonnie Thompson, a neighbor of the Copelands. She added, "She would take the Lord's name with every other word ... she could be one mean sister, that's for sure."[51]During her trial, Faye was "usually crying or mumbling to herself."[52] While she was incarcerated, she continued to protest her innocence while helping crippled and ill inmates with their personal needs.[53]

Appearance

When Faye met Ray she was a fair-haired, "pretty, shy hill girl."[54] Like Ray she seldom smiled.[55] One thing she splurged on throughout her life was getting her hair permed.[56] In court she appeared nervous and distraught.[57]

Employment

Faye was known as a hard worker. She was seldom known to smile but she was remembered as an exceptionally hard working employee who never caused the company any problems.[58] Soon after the Copelands purchased their farm Faye took a job at Midwest Quality

Gloves Corporation.[59] This was considered a "piece work job;" she also worked on the assembly line from 1966 through 1977, and from 1978 to 1988.[60]

She also worked at a motel in Chillicothe, Missouri. She began cleaning rooms for her employer, Neeta Patel, and quickly moved behind the front desk at the Holiday Motel.[61] She also performed a variety of other tasks for Patel, including baby-sitting.[62]

Health

There is little publicly known about her health ailments. Until her stroke in 2002, that is, which resulted in her early release from prison.[63] To justify the release and satisfy the bureaucrats and critics a medical pardon was granted.[64]

Battered Woman Syndrome

Ray was abusive towards Fay and his children, we already have learned. It should therefore not be surprising to learn that Faye suffered from Battered Woman Syndrome.The Public Interest Litigation Clinic declared in 2000:

> Mrs. Copeland's convictions and sentence were secured through repeated violations of her constitutional rights. The only evidence that her attorney attempted to present on her behalf to prove her innocence was the testimony of a psychologist that Mrs. Copeland suffers from Battered Woman Syndrome, supported only by testimony that her husband was verbally abusive. The court refused to permit trial counsel to present that testimony to the jury, in violation of the due process clause of the Fourteenth Amendment .... Police reports established that neighbors saw Ray Copeland beat Faye with a board, and other neighbors, friends, relatives and co-workers saw episodes of abuse or the injuries that Faye suffered as a result.[65]

"She argued to the end that she was a battered woman and did not willingly participate in Ray's schemes," one source recalled.[66] The *Los Angeles Times* reported, "Faye Copeland's defense during trial was that her husband had committed the crimes without her knowledge, and that she had been a bystander, a victim of battered woman syndrome."[67] We next turn our attention to the question of her role in the murders.

She Was Innocent of the Murders

When initially questioned by the police she was "nearly hysterical."[68] She told investigators, "I never done nuthin [*sic*]."[69] David Miller, the Livingstone County Public Defender, doubted before the trial that a jury would convict Faye Copeland let alone render the death sentence.[70]

"At first, Faye Copeland tried to plea that she didn't know anything about the murders," one source noted.[71] Holmes and Holmes recalled, "Mrs. Copeland has always denied any involvement in the case, stating simply that Ray was her husband, she loved him dearly, and she had nothing to do with the murders."[72] Faye "did not willingly participate in Ray's schemes," an Internet source observed.[73]

Some studies have concluded that Faye was not involved in the murders. For instance, the Public Interest Litigation Clinic contended, "There is little dispute that the murders were committed by her husband, Ray Copeland, and there is no competent evidence placing Mrs. Copeland anywhere near the scene of any homicide at or near the time they occurred."[74] A more guarded defense of Faye Copeland was offered by an Internet source, "It is still unknown whether or not Faye was an accomplice in the heinous murders committed by her husband. It is possible that she aided him and it is also possible that she was innocent and the evidence against her was circumstantial."[75] "It's very likely Faye never actually killed any workers," concluded *Serial Killers A-Z.*[76]

She Was Involved in the Murders

"Many officers later felt convinced that Faye Copeland had a direct role in the killings," Miller recalled. The reasons? Ray would have needed an accomplice at times, such as when he shot, wrapped and buried the victims. In addition, one victim was shot inside the Copeland house in the room next to the Copeland's bedroom. And finally, informant Jack McCormick stated that she was involved in the murders.[77]

Two facts seemed to implicate Faye Copeland in the murders, at least as an accomplice. Initially, there was the victim's list. One source noted that "The Copelands kept records, a log of all drifters that were hired. Once the Copelands killed a hired hand, they would place an "x" next to the victim's name in their log."[78] The United States Court of Appeals for the Eighth Circuit concluded, "Perhaps the strongest evidence was a list of names in the petitioner's handwriting that had x's marked next to victim names."[79]

"Also in the farm ledger book, there was a list of men who had worked on the farm. Each of the men who were killed had an x next to his name in Faye's handwriting," a cyberstudy concluded.[80] The *New York Times* reported that "a handwritten list" was found in the Copeland home, including the "employees hired by the Copelands since 1986."[81] According to *Serial Killers A-Z*, "They also came up with a crude register of the couple's past workers on the farm. Some had an "X" marked through their names."[82]

A quilt was the other incriminating item pointing towards Faye Copeland's complicity in murder. By definition a quilt is comprised of numerous pieces of cloth stitched together. In this case, "victims' clothes were used to make a quilt."[83]

"Faye made a large quilt out of the victim's clothing," one study noted.[84] Although she denied any knowledge of or involvement in the murders, "The quilt she had been working on with their clothing was telling evidence."[85] An Internet source referred to "a quilt that she had made from pieces of clothing from the victims."[86] Lohr recalled that Faye Copeland made a quilt composed of the clothing of their victims.[87]

Their Relationship

To the best of my knowledge neither killed without the other. What was it that led them to murder? Several aspects of their relationship will be examined.

Courtship

They met in 1940.[88]Ray went to his doctor for an examination and he met the nineteen-year-old Faye.[89] Miller mentioned that the two met in the Spring of 1940 as they both sat in a physician's waiting room.[90] Ray reportedly convinced Faye that he was wealthy.[91] They were married within six months.[92]

Marriage

They were married in the Fall of 1940 by a judge in Harrison County, Arkansas.[93] Their marriage was not the best as Faye explained:

I couldn't have flowers at home, he didn't like me to be tending to anything other than him. As long as I was with him or working the cattle or the tractor was OK. But flowers, no, he didn't like them.

I was raised to love my husband and support him no matter what. The man is the head of the family. The Bible says it should be that way. It wouldn't do to say if Ray was mean to me or not. Yes, he did mess up my life, but that's not to say that I wasn't a good wife to him. I was never mean to him. Maybe we'd have got along better if I had knocked the shit out of him a few times.

I've often thought since, maybe this was for the best. Where did I go wrong, if I went wrong? I know one place was getting married at all.[94]

Faye loved Ray. In a jailhouse interview with Michael McCann of the *St. Joseph News-Press/Gazzette*, she declared, "I'll always love him, but not as much now."[95]

It is unlikely that he loved her. In all the time she was awaiting trial he never once asked about her. And when told that she had been convicted and sentenced to death, he replied, "Well, those things happen to some, y'know?"[96]

Family

They had five children, four boys and a girl: Everitt, Billy Ray, Betty Lou, Alvia and William.[97] In terms of an extended family tree they had five children, seventeen grandchildren and twenty-five great-grandchildren.[98] In light of the unpleasant nature of the family homestead the Copeland kids all left home at the first chance.[99]

During her protracted legal battles and incarceration Faye Copeland enjoyed the support of and frequent contact with her family.[100] Ray did not similarly benefit from family comfort, however. He was seldom contacted by any members of his family.[101]

Transience

Ray and Faye moved the family quite a bit. They moved from Arkansas to California then back to Arkansas. They then left for Missouri before heading to Illinois where they resided before moving back to Missouri.[102] The Copeland children recall moving frequently and usually suddenly without any advance notice or preparation. The children now believe the moves were to evade the police.[103]

Poverty

The Copeland family was frequently impoverished, Miller asserted.[104] Times were particularly difficult when Ray was in prison. In the mid-1980s the Copelands owed $25,000 on farm loans and were in danger of having to declare bankruptcy.[105] Perhaps this financial desperation led to their serial slaying solution.

Who Was In Charge?

It seems fairly certain that Ray was in charge. Faye cited Scripture as the reason why he was head of the house.[106] A psychologist from Kansas City insisted that "She was controlled by him for decades."[107] According to the Copeland children's recollection, Faye Copeland did not dare cross her husband and never did.[108]

But Faye did try to exert influence when she felt it necessary. After his arrest in 1971 she bailed him out of jail in Ozark County then told him, "If you ever get in any trouble of any sort, I will not help you. I will not even be around for you, because I don't believe in getting in trouble."[109] In prison, she admitted that "I begged him time and time again to please stay out of trouble. We had our home and everything paid for. We were on Social Security. So why would he turn around and mess all that up just like he has?"[110] However, it should be noted that Faye was the brighter bulb. Faye Copeland clearly was the more intelligent of the two and the only literate one of the couple.[111]

Isolation

It may seem strange to some but the Copelands lived an isolated existence despite the presence of neighbors not far away. They kept to themselves and as a result not much was known about them.[112] They had no close friends and never visited anyone.[113] They did not attend church.[114] They avoided community social events and ceremonies.[115]

They deliberately kept to themselves. But they had Brenda Thompson to contend with. Their neighbor used binoculars to keep tabs on her murderous neighbors.[116]

OTHER CRIMES

Ray Copeland was not an innocent man before the murders began. In fact he had spent as much time in prison as he had in freedom at one point due to his continual criminality. Over the course of the next few years Copeland committed petty thefts, Lohr recalled.[117] Three main types of other crimes will be explored.

Livestock Theft

Ray stole pigs, cows and horses. He first stole two hogs from his father's farm and sold them in nearby Eureka Springs, Arkansas.[118] Copeland's criminal career and illegal activity centered on a modern version of cattle rustling.[119]

He stole horses, too. The family had to leave California because of Ray's reputation as a horse thief.[120] Older Copeland family members believe that Ray fled from California the last time he was there because he was caught stealing horses from his employer. He either dodged arrest or was offered a deal to leave the state.[121]

Forgery

He forged false signatures on blank checks or faked other people's signatures. He forged signatures on WPA checks including those of his brother John.[122] "Ray had already gotten into trouble with the law several times for cattle theft and forgery," one study concluded.[123] Another study contended that Copeland was arrested in 1936 in Harrison, Arkansas, on forged government check charges.[124]

Bad Checks

He didn't just forge signatures on other people's checks. He passed a lot of bad paper of his own, slang for writing bad checks. Beginning in 1953 the Copelands moved frequently from town to town for about eight years and Ray Copeland was arrested for writing bad checks on three or more occasions.[125] Ray Copeland was sent to a state prison farm for the three bad checks plus a forged government check.[126]

THE MURDERS

The crimes of Ray and Faye Copeland are somewhat difficult to believe. Two great-grandparents do not ordinarily murder according to the serial murder profile. Three main topics will be discussed to afford us a better grasp on these serial murders.

Number of Victims

How many people did the Copelands kill? Unfortunately there is some variance in authoritative estimates of the Copeland body count. The smallest estimate was by McCormick who told police he had seen four bodies on the Copeland farm.[127]

Most sources found five murders; that was the conclusion of studies by Egger, *The Crime Library*, and the *Los Angeles Times*.[128] There were at least five murders and possibly more according to both *Serial Killers A-Z* and the *Serial Killer Database*.[129] And there were five victims as of November 25, 1989, the *New York Times* noted.[130]

At this point the estimates escalate in victimage numbers while diminishing somewhat in specificity. The *New York Times* reported that "The police fear that as many as two dozen men were killed," because of "a handwritten list with 24 names of employees hired by the Copelands."[131] Livingston County Sheriff's Deputy Gary Calvert listed the names of people who could no longer be found.[132]

"To this day many investigators believe Ray was responsible for other murders, which have yet to be discovered."[133] Law enforcement officials strongly suspect that Copeland began killing transient workers in the 1970s but hid the bodies so they would never be discovered.[134] Gary Calvert identified three others last seen working for the Copelands—Thomas Park, Franklin Hudson and Dale Break.[135]

The Victims

There were officially five Copeland victims. They included Dennis Murphy, Paul Jason Cowart, John W. Freeman, Jimmie Dale Harvey and Wayne Warner. However, we just learned of another three likely Copeland victims: Park, Hudson and Break.

The next victim would have been Jimmy Page. The fifty-year-old disabled man had just been recruited by Copeland, who offered him $50 for driving a truck for a day, then suggested the cattle scam.[136] Page had obtained a post office box and set up his bank account, so all that remained was a cattle auction and he would have been killed.

MO

The basic MO of the lethal cattle swindle involved four basic steps. Initially, a transient or homeless person would be recruited and promised a soft, lucrative job. Step two was for the transient to obtain a post office box and checking account. The third part of the plan saw the transient purchase cattle at livestock auctions using his checks. Finally, Copeland killed the transient claiming he had stuck him with bad checks, too.

"Their modus operandi was to hire unskilled drifters as farm hands, involve them in an [*sic*] scheme to obtain loans for non-existent cows, and then kill them," asserted *Nationmaster.com* in a partly inaccurate report.[137] A more accurate version of the overall process was provided at Faye Copeland's trial by Kenny Hulshof, one of the prosecuting attorneys in the case who described the recruitment of transients, the establishment of checking accounts, obtaining post office boxes, attendance at cattle auctions and passing of bad checks culminating in murder.[138]

Shooting was the murder method and a .22 calibre rifle of Copeland's was identified by ballistics evidence as the murder weapon.[139] The place where the bodies were disposed of has been somewhat controversial, however. Some sources claim that the corpses were buried on the Copeland farm.[140] Others correctly reported that Copeland used surrounding farms to hide the bodies.[141]

Victimology is the final element of the MO worthy of our attention. In this case the victims were carefully selected for certain reasons, including their isolation from family or friends, poverty and willingness to work on a farm. The Copelands hired drifters and killed them one study asserted.[142] "Transient farm workers" were the Copeland's prey according to studies by the *Serial Killer Database* and Egger.[143] An Internet encyclopedia referred to the victims as "unskilled drifters."[144] The U.S. Court of Appeals characterized the victims as "homeless," as did Miller.[145]

COMMERCIAL MOTIVE

The Copeland murders were simple crimes. Ray was tired of imprisonment for cattle theft and bad checks so he found others willing to commit these acts, then killed them. Eight aspects of these commercially-motivated serial murders will be examined.

Profit Motive

"This case is really about greed, the hunger for money," a prosecuting attorney told the jury deliberating Faye Copeland's fate.[146]

During Ray Copeland's trial, a prosecutor remarked, "The grim reality of this case is that we have a hired killer in our midst. He might wear a pair of work boots and bib overalls, but he has a wallet where his heart should be and he's a killer for cash."[147]

The Criminal Complaint against the Copelands alleged that the murders were committed "with the purpose of promoting and facilitating the offense of stealing."[148]

The "Notice of Intent to Seek the Death Penalty" declared:

> The State intends to rely on the following aggravating circumstances as to each count herein.
>
> 1. The offender committed the offense of murder in the first degree for himself or another, for the purpose of receiving money or any other thing of monetary value from the victim of the murder or another; and
> 2. The murdered individual was a witness or potential witness in a past or pending investigation or past or pending prosecution, and was killed as a result of his status as a witness or potential witness.[149]

Lethal Check Fraud

In the most simple terms the Copeland crimes were check frauds concealed by murder. The *Los Angeles Times* reported, "Authorities contended that Ray and Faye Copeland had used transients in a late-1980s scheme to buy cattle with bad checks, then killed five men and buried them in shallow graves."[150] Another study noted that "The senior citizen duo had developed a fraudulent check scheme using drifters to illegally purchase livestock and resell it, making the drifters disappear after the scheme was complete."[151] The U.S. Court of Appeals decided that "The petitioner and her husband, Ray Copeland, were involved in a fraudulent check and cattle-buying scheme that ultimately led to the shootings of five homeless men."[152]

Version #1

Ray tinkered with his cattle fraud schemes, perfecting them over time. In the first version of the crime:

> He began showing up at cattle auctions with hitchhikers and drifters. The two men would sit on opposite sides of each other during the sales and Ray would signal whenever he wanted a particular group of livestock. When it came time to complete the purchase, Ray would have the man write out a check from Ray's book and sign his name to it.

> The check would eventually bounce, but by then Ray would have already sold the cattle.[153]

When confronted by the police Copeland professed ignorance, noting that the checks bore someone's else's signature. He was able "to pull it off dozens of times. Ray used several different drifters and all of them would disappear after the sales."[154] Hitchhikers disappeared from Chillicothe after a couple of rounds of check-writing ventures.[155]

Version #2

A drifter named Gerald Perkins worked with Copeland on his second check fraud system. In this method, Copeland would have checks made up with other people's names on them, which the drifters would then use to purchase cattle.[156] Some of these bogus names included Ray Moore, Roy Rollins, Stanley Rostron and William Hull.[157]

Version #3

This was the refined and developed final version of the scam. Copeland would find a drifter and a post office box and checking account would be opened in his name. He would attend farm auctions and sales, bid on and purchase cattle and then vanish.[158]

Individual Cases

Copeland profited in the amount of slightly more than $6,000 from Wayne Warner's cattle purchases.[159] Similarly, the scheme as implemented by Dale Harvey netted $1,200.[160] $1,400 was obtained by John Freeman's illegal cattle purchases.[161]

Overall Commercial Significance

It is difficult to offer an overall estimate of Copeland's proceeds from his fraudulent cattle schemes. Prosecuting attorney Doug Roberts told the jury, "$32,000. That's what they were killed for." Authorities think that Copeland made from $30,000 to $32,000 over three years. A pipe containing $1,800 was found buried on Copeland's farm.[162] And a dozen drifters had opened post office boxes and checking accounts.[163]

Deaths Concealed the Frauds

The murders resulted from Copeland's need to distance himself from the bad check writers. If he did not sign the bad checks and if the signer could not be found the investigation would be at a dead end. *Serial Killer Database* asserted that the Copelands "murdered some of their transient farm workers to keep them from telling about their cattle fraud schemes."[164] Miller recalled that a dozen or more workers had attended auctions with Copeland, purchased cows and then disappeared.[165]

CONCLUSION

Ray Copeland was tired of being arrested and sentenced to prison terms for cattle swindles, forgery and bad checks. He sought a way to continue with his larcenous activity but without the risk of being caught. He arrived at his criminal system where his proxies would make the bids, purchase the cattle and write out checks on their own accounts but give Copeland the proceeds. He killed them in return for their assistance.

These serial murders were entirely commercial in nature. There was no sex-depraved killer, no psychotic torturer, nothing of the sort. Just two geriatric farmers trying to make as much money as easily as possible. Even at the cost of human life.

CHAPTER 12

Dana Sue Gray

"I felt this overwhelming need to shop."[1] With these words Dana Sue Gray confessed the motive behind her crimes. She killed elderly ladies for credit cards. Crime scene investigators proclaimed that these murders were among the most brutal they had ever observed.[2] Riverside County (California) Sheriff's Department Detective Chris Antoniadas asserted that Gray's vicious assault on Dora Beebe ranked among the worst of the one hundred homicides he had investigated.[3] Judge Patrick Magers declared during Gray's sentencing, "It's hard to find words to describe the atrocity in this case. The crimes were horrendous, callous and despicable."[4]

Gray stood five-foot-two and weighed less than 150 pounds. Despite her relatively small size she did "great violence to the victim," during her acts of "extreme violence."[5] One victim was nearly decapitated.[6]

This case did not attract substantial national news coverage; it was not widely publicized locally and it failed to warrant mention in the nearby Los Angeles news market, a 2008 study noted.[7] There was significant local media interest according to Gray's biographer Kathy Braidhill, "In Dana's case, each new murder and attack was well publicized, and with the publicity came a steady increase in public fear."[8]

The public outcry over the murder of one victim caused fear among his constituents, Riverside County Sheriff Cois Byrd observed.[9] The

Canyon Lake City Council convened a Special Meeting to address public concerns and provide important public safety information.[10] Canyon Lake residents, the elderly in particular, were worried that a serial murderer was wandering around their neighborhood seeking a way to enter their homes and kill them.[11] Local residents were "frightened and angry," Braidhill claimed, and others "bordered on hysteria."[12] "One group of card-playing women" created a geriatric dorm room in one's condo, hoping for safety in numbers.[13]

This analysis of Gray's crimes is intended to advance our understanding of the commercial nature of these murders.

THE MURDERESS: DANA SUE GRAY

Birth

We know surprisingly little about her birth. She told the police that she was born in Pasadena, California. Her birthday was December 6, 1957.[14]

Parents

Her parents were Russell and Beverly Armbrust.[15] Gray had a good relationship with her father Russell Armbrust, who worked as a hairstylist and had been married four times.[16] Yet later in her life when Russell was married to his fourth wife Gray seldom visited them although they lived nearby, repeatedly declining invitations for family Thanksgiving, Christmas and birthday get-togethers.[17]

Gray and her mother quarreled as mothers and daughters often do. She argued incessantly with her mother, one source recalled.[18] One year Dana gave her mother a snake for Christmas.[19]

Beverly Gray was a former beauty queen who still enjoyed the attention. She liked being pampered by assistance with make-up and dressing.[20] She modeled at Bullock's, did print ads for Hamilton watches and was a Rose Princess in the Tournament of Roses Parade.[21]

Beverly was fun and funny, and made a big deal out of holiday decorations. One study claimed that "Beverly Gray was an aggressive, vain woman who frequently maxed out her husband's credit cards."[22] The glamorous mother of this serial killer died of aggressive breast cancer between Gray's first and second years of high school.[23]

Childhood

Gray lacked the abusive childhood of many serial killers. Besides the typical problems affecting the American families, Gray's childhood failed to suggest that she would develop into a serial killer.[24] However, stepbrother Cedric Ward, who was estranged from Gray, declared to reporters, "It was not happy growing up."[25]

After the death of her mother Gray went to live with her father and his new wife Yvonne and her stepsister Cathy but she moved out within two years.[26] Several studies state that Gray was invited to leave when marijuana was found hidden in the room shared by the girls.[27] Gray believed that Beverly showed more affection to and interest in her older stepbrothers Rick and Craig, so she retaliated by talking an afternoon nap in Rick's room every day and wetting the bed, from the time she was five until she was eight.[28] The quality of Gray's relationships with her brothers varied over the years.[29]

She liked scary movies and read Grimm's Fairy Tales many times. She would stay up past her bedtime reading scary books or watching frightening movies.[30] When she was a teenager she and a neighbor built a catapult. The device was intended to hurl cats into the air whereupon their tiny parachutes would open and gently carry them down to swimming pools.[31] Would this be considered cruelty to animals?

School

She was a suboptimal student at least until nursing school. She told police that she was a B student.[32] She attended Newport Harbor High School infrequently but graduated in 1976.[33] She was often disciplined and in trouble for fights and forging notes, "In school she didn't get along well with other students, and did poorly in all her classes. She was suspended from school many times for forging notes to get out of class."[34]

Marriage

Gray married Tom Gray in October of 1987 at an elaborate seaside ceremony followed by a lavish reception and three months in Hawaii.[35] One source declared that she married Bill Gray.[36] Two others contend that the groom was Tom Davis.[37] Whatever his name was (and it was Tom) he and Dana filed for bankruptcy and divorce in 1993.[38]

Disobedience

"Dana was temperamental and demonstrative," her biographer concluded, adding that telling her no was likely to lead to a screaming match, followed by her inevitable misbehavior.[39] Richard Singer, a former boyfriend of Beverly, recalled that "Dana has a problem. She does not want to be told no. She has her own thing, and nobody could tell her any different. You could not tell Dana what to do."[40]

Personality

Aspects of her personality have been singled out for criticism. Her prosecutor, Richard Bentley, called her very moody and irrational with an argumentative personality.[41] Jim Wilkins, her boyfriend, noticed extreme shifts in mood.[42]

Gray was a controlling person with a complete lack of sensitivity, Braidhill noted.[43] Her stepbrother Rick agreed, writing to her in a letter that "You have little consideration for anyone else's feelings or comfort."[44] She reacted angrily when it was suggested that she sell some belongings to pay accumulating bills, "You know the way everyone's so anxious to cash me out makes me feel like I'm already dead! IT FUCKING INSULTS AND HURTS ME! So please honor my wishes till further notice."[45]

A final personality trait might be mentioned—sarcasm. "She is sarcastic," said Darlene Addison, a former Nursing Supervisor who terminated Gray for stealing drugs. Addison added, "She does get her point across if she's crossed or doesn't get her way."[46]

Appearance

Her looks varied over time. But her sense of style never relaxed; one source described her elegant appearance and sense of style, and observed that she dressed in glamorous clothes and groomed herself with manicures and pedicures.[47] Gray kept up her appearance with regular pedicures and manicures every week resulting in an image of looking neat, well-groomed and professional.[48]

Gray was called "blonde and striking" by an Internet source.[49] She was a beautiful woman with wavy blonde hair, Braidhill declared.[50] A surviving victim described her as blonde and in her thirties, about five foot two inches tall.[51]

One surviving victim saw no anger in her attacker's eyes, merely a look of determination, "Her eyes were flat. I could tell she had killed before."[52] A clerk recalled Gray's "intense blue eyes."[53] At her arrest policemen recalled "her ice-blue eyes."[54]

By the age of thirteen, she had become a beautiful young girl.[55] She told the police nurse that she was 5' 2" tall and weighed 135 pounds.[56] A witness described Gray as being relatively short and stocky in appearance, five feet, two inches tall, with dark blonde hair to her shoulders.[57] Gray's friends and acquaintances noted that Gray frequently had a "hard" appearance and demeanor which they attributed to the demanding and stressful life of a medical-surgical nurse.[58]

Athletic and Muscular

Gray was muscular and athletic, an expert swimmer and excellent softball player.[59] "She was a hard-core athlete," her husband Tom recalled. Gray was a skydiver, wind-surfer, mountain bike enthusiast and snorkler, and she was skilled in each sport.[60]

Gray was proud of her muscular development and physique and would from time to time roll her sleeve up revealing her flexed bicep muscle. She would say, "See how strong I am?"[61] Crime scene analysts described Dora Beebe's murderer as "a very physical person," based on crime scene forensic examination.[62] Braidhill asserted that Gray's playtime with her husband Tom became very physical. Gray liked rough play and would run at Tom and launch herself at him, tackling and sometimes knocking him down. On occasion she would punch Tom in the face while they wrestled.[63]

Substance Abuse

Alcohol seemed to be her drug of choice but hers was a versatile substance addiction. Prior to the murders she was abusing alcohol and had discontinued her medications the defense experts said.[64] Gray spent impulsively and indulged in bouts of binge drinking.[65] *Reference.com* asserted that "The marriage quickly disintegrated, however, when Gray began drinking heavily and abusing her husband's credit card."[66]

She had three or four glasses of wine while cooking dinner and more with dinner. Her drinking was a significant aspect of her lifestyle as weekends dissolved into a foggy haze of bourbon whiskey, 7Up and tequila shooters.[67] Her response to bad news was depression leading to binge drinking.[68] She admitted having two drinks daily.[69]

She smoked marijuana as a teenager and later in life.[70] The discovery of this drug in her bedroom led to her eviction from her father and stepmother's home the reader may recall from earlier in this chapter. She admitted to occasional marijuana and cocaine use in separate interviews with law enforcement personnel and psychologists.[71]

Employment

Gray graduated from nursing school then was employed in a number of lucrative hospital positions, *Crimeshots* claimed.[72] She attended nursing school at Saddleback College in Mission Viejo, California, and was assisted by her live-in beau and skydiving instructor, Rob Beaudry.[73] As soon as she received her nursing license she took a job at Corona Community Hospital.[74] She soon landed a relatively high-paying ($46,000/yr) position as an Operating Room Nurse at Inland Valley Regional Medical Center.[75] She was almost universally described as a very effective nurse.[76]

Gray was industrious and made money in more than one way. She had worked as a waitress to help put herself through nurses training.[77] She also self-taught herself screen-printing techniques and was skilled at creating attractive screen-printed items.[78]

Health

Gray was in generally good health. She had not suffered from any acute illnesses and was not afflicted with any chronic maladies. During her various medical intake sessions with law enforcement, jail and prison authorities, she complained of insomnia, chronic diarrhea, weakness, lethargy, night sweats and loss of appetite.[79]

Mental Health

There was and remains considerable controversy about her state of mind at the time of these crimes. Equally expert medical professionals disagreed as they typically do. The psychiatric team employed by the defense concurred that Gray did not fully understand the consequences of her crimes but they failed to agree on a diagnosis of what she suffered from.[80] Her attorney hired mental health professionals to document his claim that Gray manifested a state of diminished capacity caused by the series of traumatic circumstances in her life at that time.[81]

One psychiatrist, Michael Kania, observed her depression and stress and concluded that she was "disassociated" during the crimes. Dr. Lorna Forbes (a second psychiatrist) concluded that "Gray had no awareness of the significance of her actions during the times she committed each offense." But a prosecution expert, Dr. Martha Rogers, testified that "Despite stress, she had planned, prepared for and carried out the duties in full awareness that they were wrong."[82]

Gray volunteered to the police that she was depressed which she attributed to her divorce.[83] During her pre-trial incarceration she repeatedly expressed suicidal ideation.[84] She reportedly was in a deep depression for a year after her mother's death.[85] She began seeing a psychiatrist in March of 1992 and was prescribed Paxil.[86] Gray was prone to breaking out into "hysterical tears" according to her boyfriend Wilkins.[87]

Her sanity evaluation included a number of diagnostic tests. These included the Wechsler Adult Intelligence Scale, the Rorschach inkblot test, the Minnesota Multiphasic Personality Inventory, the Personality Assessment Inventory, the Beck Depression Inventory, the Thematic Apperception Test and the Clinton Multi Axial Inventory III.[88]

Interviews with the defense psychiatrists gave Gray a chance to develop her insanity defense. They also were bizarre interactions as Gray altered her basic story and changed the details of her story with each telling.[89] Dr. Kania and Dr. Forbes decided that Gray was insane during the murders. Alcoholic psychotic depression was the diagnosis of Dr. Kamia, and Dr. Forbes mentioned an unspecified emotional disassociative disorder.[90]

Sexual Precocity

Gray was an early bloomer in that she became sexually active at a relatively early age. At fifteen she moved out from the home of her father and stepmother and cohabitated with Beaudry, her twenty-three-year-old skydiving "jumpmaster."[91] She reportedly became pregnant twice and Rob convinced her to have abortions.[92] Gray had lost her virginity at twelve to a man living in a mobile home on her mother's property.[93]

Good Dana

It seemed almost as if there were two Dana Grays. The nice Dana, for instance, was described as "very caring" by a former nursing supervisor.[94] An acquaintance, Dave Dressecker, claimed "He had known Gray as an R.N., recalling how educated she had been, and had done some real estate transactions with her. She was a very nice girl."[95] As her life became problematic her demeanor changed as well. A few neighbors remarked how Gray was a friendly neighbor until her life started to become dysfunctional at which point she become unpleasant and withdrew from the presence of others.[96]

Bad Dana

The bad Dana was bad indeed. She had the condescending belief that she was smarter than everyone else. During her initial police interrogation it was obvious to police interviewers that Gray believed that she could fool them and talk her way out of trouble.[97] She was a destructive person as well who cut holes in her mother's clothes and hurt other children on purpose.[98] She was so controlling on the job that others had to accept her domineering demeanor and she displayed the same trait in her personal life.[99]

She and Tom filed for bankruptcy, owing about $177,500 on a house valued at only $125,000 because of double mortgages.[100] The problem was a deep-seated attitude; according to a sister-in-law, Gray was "Nuts. Not even normally greedy. Crazy."[101] When Gray requested that her Great-Aunt include her in the elderly woman's will in addition to her stepbrothers Craig and Rick, hard feelings arose and were acted out on several occasions in public and private.[102] "At this point she was also estranged from her remaining family, having burned many bridges."[103] She and Tom took out a loan for $47,000 and another for $20,000 within the first nine months of marriage.[104]

"Gray is missing a conscience," her sister-in-law claimed. She added, "I do not think it is there. When you talk to her, she has no concept of other human beings."[105] She had a tendency to deliver "zingers," especially-nasty personalized insults and hurtful comments. In a dispute over some furniture she asked her brother Rick, "Are you pissed off enough to stroke off and die? I hope so!"[106] Rick was so unnerved by the experience that he called the police who demurred at the invitation to investigate the incident.[107]

A final dimension of the bad Dana—she was frequently designated as a bitch. Her biographer declared, "Dana had no problem being called a bitch. She prided herself on earning the title."[108] Lynn Fogelman, a sky-diving associate, called Gray "a bitch."[109] Her former husband Tom's term for tirades seemingly from nowhere was "insta-bitch."[110] A former co-worker called Gray "a bitch on wheels."[111]

OTHER CRIMES

Despite her record, D.A. Bentley publicly stated that the reason behind the plea bargained deal was Gray's lack of a criminal record before the murders, along with the desirability of providing relatively quick closure while sparing victim families the agony of hearing details of the killings.[112]

Stealing

She stole as a child. One evening she crashed on the couch of Joanie Fulton, a friend of hers. The next day Fulton was missing one twenty dollar bill.[113] Potential insight into Gray's motives was hypothesized by one source, "Whenever Beverly would discipline her daughter, Dana would retaliate by stealing money to buy candy, and occasionally fly into fits of violence."[114] Step-brother Cedric Ward noted, "She had a habit of asking others to give her money, as well as of stealing it when it suited her."[115]

Moped Mischief

Gray and her best friend Carrie Ann loved to zoom around on Dana's moped. One day they were interrupted in their fun by a policeman who took them home in his squad car. When he let Beverly take custody of her daughter he reportedly told her, "If you're not careful, she'll lead a life of crime."[116]

Shoplifting

Another profit-motivated crime. In the seventh grade Gray tried to steal a pair of earrings from the May Company store. Her mother Beverly was called after her arrest.[117]

Illegal Skydiving

The Grand Canyon is restricted air space and therefore an inviting target for adventuresome skydivers. Gray and her co-divers practiced for the jump in Colorado. Arrest greeted them upon their landing and their gear was confiscated in addition to the imposition of hefty fines.[118]

Drug Theft

This was quite likely her most serious offense. She was forced to resign her R.N. position after twenty-one doses of narcotic drugs were unaccounted for and improperly documented.[119] "She found work as a nurse," claimed one study, "but was eventually fired for stealing drugs."[120] She began stealing the drugs in April of 1993, most often taking Demerol, Sublimaze and Astramorph. She was suspended at a November 18th meeting and terminated a week later.[121]

THE MURDERS

Dana Sue Gray killed because she loved to shop as difficult to believe as that may be for some. On the one hand fairly simple these crimes were also complex criminal acts.

Number of Victims

There is some disagreement over the precise number of Gray murder victims. However, the total number did not exceed a half-dozen and may have been just three. A number of geriatric-aged women were victimized according to one source.[122]

Gray pled guilty to two murders and one attempted murder several sources suggested.[123] She was sentenced for two murders and one attempted murder and suspected of three additional homicides Egger claimed.[124] She admitted to three murders, independent studies by Ramsland and *Crimeshots* concluded.[125] "She killed three elderly women," *SKCentral.com* observed, and another Internet reference source concurred.[126]

There are signs of more victims. Ramsland noted there were two fatal assaults before the failed attempt on Dorinda Hawkins, followed by one other successful homicide.[127] One study suggested that Gray had killed some patients but was never even suspected, inflating her death total. Dr. Patricia Kirby, a Baltimore-area psychologist, contended that "My feeling is that she was, in fact, killing within her occupation."[128]

Were there two additional victims? Laureen Johnson, a stylist at A Cut Above, recalled Gray wondering during a manicure if the Canyon Lake homicides were connected to two previous deaths.[129] A second study confirmed this incident.[130]

The Victims

There were two "official" Gray victims, June Roberts and Dora Beebe. There was reportedly sufficient evidence in the Norma Davis case to convict her for that murder as well, but it was decided that the trial was not needed since Gray was already sentenced to life without possibility of parole in the first two cases. Dorinda Hawkins was left for dead by Gray in the Main Street Trading Post, an antique store.[131]

There may have been a fifth intended victim—her former husband Tom Gray. He recalls that she made a date to meet with him about their divorce paperwork, but he skipped at the last minute. It was the day Gray murdered Norma Davis.[132]

MO

Gray's murders were defined by their recurrent characteristics. They had a very similar MO, in terms of their timing, the geographic area and victimology.[133] Her MO was also marked by the violent nature of her preferred murder methods. One study noted the unusually intimate method of strangulation, first manually then with a phone cord, followed by the use of a convenient object to bludgeon the victim with.[134] Braidhill referred to the *in-your-face* murder method of manual strangulation.[135] But Gray was calculating, too—she always wore gloves.[136]

Norma Davis was strangled and then stabbed to death, the police and medical examination concluded.[137] June Roberts was tied to a chair, strangled and then bludgeoned to death.[138] Dora Beebe was strangled by a phone cord and beaten to death.[139]

Overkill

One additional dimension of the Gray MO warrants discussion—the ferocity and overkill nature of the murders. In the Davis murder the body was nearly decapitated.[140] Her autopsy revealed that Norma was stabbed eleven times with the killer leaving the knives stuck in her body. She had also been strangled by hand with tremendous physical force.[141] "Davis had been repeatedly stabbed."[142]

June Roberts' murder was similarly gruesome and violent. Her autopsy noted a "moderately deep ligature furrow," and a "6 x 3 purple contusion."[143] The cranium contusion was caused by a heavy glass wine decanter swung with considerable force.[144] The volume of blood in and near the bathroom door, on the walls and pooled near the body made it impossible to estimate the victim's age.[145]

Beebe was also battered and treated quite shabbily by her assailant.[146] The carnage was considerable; so much splatter remained on the walls and floor that an outline of her body in blood was left.[147] Gray hit Beebe so hard and so often with a Black and Decker iron that the appliance bent and broke.[148]

We know that Gray left the murder crime scenes and immediately went shopping. What is unclear is how she was able to commit such violent, physical and bloody tasks without being covered in blood, or scratched or having a nail broken. Prosecutor Bentley was unable to determine how Gray left the bloody crime scenes and then shopped for hours without a speck of blood on her, nor any other signs of a fatal struggle.[149] Clerks and waitstaff who served her reported no muss and nothing out of the usual.[150]

COMMERCIAL MOTIVE

In this case other (secondary) motives may have co-existed. But the primary purpose behind the killings was profit. .

Profit Motive

"Within minutes of each murder or attack, Gray was indulging her 'shopaholic' tendencies, running up bills of thousands of dollars with the money and credit cards of her victims," Egger concluded.[151] "Her obsession with shopping" motivated the murders, suggested *SKCentral*.[152] The Reverend Frank Logue sermonized to his congregation at the King of Peace Episcopal Church in Kingsland, Georgia:

> Envy turned to murder was exactly why an 87-year-old California woman was beaten to death for her credit cards. Her 30-something killer, Dana Sue Gray, was arrested later that day. Between the murder

and the arrest, Gray had gone on a shopping spree. Police found Beebe's credit cards in Gray's home. They also found a closet full of new clothes with the price tags still attached. There were unopened bottles of Opium perfume, an expensive mountain bike and a purple boogie board.[153]

"Gray says she committed these murders to support her spending habits," according to *Reference.com*[154] "She had garroted and bludgeoned to death a number of elderly women, then gone on binges with their credit cards," another study noted.[155] The day after killing Roberts, Gray purchased some suntan oil, treated herself to a massage at the Murrieta Hot Springs resort, then spent the afternoon "power shopping," with the entire shopping excursion financed by her victim.[156] She told the police that after one murder she "went out and proceeded to shop up a storm."[157]

Alternate Motivation

Gray may have had mixed motives. An examining psychiatrist concluded that Gray had a trio of "psychological triggers:" the desire to shop, the need to possess power and dominate others and unresolved family issues.[158] Gray claimed that her victims had nauseated her, either because they reminded her of her mother or because she found their behavior condescending or demeaning, and that shopping made her feel better.[159]

The Davis Murder

It is possible that nothing was taken from Norma Davis other than her life. Ramsland claimed that nothing of value was stolen from the Davis residence, nor was any money taken from Norma Davis' purse which was in plain view. A valuable ring was left untouched on her finger.[160] Her purse contained approximately $270 and was left undisturbed.[161] There is disagreement over Davis' Social Security check which was reported missing from the house.[162] Another account reported that the $148 check was found in Davis' dwelling and was not taken.[163]

The Roberts Murder

Gray took two of Roberts' credit cards, a Mervyn's store card and a Visa card, leaving cards for stores like Broadway and JCPenney.[164]

Soon after Roberts' death police noticed activity on her credit cards.[165] Gray's boyfriend Jim noticed all of the new stuff, too, and told her to take it back.[166]

The post-Roberts spree began with a stop at Bally's Wine Country Café followed by a moustache wax and perm for her and a haircut for Jim's son Jason for $164.71. She spent $511 at West Dallas on a black fringed leather jacket and a pair of black, yellow and red cowboy boots. At Jewelry Mart she purchased a $161 pair of diamond-and-sapphire earrings. From Mervyn's she obtained a dozen pairs of Jockey women's underwear and three pair of shoes for Jason for $169.67, along with five pairs of boy's jeans and a few sets of boys underwear and socks for $240.80 and a new set of sheets costing $40.93. Then she spent $74.62 on Tootsie-Rolls, Skittles, Gatorade, dog shampoo, rawhide dog treats, dog biscuits, a couple of cartons of Marlboro Lights, two bottles of Smirnoff vodka, a purple boogie board and a child's toy helicopter.[167]

She dined on shrimp scampi and crab cakes within minutes of murdering Roberts.[168] Her hair and eyebrow wax were done at Ethiques, a trendy and expensive beauty shop.[169] Gray had Roberts' bankbook and withdrew about $2,000.[170] "By the end of the day, she had charged $1,700 on two cards."[171] One study asserted that Gray had Roberts' bankbook.[172] Yet Braidhill claims that police found it in Roberts' lodging.[173]

The Hawkins Attempted Murder

Gray believed that Hawkins was dead when she left her on the floor of her store. Taken by Gray was approximately $25 from the cash register.[174]She took a five-dollar bill from Hawkins' purse but left a $20 bill.[175] She also took the keys to the store.[176]

The Beebe Murder

Beebe was murdered between 11:10 a.m. and noon on March 16, 1994. Gray was arrested later that day at 5:45 p.m. so there wasn't time for much shopping. Detectives noted Beebe's purse being open upon their arrival.[177] Nevertheless, "Gray managed to find Beebe's bank and withdraw $2,000 in cash. Her splurge this time was a smoothie and assorted supplements at a health food store, a briefcase and gourmet groceries. She became so blithe about forging Beebe's checks that she signed one 'Dana Beebe'."[178]

The Victims Appeared Not to Have Been Robbed

One thing puzzling detectives in the early stages of this investigation was motive. Gray's selective thefts were subtle, "It appeared that neither had been significantly robbed," one source noted.[179] After the Roberts slaying Detective Greco wondered why the cash had been left in her purse and jewelry and other valuables left behind.[180]

Purchased Items Incriminated Gray

Items purchased as a result of the murders wound up providing investigative leads and incriminating evidence against Gray. Roberts' bank had informed police of activity on her account and interviews with the retail clerks involved had provided valuable information.[181] "She was caught when a bank clerk had notified Roberts's relatives that her credit cards had been used after her death, and they in turn had told the police."[182]

After her arrest police searched her home. "They found jewelry, food, liquor, a ski mask, a purse with nearly $2,000 stuck in the washing machine, and many items of clothing," one study asserted.[183] District Attorney Bentley "had a wealth of evidence: Gray's use of credit cards, clerks who had seen her directly after each murder, handwriting experts who identified her signatures on various items."[184] The importance of this evidence was emphasized by Braidhill, "Their case consisted of showing jurors that Dana had spent June's credit cards and used Dora's bankbook less than an hour after each of them had been murdered."[185] Another study added, "The search of Gray's home revealed property belonging not only to Roberts, but also to Beebe, and a third victim, Dorinda Hawkins, who survived her attack and later identified Gray."[186]

Psychological Significance of Purchases

Many serial killers retain personal items from their victims to serve as mementos. These trophies were evident in the Gray case. "She had stashed items from her post-murder spending binges all over her house like trophies," one study noted.[187]

"I got desperate to buy things. Shopping puts me to rest," she told police.[188] Police interrogators noted that Gray dispassionately discussed killing elderly women but she began to cry when discussing her shopping.[189] Psychologist Patricia Kirby decided that "The shopping then provides her with something to do to celebrate the killing."[190]

Gray's Explanations and Rationalizations

She never confessed or completely admitted to her deeds despite dedicated police efforts to encourage her to talk. Her initial alibi to explain her possession of items taken from recently murdered elderly ladies? She found them, she claimed, in a tale familiar to any parent.[191] When interrogators tried to make Gray feel guilty about making the purchases, her rationalization was, "I just wanted to get stuff for Jason and us."[192]

CONCLUSION

Dana Sue Gray lived and loved to shop. Nothing else made her feel better about herself, her life and her world than spending money. But after bankrupting a marriage with her obsessive shopping, she lost her job and was in financial difficulty.

Her solution was to strangle and batter elderly women to death. She then absconded with credit cards or a bankbook. Gray placed her greed and need for material goods over the lives of sweet little old ladies. The crime scenes were reminiscent of slaughterhouses, the carnage considerable and criminal in conduct. Gray was an angry person whose murders reflected that anger and her inherent dominating greed.

Conclusion

What have we learned about the phenomenon of commercial serial murder? The purpose behind this book was to explain, document and exemplify the existence of a genre of serial murder where the motive was money. We have examined a dozen cases of commercial serial murder, and while they naturally differ in circumstances it is possible to discern some common and transcendent themes.

These recurrent factors will be discussed in this concluding chapter. We will conclude that commercial serial murder is a valid, existant phenomenon.

AGGREGATE ANALYSIS OF THE MURDERERS

Although our main focus has been understanding the nuances of commercial serial murder, it is nevertheless important to contextualize this understanding through study of the killers themselves. To accomplish this we have devoted a considerable part of each chapter to analysis of the prominent aspects of these individuals' lives. Certain patterns and tendencies have been observed and are perhaps worthy of consideration.

The killers in our study shared certain traits and life patterns. For instance, they experienced painful childhoods and many suffered from physical and mental health maladies. They all had extensive criminal records. And they were older than you might think.

Bad Childhoods

Many people suffer from suboptimal childhoods. The overwhelming majority do not turn to serial murder later in life. However there may be some childhood issues involved in the development of serial murderers. Blanche Moore was forced to become a prostitute by her alcoholic father in her early adolescence and Richard Ramirez watched his favorite cousin shoot his wife in the face. H. H. Holmes was frightened out of his wits when neighborhood bullies scared him with a real human skeleton. Martha Beck was raped by her brother and Raymond Fernandez's parents did not care for him. Table 1 quantifies and reveals the significance of bad childhoods in our study.

Physical and Mental Health

Most people experience some physical ailments during their lives. It is also quite likely that most or all of us have been afflicted with an

Table 1 Bad Childhoods

Killer(s)	Child Abuse	Rape	Poverty	Parental Problems	Incest	Traumatic Event	Substance Abuse
Benders	Y	N	N	Y	Y	N	N
Holmes	N	N	N	N	N	Y	N
Gunness	N	N	Y	N	N	Y	N
Haarmann	Y	N	Y	N	N	Y	N
Becker	N	N	N	N	N	N	N
Singh	N	N	Y	Y	N	Y	N
Fernandez & Beck	N N	N Y	N N	Y Y	N Y	Y Y	N N
Ramirez	N	N	N	Y	N	Y	Y
Moore	Y	N	Y	Y	N	Y	N
Beets	N	N	Y	Y	N	Y	Y
Ray & Faye Copeland	N N	N N	Y Y	N N	N N	N N	N N
Gray	N	N	N	Y	N	Y	Y
TOTALS	3	1	7	8	2	10	3

emotional or mental disorder at some point. And the killers in my study were no different, except perhaps in the frequency and severity of their medical and mental maladies.

Physical Health

Ramirez and Fritz Haarmann had epilepsy, Haarmann also suffering from meningitis as a youth. Betty Beets had the measles which led to ear infections and eventual partial deafness. Holmes, Haarmann, Fernandez, Ramirez and Beets all suffered possible neurological damage from head injuries. Kate Bender, Haarmann, Boysie Singh and Fernandez all had sexually transmitted diseases. The medical issues confronting these killers are summarized in Table 2 and Table 3.

Mental Health

The incidence of serious mental and emotional disorders among our sample was significant. Holmes, Haarmann, Ramirez and Dana

Table 2 Serial Killer Physical Health

Killer(s)	Head Injury	Deafness	Epilepsy	Sexual Diseases	Insomnia	Overweight
Benders	N	N	N	Y	N	N
Holmes	Y	N	N	N	N	N
Gunness	N	N	N	N	N	Y
Haarmann	Y	N	Y	Y	N	N
Becker		N	N	N		N
Singh	N	N	N	Y	N	N
Fernandez & Beck	Y N	N N	N N	Y N	N N	N Y
Ramirez	Y	N	Y	N	Y	N
Moore	N	N	N	N	Y	N
Beets	Y	Y	N	N	Y	N
Ray & Faye Copeland	N N	Y N	N N	N N	N N	N N
Gray	N	N	N	N	Y	N
TOTALS	5	2	2	4	4	2

Table 3 Serial Killer Physical Health

Killer(s)	Diarrhea	Diabetes	Meningitis	Asthma
Benders	N	N	N	N
Holmes	N	N	N	N
Gunness	N	N	N	N
Haarmann	Y	N	Y	N
Becker	N	N	N	N
Singh	N	Y	N	N
Fernandez & Beck	N N	N N	N N	N N
Ramirez	N	N	N	N
Moore	Y	N	N	Y
Beets	Y	N	N	N
Ray & Faye Copeland	N N	Y N	N N	N N
Gray	Y	N	N	N
TOTALS	4	2	1	1

Gray were all probably psychopathic. Sociopaths included the Benders, Holmes, Belle Gunness, Haarmann, Martha Beck, Ray and Faye Copeland and Gray. They were all described as emotionally unstable except Holmes, Gunness and the Copelands. Half of these killers reported depression throughout their lives. Table 4 and Table 5 systematically indicate the scope of the emotional and mental health issues manifested in our sample of serial murderers.

Extensive Criminal Records

The killers described in this book were veteran criminals, for the most part. An extensive criminal background for each of these offenders was discovered with the exception of the Benders. This may be the most noteworthy characteristic of the sample as a whole, the universal criminal history of relatively serious crimes.

Theft was a common offense, as each killer included in this study was a thief save for Beets. Robbery was also quite prevalent as all of these killers except for Moore and Beets robbed someone. Fraud was another popular crime, as each of these killers engaged in some fraudulent scheme except Marie Becker, Ramirez and Gray. More than half of these killers also engaged in forgery.

Table 4 Serial Killer Mental Health

Killer(s)	Psychotic	Sociopath	Depression	Retarded	PTSD	Battered Woman's Syndrome
Benders	N	Y	N	N	N	N
Holmes	Y	Y	N	N	N	N
Gunness	N	Y	N	N	N	N
Haarmann	Y	Y	Y	Y	N	N
Becker	N	N	Y	N	N	N
Singh	N	N	Y	N	N	N
Fernandez & Beck	N N	N Y	N Y	N	N N	N N
Ramirez	Y	N	Y	N	Y	N
Moore	N	N	Y	N	N	Y
Beets	N	N	Y	N	Y	Y
Ray & Faye Copeland	N N	Y Y	N N	N	N Y	N Y
Gray	Y	Y	Y	N	N	N
Totals	4	8	8	1	3	3

Not only were some crimes common to our sample but virtually all of these murderers engaged in a large number of criminal acts. Singh engaged in more than a dozen other types of criminality. Haarmann had nine types of crime and Holmes had eight other types of offenses. Fernandez had seven types of crime on his record, and Ramirez had six. Beck and Gray had five other offenses, Becker and Moore accumulated four each, but Beets only had three other offenses. The details of this diverse criminal activity are included in Table 6 and Table 7.

We might consider a final collective dimension of the serial killers discussed in this book—they were not as young as you might expect. Singh, Holmes, Beck, Ramirez, John Jr. and Kate Bender were in their twenties when they killed, with Fernandez, Moore and Gray in their thirties. But Gunness, Haarmann and Beets were in their forties, and Becker and "Ma" Bender were in their fifties. Faye Copeland and Pa Bender were in their sixties, and the oldest was Ray Copeland, in his mid-seventies. The average age of these seventeen killers was 40.47

Table 5 Serial Killer Mental Health

Killer(s)	Megalomania	Incest	Cannibalism	Vampirism	Emotionally Unstable
Benders	N	Y	N	N	Y
Holmes	Y	N	N	N	N
Gunness	N	N	N	N	N
Haarmann	N	N	Y	Y	Y
Becker	N	N	N	N	Y
Singh	Y	N	N	N	Y
Fernandez & Beck	N N	N Y	N N	N N	Y Y
Ramirez	N	N	N	N	Y
Moore	N	Y	N	N	Y
Beets	N	N	N	N	Y
Ray & Faye Copeland	N N	N N	N N	N N	N N
Gray	N	N	N	N	Y
TOTALS	2	3	1	1	10

years; the men averaged 38.5 years of age, and the women had an average age of 42.22.

AGGREGATE ANALYSIS OF THE TYPES OF COMMERCIAL MURDER

The focus of this study has been the phenomenon of profit-motivated serial slaying. Now that we are equipped with an understanding of the individual serial murder cases as well as the recurrent or transcendent themes reflected in the lives of these criminals, we are ready to assess the commercial behavior manifest in these serial murders. Systematic assessment of these crimes reveals significant commercial aspects.

Profit Motive

There are seven main ways murderers may make money from their murders: 1) insurance, 2) pensions, 3) bank accounts and property, 4)

Table 6 Diverse Criminal Background

Killer(s)	Pick-pocket	Theft	Rape	Arson	Smuggling	Fraud	Forgery	Drugs
Benders	N	Y	N	N	N	Y	N	N
Holmes	N	Y	Y	Y	N	Y	Y	N
Gunness	N	Y	N	Y	N	Y	N	N
Haarmann	Y	Y	Y	Y	Y	Y	N	N
Becker	N	Y	N	N	N	Y	Y	N
Singh	Y	Y	N	Y	Y	N	N	Y
Fernandez & Beck	N N	Y Y	N N	N N	N N	Y Y	Y Y	N N
Ramirez	N	Y	Y	N	Y	N	N	Y
Moore	N	Y	N	Y	N	Y	Y	N
Beets	N	N	N	Y	N	Y	Y	N
Ray & Faye Copeland	N N	Y Y	N N	N N	N N	Y Y	Y Y	N N
Gray	N	Y	N	N	N	N	Y	Y
TOTALS	2	13	3	6	3	11	9	3

robbery and theft, 5) convincing victims to sign over possessions, 6) selling bodies and parts, and 7) paid killings.

Murder-related robbery and theft was the most prevalent type of commercial activity with twelve of the fourteen killers active in this category, as shown in Table 8. Three types of profit-taking were engaged in by half of the killers studied. Pensions were involved in four cases, and there were two cases of bodies being sold and one instance of a killer being paid for the murder.

These killers typically participated in multiple types of commercial activity. For instance Holmes engaged in six of the seven types of profit-taking, only failing to serve as a "hit man." Gunness and Becker both participated in five of the seven types of commercial gain. Moore and Fernandez and Beck were guilty of four kinds of murder-related monetary gain. Beets was active in three profitable ways and there were two commercial behaviors manifested by Haarmann, Singh and the Copelands. The Benders, Ramirez and Gray were involved in just one type of profit-taking.

Table 7 Diverse Criminal Background

Killer(s)	Bigamy	Con Games	Robbery	Shop-lifting	Child Molesting	Prostitu-tion	Horse Theft
Benders	N	Y	Y	N	Y	N	Y
Holmes	Y	Y	Y	N	N	N	Y
Gunness	N	N	Y	N	N	N	Y
Haarmann	N	N	Y	N	Y	Y	N
Becker	N	N	Y	N	N	N	N
Singh	N	N	Y	N	N	Y	N
Fernandez & Beck	Y N	Y Y	Y Y	N N	N N	Y N	N
Ramirez	N	N	Y	N	Y	N	N
Moore	N	N	N	N	N	N	N
Beets	N	N	N	N	N	N	N
Ray & Faye Copeland	N N	N N	Y Y	N N	N N	N N	Y N
Gray	N	N	Y	Y	N	N	N
TOTALS	2	4	12	1	3	3	4

Self-Incrimination

The central irony of commercial serial murder is the fact that the temporal goods motivating such crime typically wind up incriminating the killer(s). This works in two ways. Investigative leads are frequently generated by the commercial activity of the killers. And perhaps more importantly the tangible items resulting from serial murder-related profit-taking often are used as evidence of the guilt of the offenders.

The Benders were allegedly stopped as they fled, and a considerable sum of money testified to their crimes. Haarmann's apartment yielded items stolen from his murder victims, Gray's trailer home was filled with recently-purchased products, most with price tags still attached, and police found stolen cargo and marine motors at Singh's residence. Beets' attempt to purchase additional insurance on Jimmy Don was a signal to the police, as was the quilt made from victims' clothing discovered at the Copeland farm. The fence used by Ramirez turned over

Table 8 Types of Commercial Serial Murder

Killer(s)	Life Insurance	Pensions	Bank Accounts	Robbery & Theft	Convinced to Sign Over Possessions	Sold Bodies	Paid Killer
Benders	N	N	N	Y	N	N	N
Holmes	Y	N	Y	Y	Y	Y	N
Gunness	Y	Y	Y	Y	Y	N	N
Haarmann	N	N	N	Y	N	Y	N
Becker	Y	Y	Y	Y	Y	N	N
Singh	N	N	N	Y	N	N	Y
Fernandez & Beck	Y Y	N N	Y Y	Y Y	Y Y	N N	N N
Ramirez	N	N	N	Y	N	N	N
Moore	Y	Y	Y	N	Y	N	N
Beets	Y	Y	Y	N	N	N	N
Ray & Faye Copeland	N N	N N	N N	Y Y	Y Y	N N	N N
Gray	N	N	N	Y	N	N	N
TOTAL	7	4	7	12	8	2	1

to police most of the items he stole and Holmes was trapped by his insurance fraud proceeds.

The Importance of Advertising

A final commercial aspect of profit-oriented serial murder might be considered—the significance of advertising. In four cases victims were obtained through advertising. In a sense, ads were an investment aimed at marketing their criminal activity through attracting victims.

Kate Bender advertised her clairvoyant services as a means of attracting visitors to the Bender Inn. Gunness used two different kinds of ads, one aimed at eliciting suitors (potential murder victims) and the other to attract farm hands to work for her. Holmes advertised for hotel workers who frequently became murder victims. And Fernandez and Beck used ads in lonely-hearts columns of newspapers and magazines to recruit victims.

SUMMARY

Serial murderers kill for different reasons. Sometimes more than one motive may be present in a serial killing case, and motives may change over time. Nevertheless, it is reasonable to postulate that there is a type of serial murder motivated by money where the primary or sole reason for the killing is commercial. This book has hopefully described and documented commercial serial slaying as a valid and legitimate concept.

If we understand the reasons behind serial murder we are one step closer to creating more effective means of preventing and dealing with this type of crime. Law enforcement profiling and investigation, judicial deliberations and sociological intervention strategies might all benefit from a more accurate understanding of the mindset of commercially-motivated serial murderers. Recognition of the profit motive underlying some cases of serial murder can only enhance our chances of adopting more appropriate and effective social solutions to this sort of serial slaying.

Notes

INTRODUCTION

1. Constance McKenzie, "A Study of Serial Murder," *International Journal of Offender Therapy and Comparative Criminology* **39**, No. 1 (1995), p. 273.
2. Belea T. Keeney and Kathleen M. Heide, "Gender Differences in Serial Murderers: A Preliminary Analysis," *Journal of Interpersonal Violence***19**, No. 3 (1994), p. 492.
3. John A. Liebert, "Contributions of Psychiatric Consultation in the Investigation of Serial Murder," *International Journal of Offender Therapy and Comparative Criminology* **29**, No. 3 (1985), p. 187.
4. Ronald Hinch and Crystal Hepburn, "Researching Serial Murder: Methodological and Definitional Problems," *Electronic Journal of Sociology* (1998), http://www.sociology.org/content/vol003.002/hinch.html, pp. 8–9. Accessed on January 13, 2003.
5. Hinch and Hepburn, "Researching Serial Murder," p. 8.
6. Steven A. Egger, *The Need to Kill: Inside the World of the Serial Killer* (Upper Saddle River, New Jersey: Prentice Hall, 1990), p. 4.
7. Ronald M. Holmes and Stephen T. Holmes, *Serial Murder* (Thousand Oaks, California: Sage Publications, 1998), p. 33.
8. Hinch and Hepburn, "Researching Serial Murder," p. 4.
9. Hinch and Hepburn, "Researching Serial Murder," p. 3.
10. Hinch and Hepburn, "Researching Serial Murder," p. 4.
11. T.F. Jesse, *Murder and Its Motive* (New York: Knopf, 1924).
12. Egger, *The Need to Kill*, p. 33.
13. Holmes and Holmes, *Serial Murder*, p. 119.
14. Hinch and Hepburn, "Researching Serial Murder," p. 9.
15. Holmes and Holmes, *Serial Murder*, p. 123.

16. David Lester, *Serial Killers: The Insatiable Passion* (Philadelphia: The Charles Press, Publishers, 1995), p. 13.
17. David Schmid, *Natural Born Celebrities* (Chicago: University of Chicago Press, 2005), p. 78.

CHAPTER 1

1. Katherine Ramsland, *The Human Predator: A Historical Chronicle of Serial Murder and Forensic Investigation* (New York: Berkley Books, 2005), p. 68; David Everitt, *Human Monsters: An Illustrated Encyclopedia of the World's Most Vicious Murderers* (Chicago: Contemporary Books, 1993), p. 40; and Robert H. Adleman, *The Bloody Benders* (New York: Stein & Day, 1970), p. 33.
2. State of Kansas, Executive Department, "Governor's Proclamation: $2,000 Reward," May 17, 1878.
3. William Bolitho, "Old Man Bender's Orchard," in Jonathan Goodman (Ed.), *Masterpieces of Murder* (London: Magpie Books, 2004), p. 482.
4. Bolitho, "Old Man Bender's," p. 482. One study asserted, "They arrived in the township of Cherryvale, Kansas in 1870 as part of a small cult of spiritualists." See Mike Mayo, *American Murder: Criminals, Crime and the Media* (Canton, Missouri: Visible Ink Press, 2008), p. 30.
5. Bolitho, "Old Man Bender's," pp. 482–83.
6. Richard G. Jones, "Kate Bender: Bumps in the Night," *The Mammoth Book of Women Who Kill* (New York: Carroll & Graf, 2002), p. 81.
7. Everitt, *Human Monsters*, p. 40.
8. Adleman, *Bloody Benders*, pp. 136–38.
9. Bolitho, "Old Man Bender's," p. 482. The elder Bender was named "Old Man William John," according to a 2008 study. See Mayo, *American Murder*, p. 30.
10. Harold Schechter, *The Serial Killer Files* (New York: Ballantine Books, 2003), p. 138; Everitt, *Human Monsters*, p. 40.
11. Jones, "Kate Bender," p. 81.
12. Jones, "Kate Bender," p. 82.
13. Jones, "Kate Bender," p. 82.
14. Adleman, *Bloody Benders*, p. 35.
15. Adleman, *Bloody Benders*, pp. 101–2.
16. Adleman, *Bloody Benders*, p. 144.
17. Bolitho, "Old Man Bender's," p. 482.
18. Schechter, *Serial Killer Files*, p. 138.
19. Everitt, *Human Monsters*, p. 40.
20. Jones, "Kate Bender," p. 82.
21. Adleman, *Bloody Benders*, p. 46.
22. Schechter, *Serial Killer Files*, p. 138.
23. Everitt, *Human Monsters*, p. 40.
24. Bolitho, "Old Man Bender's," p. 482.

25. Jones, "Kate Bender," p. 81.
26. Jones, "Kate Bender," p. 82.
27. Adleman, *Bloody Benders*, p. 34.
28. Jones, "Kate Bender," p. 83.
29. Jones, "Kate Bender," p. 81; Everitt, *Human Monsters*, p. 40.
30. Adleman, *Bloody Benders*, p. 240.
31. Everitt, *Human Monsters*, p. 41.
32. Jones, "Kate Bender," p. 81.
33. Jones, "Kate Bender," p. 82.
34. Adleman, *Bloody Benders*, p. 238.
35. *Internet Crime Archive*, "The Bender Family" (n.d.), http://www.mayhem.net/Crime/serial2.html, p. 34. Accessed on August 29, 2006.
36. Adleman, *Bloody Benders*, p. 48.
37. Bolitho, "Old Man Bender's," p. 482. Indeed, Kate Bender may not have been such a beauty, after all. Everitt noted that she was easily the most romanticized and mischaracterized of the four Benders. He concluded that she most likely was not the beautiful and alluring temptress of some writers' imagination. See Everitt, *Human Monsters*, p. 41.
38. Schechter, *Serial Killer Files*, p. 138.
39. *Internet Crime Archive*, "The Bender Family," p. 32; Ramsland, *Human Predator*, p. 68; Everitt, *Human Monsters*, p. 41; and Jones, "Kate Bender," p. 82.
40. *Internet Crime Archive*,"The Bender Family," p. 32; Bolitho, "Old Man Bender's," p. 482; Schechter, *Serial Killer Files*, p. 138; and Adleman, *Bloody Benders*, pp. 55–56, 170.
41. Everitt, *Human Monsters*, p. 41.
42. Jones, "Kate Bender," p. 82.
43. Adleman, *Bloody Benders*, p. 178.
44. *Internet Crime Archive*, "The Bender Family," p. 34.
45. Adleman, *Bloody Benders*, p. 14.
46. Ramsland, *Human Predator*, p. 68; Schechter, *Serial Killer Files*, p. 139.
47. Harold Schechter and David Everitt, *The A-Z Encyclopedia of Serial Killers* (New York: Simon and Schuster, 1996), p. 209.
48. Michael Newton, *The Encyclopedia of Serial Killers* (New York: Checkmark Books, 2000), p. 101; Peter Vronsky, *Serial Killers: The Method and Madness of Monsters* (New York: Berkley Books, 2004), p. 71.
49. Jones, "Kate Bender," pp. 87–88.
50. Adleman, *Bloody Benders*, pp. 86–89.
51. Kansas State Historical Monument, "The Bloody Benders." Mayo's 2008 study suggested a time frame for the murders between the Winter of 1871 and the Spring of 1873. See Mayo, *American Murder*, p. 31.
52. Newton, *The Encyclopedia*, p. 101; Vronsky, *Serial Killers*, p. 71.
53. Jones, "Kate Bender," p. 84.
54. Schechter and Everitt, *A-Z Encyclopedia*, p. 209.
55. Schechter, *Serial Killer Files*, p. 138.
56. Bolitho, "Old Man Bender's," p. 482.

57. Ramsland, *Human Predator*, p. 68.

58. Bolitho, "Old Man Bender's," p. 483; Schechter, *Serial Killer Files*, p. 138; and Jones, "Kate Bender," p. 83.

59. Adleman, *Bloody Benders*, pp. 36–37. Mayo mentioned that the room divider was made from a covered wagon cover. See Mayo, *American Murder*, p. 31.

60. *Internet Crime Archive*, "The Bender Family," p. 32.Despite an optimal location and even newspaper ads and posters, the Benders were generally ineffective in luring victims to their home. Bolitho recalled that "Apparently the advertisement did not attract many to the inn. The journey was long and difficult, and it is not recorded that more than two or three sufferers came . . . Occasionally a stray visitor ate there." See Bolitho, "Old Man Bender's," p. 483.

61. Bolitho, "Old Man Bender's," p. 482.

62. Schechter, *Serial Killer Files*, p. 138.

63. Jones, "Kate Bender," p. 83.

64. Adleman, *Bloody Benders*, pp. 7, 56–57.

65. Bolitho, "Old Man Bender's," p. 483; Adleman, *Bloody Benders*, pp. 151, 229; and Everitt, *Human Monsters*, p. 41.

66. Schechter and Everitt, *A-Z Encyclopedia*, p. 209.

67. Ramsland, *Human Predator*, p. 68.

68. *Internet Crime Archive*, "The Bender Family," p. 32.

69. Bolitho, "Old Man Bender's," p. 484.

70. Schechter, *Serial Killer Files*, p. 139.

71. Everitt, *Human Monsters*, p. 41.

72. Jones, "Kate Bender," pp. 88–89.

73. Adleman, *Bloody Benders*, pp. 177–79.

74. *Internet Crime Archive*, "The Bender Family," p. 32.

75. Schechter and Everitt, *A-Z Encyclopedia*, p. 209.

76. Schechter, *Serial Killer Files*, p. 138; Everitt, *Human Monsters*, pp. 41–42; and Jones, "Kate Bender," pp. 87–88.

77. Everitt, *Human Monsters*, pp. 41–42.

78. Bolitho, "Old Man Bender's," p. 484; Schechter, *Serial Killer Files*, p. 138; Jones, "Kate Bender," p. 89; and Adleman, *Bloody Benders*, p. 178.

79. Adleman, *Bloody Benders*, pp. 181–89.

80. Jones, "Kate Bender," p. 87.

81. Schechter and Everitt, *A-Z Encyclopedia*, p. 209.

82. Ramsland, *Human Predator*, p. 68.

83. Bolitho, "Old Man Bender's," p. 484.

84. Schechter, *Serial Killer Files*, p. 42.

85. Everitt, *Human Monsters*, p. 42.

86. Bolitho, "Old Man Bender's," p. 485.

87. Adleman, *Bloody Benders*, pp. 16–18.

88. Adleman, *Bloody Benders*, p. 195.

89. Adleman, *Bloody Benders*, pp. 175, 232.

90. Ramsland, *Human Predator*, p. 68.

91. Everitt, *Human Monsters*, p. 40.
92. Adleman, *Bloody Benders*, pp. 88–90, 188.
93. Ramsland, *Human Predator*, p. 68; Newton, *The Encyclopedia*, p. 101.
94. *Internet Crime Archive*, "The Bender Family," p. 32; Bolitho, "Old Man Bender's," pp. 484–85.
95. J. Kramer. Personal communication. 1910. Adleman provided an extended description of such a vigilante justice scenario. See Adleman, *Bloody Benders*, pp. 187–225. Mayo also recalled this alternate version, "The posse had found the family. They shot Pa, Ma, and young John, and burned Kate alive before they threw the bodies down a 20-foot well." See Mayo, *American Murder*, p. 31.
96. Schechter, *Serial Killer Files*, pp. 139–40.
97. Jones, "Kate Bender," pp. 87–89.
98. Ramsland, *Human Predator*, p. 68.
99. Vronsky, *Serial Killers: Method*, p. 71.
100. Bolitho, "Old Man Bender's," p. 485.
101. Everitt, *Human Monsters*, p. 41. Mayo noted that "The Benders had been carrying several thousand dollars and the posse had split the money." See Mayo, *American Murder*, p. 31.
102. Everitt, *Human Monsters*, p. 41.
103. Jones, "Kate Bender," p. 90.
104. Jones, "Kate Bender," p. 87.
105. Adleman, *Bloody Benders*, pp. 20–21; 170; 176–77; 181; 224; 236–37.
106. John Harris, "Miss Kate Bender," *Kansas*, 1936.
107. Bolitho, "Old Man Bender's," p. 482; Jones, "Kate Bender," pp. 82–83.
108. Adleman, *Bloody Benders*, pp. 96–97.
109. Adleman, *Bloody Benders*, p. 236.
110. Adleman, *Bloody Benders*, p. 191.
111. Adleman, *Bloody Benders*, p. 238.
112. Adleman, *Bloody Benders*, p. 131.
113. Everitt, *Human Monsters*, p. 42.

CHAPTER 2

1. Colin Wilson and Damon Wilson, *The Killers Among Us: Sex, Madness & Mass Murder* (New York: Warner Books, 1995), p. 148; Brian Lane and Wilfred Gregg, *The Encyclopedia of Serial Killers* (New York: Berkley Books, 1995), p. 217.
2. Philip Jenkins, *Using Murder: The Social Construction of Serial Homicide* (New York: Aldine De Gruyter, 1994), p. 33; Harold Schechter, *The Serial Killer Files* (New York: Ballantine Books, 2003), p. 142.
3. David Everitt, *Human Monsters: An Illustrated Encyclopedia of the World's Most Vicious Murderers* (Chicago: Contemporary Books, 1993), p. 56.
4. Schechter, *Serial Killer Files*, p. 183.
5. Schechter, *Serial Killer Files*, p. 273.

6. Katherine Ramsland, *The Human Predator: A Historical Chronicle of Serial Murder and Forensic Investigation* (New York: Berkley Books, 2005), p. 89.

7. "Detectives Search Murder Castle," *Chicago Daily News*, July 29, 1895, p. 3.

8. "Herman Mudgett," *Serial Killers* (n.d.). http://home.cfl.rr.com/hagar/Mudgett.htm, p. 2. Accessed on September 3, 2006; David Lester, *Serial Killers: The Insatiable Passion* (Philadelphia: The Charles Press, Publishers, 1995), p. 22; Schechter, *Serial Killer Files*, p. 356; and Time-Life Books, *True Crime: Serial Killers* (Alexandria, Virginia: Time-Life Books, 1992), p. 95.

9. Lane and Gregg, *The Encyclopedia*, p. 267.

10. Lane and Gregg, *The Encyclopedia*, p. 267.

11. Wilson and Wilson, *Killers Among Us*, p. 148; Everitt, *Human Monsters*, p. 56; and Schechter, *Serial Killer Files*, p. 180.

12. Wilson and Wilson, *Killers Among Us*, p. 148.

13. Everitt, *Human Monsters*, p. 56; Schechter, *Serial Killer Files*, p. 180.

14. Everitt, *Human Monsters*, p. 56; Schechter, *Serial Killer Files*, p. 180.

15. Everitt, *Human Monsters*, p. 56; Schechter, *Serial Killer Files*, p. 180.

16. Schechter, *Serial Killer Files*, p. 180.

17. Everitt, *Human Monsters*, p. 56.

18. See Michael Newton, *The Encyclopedia of Serial Killers* (New York: Checkmark Books, 2000), p. 120; Schechter, *Serial Killer Files*, p. 180; and Everitt, *Human Monsters*, p. 56.

19. Publications International Ltd., *Murder & Mayhem* (Lincolnwood, Illinois: Publications International Ltd., 1991), p. 205. Also see Everitt, *Human Monsters*, p. 56.

20. Schechter, *Serial Killer Files*, p. 181.

21. Time-Life Books, *True Crime*, p. 95.

22. Helen Morrison and Harold Goldberg, *My Life Among the Serial Killers* (New York: Harper Collins, 2004), p. 61.

23. Robert W. Dolan, *Serial Murder* (Philadelphia: Chelsea House Publishers, 1997), p. 16; Newton, *The Encyclopedia*, p. 101.

24. Everitt, *Human Monsters*, p. 56; Schechter, *Serial Killer Files*, p. 181.

25. Robin Odell and Wilfred Gregg, *Murderer's Row: An International Murderers' Who's Who* (London: Headline Book Publishing, 1996), p. 216.

26. Cara J. Spindler, "U-M's Most Murderous Alumni: Mr. Herman Mudgett, aka H.H. Holmes," *Michigan Today* (Summer 1999). http://www.umich.edu/'newsinfo/MT/99/Sum99/mt15j99.html, p. 1. Accessed on September 4, 2006.

27. *CrimeLife.com*, "H.H. Holmes" (n.d.). http://www.crimelife.com/killers/holmes.html, p. 1. Accessed on September 6, 2006.

28. Schechter, *Serial Killer Files*, p. 180.

29. Mark Seltzer, *Serial Killers: Death and Life in America's Wound Culture* (New York: Routledge, 1995), p. 7.

30. Seltzer, *Wound Culture*, p. 218.

31. Lane and Gregg, *The Encyclopedia*, p. 267; Time-Life Books, *True Crime*, p. 95.

32. Lane and Gregg, *The Encyclopedia*, p. 267.

33. Time-Life Books, *True Crime*, p. 95.

34. See Wilson and Wilson, *Killers Among Us*, p. 148; Publications International Ltd., *Murder and Mayhem*, p. 205.

35. Publications International Ltd., *Murder and Mayhem*, p. 205.

36. Publications International Ltd., *Murder and Mayhem*, p. 205; Wilson and Wilson, *Killers Among Us*, p. 149.

37. Seltzer, *Wound Culture*, p. 217; Schechter, *Serial Killer Files*, p. 103.

38. Schechter, *Serial Killer Files*, p. 183.

39. Eric W. Hickey, *Serial Murderers and Their Victims* (Belmont, California: Wadsworth Publishing Company, 1997), p. 132; Everitt, *Human Monsters*, p. 55.

40. Ramsland, *Human Predators*, p. 88.

41. Ramsland, *Human Predators*, p. 89.

42. Morrison and Goldberg, *My Life*, p. 61; Everitt, *Human Monsters*, p. 56; and Lane and Gregg, *The Encyclopedia*, p. 267.

43. Colin Wilson and Donald Seaman, *The Serial Killers: A Study in the Psychology of Violence* (New York: Carol Publishing Group, 1992), p. 7; Everitt, *Human Monsters*, p. 55.

44. *CrimeLife.com*, "H.H. Holmes," p. 1; A History of Madness, "H.H. Holmes" (n.d.). http://ajas29.tripod.com/serialbio.html, p. 5. Accessed on September 3, 2006.

45. Wilson and Wilson, *Killers Among Us*, p. 148.

46. Publications International Ltd., *Murder and Mayhem*, p. 205.

47. Spindler, "U-M's Most Murderous Alumni," p. 1; Seltzer, *Wound Culture*, p. 213; and Time-Life Books, *True Crime*, p. 95.

48. Ramsland, *Human Predator*, p. 88. See also Katherine Ramsland, "H.H. Holmes: Master of Illusion: Swindler," *Court TV Crime Library* (2006). http://www.crimelibrary.com/features/fea_printPage.asp?curPage=&thisFile=serial_killers/..., pp. 1–2. Accessed on September 4, 2006; and "Serial Killers" (n.d.). http://members.tripod.com/ahrens/serial/serial.html, p. 1. Accessed on September 4, 2006.

49. Odell and Gregg, *Murderers Row*, p. 216; Everitt, *Human Monsters*, p. 58; and Schechter, *Serial Killer Files*, p. 182.

50. Spindler, "U-M's Most Murderous Alumni," p. 1; Publications International Ltd., *Murder and Mayhem*, p. 205.

51. Schechter, *Depraved*, pp. 171, 180.

52. Schechter, *Serial Killer Files*, p. 334; Spindler, "U-M's Most Murderous Alumni," p. 2; and Time–Life Books, *True Crime*, p. 95.

53. Steven A. Egger, *The Need to Kill: Inside the World of the Serial Killer* (Upper Saddle River, New Jersey: Prentice-Hall, 2003), pp. 3–4; Peter Vronsky, *Serial Killers: The Method and Madness of Monsters* (New York: Berkley Books, 2004), p. 71; Hickey, *Serial Murderers*, p. 139; and Odell and Gregg, *Murderers Row*, p. 216.

54. Jenkins, *Using Murder*, p. 33; Chicago Public Library, "1890–1894: The Monster of 63rd Steet [*sic*], a Serial Killer" (March, 1997). http://www.chipublib.org/004chicago/disasters/63rd_killer.html, p. 1. Accessed on September 4, 2006.

55. Odell and Gregg, *Murderers Row*, p. 216.

56. Schechter, *Serial Killer Files*, p. 183.

57. Lester, *Serial Killers*, p. 22; Time-Life Books, *True Crime*, p. 95.

58. Morrison and Goldberg, *My Life*, p. 61; Lane and Gregg, *The Encyclopedia*, p. 267; Ramsland, *Human Predator*, p. 90; Hickey, *Serial Murderers*, p. 139; and Everitt, *Human Monsters*, p. 58.

59. Schechter, *Serial Killer Files*, p. 142; Chicago Public Library, "1890–1894," p. 1; and A History of Madness, "H.H. Holmes," p. 1.

60. Wilson and Wilson, *Killers Among Us*, pp. 148–49; Lane and Gregg, *The Encyclopedia*, p. 267; and Odell and Gregg, *Murderers Row*, p. 216.

61. Wilson and Wilson, *Killers Among Us*, pp. 149–50; Ramsland, *Human Predator*, p. 88; Everitt, *Human Monsters*, p. 58; and Wilson and Seaman, *The Serial Killers*, p. 7.

62. Everitt, *Human Monsters*, p. 57; *Southcoast Today*, "Doctor's Victims" (May 26, 1997). http://www.geocities/daily/05-96/05e26106mblwn212.htm, p. 1. Accessed on September 4, 2006.

63. Lester, *Serial Killers*, p. 22; Everitt, *Human Monsters*, p. 58; and *CrimeLife.com*, "H.H. Holmes," p. 2.

64. Seltzer, *Wound Culture*, pp. 205, 247; Vronsky, *Serial Killers: Method*, pp. 71, 163–64. Also see Lane and Gregg, *The Encyclopedia*, p. 267.

65. Dolan, *Serial Murder*, p. 16; Ramsland, *Human Predator*, p. 88; and *CrimeLife.com*, "H.H. Holmes," p. 2.

66. Morrison and Goldberg, *My Life*, p. 61; Spindler, "U-M's Most Murderous Alumni," p. 1; Publications International Ltd., *Murder and Mayhem*, p. 205; and *Serial Killers*, "Herman Mudgett," p. 1.

67. Seltzer, *Wound Culture*, p. 217; Lane and Gregg, *The Encyclopedia*, p. 267; and Newton, *The Encyclopedia*, p. 101.

68. Schechter, *Serial Killer Files*, p. 248; Jenkins, *Using Murder*, p. 33; and Everitt, *Human Monsters*, p. 57.

69. Time-Life Books, *True Crime: Serial Killers* (Alexandria, Virginia: Time-Life Books, 1992), p. 95.

70. Hickey, *Serial Murderers*, p. 139; *CrimeLife.com*, "H.H. Holmes," pp. 1–2; and Time-Life Books, *True Crime*, p. 95.

71. Publications International Ltd., *Murder and Mayhem*, p. 205; *Southcoast Today*, "Doctor's Victims," p. 1.

72. Publications International Ltd., *Murder and Mayhem*, pp. 205–6; Schechter, *Serial Killer Files*, p. 182; Everitt, *Human Monsters*, p. 57; Odell and Gregg, *Murderers Row*, p. 216; and *Southcoast Today*, "Doctor's Victims," p. 1.

73. *Southcoast Today*, "Doctor's Victims," p. 1.

74. *Southcoast Today*, "Doctor's Victims," p. 1.

75. Wilson and Seaman, *The Serial Killers*, p. 7; *Southcoast Today*, "Doctor's Victims," p. 1.

76. *Southcoast Today*, "Doctor's Victims," p. 1; Wilson and Seaman, *Serial Killers*, p. 7.

77. Everitt, *Human Monsters*, pp. 57–58; *Southcoast Today*, "Doctor's Victims," p. 1; Ramsland, *Human Predator*, p. 88; Wilson and Seaman, *The Serial Killers*, p. 7; and Wilson and Wilson, *Killers Among Us*, pp. 149–50.

78. Schechter, *Depraved*, pp. 259; 347–51.

79. Everitt, *Human Monsters*, p. 56.

80. *Southcoast Today*, "Doctor's Victims," p. 1; Everitt, *Human Monsters*, p. 57.

81. Herbert Ashbury, *Gem of the Prairie: An Informal History of the Chicago Underworld* (New York: Knopf, 1940), p. 116.

82. Chicago Public Library, "1890–1894," p. 1.

83. Ramsland, *Human Predator*, p. 89.

84. Chicago Public Library, "1890–1894," p. 1.

85. *Southcoast Today*, "Doctor's Victims," p. 1.

86. Charles Boswell and Lewis Thompson, *The Girls in Nightmare House* (New York: Fawcett, 1955), p. 90.

87. *Southcoast Today*, "Doctor's Victims," p. 1.

88. Morrison and Goldberg, *My Life*, p. 61; Everitt, *Human Monsters*, p. 58.

89. Lester, *Serial Killers*, p. 22; Seltzer, *Wound Culture*, p. 209.

90. Ramsland, *Human Predator*, p. 89; Time-Life Books, *True Crime*, p. 95; and Chicago Public Library, "1890–1894," p. 1.

91. Time-Life Books, *True Crime*, p. 95.

92. Lane and Gregg, *The Encyclopedia*, pp. 267–68; Schechter, *Serial Killer Files*, p. 182; and Odell and Gregg, *Murderers Row*, p. 162.

93. Morrison and Goldberg, *My Life*, p. 61; A History of Madness, "H.H. Holmes," p. 6.

94. Seltzer, *Wound Culture*, pp. 205, 215; Chicago Public Library, "1890–1894," p. 1; Lester, *Serial Killers*, pp. 21–22; and Schechter, *Serial Killer Files*, p. 182.

95. Morrison and Goldberg, *My Life*, p. 61; Lane and Gregg, *The Encyclopedia*, p. 267; Chicago Public Library, "1890–1894," p. 1; Seltzer, *Wound Culture*, pp. 205–6; and Time-Life Books, *True Crime*, p. 95.

96. Lester, *Serial Killers*, p. 22; Schechter, *Serial Killer Files*, p. 182; and Everitt, *Human Monsters*, p. 57.

97. Wilson and Wilson, *Killers Among Us*, p. 149.

98. Lane and Gregg, *The Encyclopedia*, p. 267; Odell and Gregg, *Murderers Row*, p. 216.

99. Lane and Gregg, *The Encyclopedia*, p. 268.

100. Schechter, *Serial Killer Files*, pp. 142, 334.

101. Seltzer, *Wound Culture*, p. 206; Publications International Ltd., *Murder and Mayhem*, p. 204; Lane and Gregg, *The Encyclopedia*, p. 267; and Time-Life Books, *True Crime*, p. 95.

102. Odell and Gregg, *Murderers Row*, p. 216; Time-Life Books, *True Crime*, p. 95.

103. Seltzer, *Wound Culture*, p. 206.

104. Vronsky, *Serial Killers: Method*, p. 71; Odell and Gregg, *Murderers Row*, p. 216; and Seltzer, *Wound Culture*, p. 206.

105. Lester, *Serial Killers*, p. 22.

106. Odell and Gregg, *Murderers Row*, p. 216.

107. Morrison and Goldberg, *My Life*, p. 61.

108. Spindler, "U-M's Most Murderous Alumni," p. 1.

109. Seltzer, *Wound Culture*, pp. 206–7.

110. Vronsky, *Serial Killers: Method*, pp. 163–64.

111. Schechter, *Serial Killer Files*, pp. 268–69; and Egger, *The Need to Kill*, p. 56.

112. Morrison and Goldberg, *My Life*, p. 61; Publications International Ltd., *Murder and Mayhem*, p. 206.

113. Odell and Gregg, *Murderers Row*, p. 216; Schechter, *Serial Killers File*, p. 291; Lester, *Serial Killers*, p. 22; Everitt, *Human Monsters*, p. 57; and Publications International Ltd., *Murder and Mayhem*, p. 205.

114. *Southcoast Today*, "Doctor's Victims," p. 1; Everitt, *Human Monsters*, p. 57; and Time-Life Books, *True Crime*, p. 95.

115. Ramsland, *Human Predator*, p. 89; Morrison and Goldberg, *My Life*, p. 61.

116. *Southcoast Today*, "Doctor's Victims," p. 1.

117. Publications International Ltd., *Murder and Mayhem*, p. 205.

118. Morrison and Goldberg, *My Life*, p. 61.

CHAPTER 3

1. Richard Jones, *The Mammoth Book of Women Who Kill* (New York: Carroll & Graf, 2002), p. 232.

2. Colin Wilson and Damon Wilson, *The Killers Among Us: Sex, Madness & Mass Murder*. Volume II (New York: Warner Books, 1995), p. 153.

3. Michael D. Kelleher and C.L. Kelleher, *Murder Most Rare: The Female Serial Killer* (New York: Dell Books, 1998), p. 32.

4. Margaret Lyons, "DNA Tests on Possible Skeleton of Belle Gunness, Serial Killer from 1900s," *Chicago1st* (February 12, 2008). http://chicagoist.com/2008/02/12/dna_tests_on_po.php, p. 1.Accessed on October 31, 2008.

5. "Notorious Hoosiers: Belle Gunness," *INDYSTAR.COM* (October 31, 2008). http://www.indystar.com/apps/pbcs.dll/article?AID=/99999999/N..., p. 1. Accessed on October 31, 2008.

6. Brian Lane, *The Butchers: A Casebook of Macabre Crimes and Forensic Detection* (Kettering, U.K.: Index House, 1991), p. 115; R. Jones, *Mammoth Book*, p. 238.

7. *Bedlam Asylum Crime Files*, "Belle Gunness: The Black Widow of La Porte" (n.d.). http://usersites.horrorfind.com/home.horror/bedlambound/library/g..., p. 1. Accessed on October 31, 2008.

8. Joseph Geringer, "Mrs. Sorenson," *The Crime Library* (n.d.). http://www.trutv.com/library/crime/serial_killers/history/gunness/4..., p. 1. Accessed on October 31, 2008.

9. Kelleher and Kelleher, *Murder Most Rare*, p. 32.

10. Wilson and Wilson, *Killers Among Us*, p. 156.

11. R. Jones, *Mammoth Book*, p. 232.

12. Lane, *Butchers*, p. 112.

13. Ann Jones, *Women Who Kill* (New York: Fawcett Columbine Publishers, 1980), p. 129.

14. *The Biography Channel*, "Belle Gunness" (n.d.). http://www.biography.com/notorious/crimefiles.do?catId=259457&a..., p. 1. Accessed on October 31, 2008.

15. La Porte County Historical Society, "Belle Gunness, La Porte's 'Lady Bluebeard,'" (1999). http://www.laportecountyhistory.org/belleg1.htm, p. 1. Accessed on October 31, 2008.

16. *The Serial Killer Database*, "Belle Gunness" (n.d.). http://www.serialkillerdatabase.net/bellegunness.html, pp. 1–2. Accessed on October 31, 2008.

17. La Porte County Public Library, "The Legend of Belle Gunness" (n.d.). http://www.alco.org/libraries/lepl/belle.html, p. 3. Accessed on October 31, 2008.

18. Michael Newton, *The Encyclopedia of Serial Killers* (New York: Checkmark Books, 2000), p. 88.

19. *Bedlam Asylum Crime Files*, "Belle Gunness," p. 2.

20. *Biography Channel*, "Belle Gunness," p. 1; Geringer, "Mrs. Sorenson," p. 1; Newton, *The Encyclopedia*, p. 88.

21. Newton, *The Encyclopedia*, p. 88; Wilson and Wilson, *Killers Among Us*, p. 156.

22. Kelleher and Kelleher, *Murder Most Rare*, p. 32.

23. Kelleher and Kelleher, *Murder Most Rare*, p. 32; La Porte County Public Library, p. 3.

24. Kelleher and Kelleher, *Murder Most Rare*, p. 32.

25. *Bedlam Asylum Crime Files*, "Belle Gunness," p. 2.

26. *Bedlam Asylum Crime Files*, "Belle Gunness," p. 2.

27. Kelleher and Kelleher, *Murder Most Rare*, p. 33.Newton, *The Encyclopedia*, p. 88.

28. Wilson and Wilson, *Killers Among Us*, p. 156; Newton, *The Encyclopedia*, p. 88; and R. Jones, *Mammoth Book*, p. 129. Belle emigrated in 1886, according to the La Porte County Historical Society. See La Porte County Historical Society, "La Porte's 'Lady Bluebeard,'" p. 1.

29. Kelleher and Kelleher, *Murder Most Foul*, p. 33; La Porte County Public Library, "The Legend," p. 3.

30. La Porte County Public Library, "The Legend," p. 3.

31. Newton, *The Encyclopedia*, p. 88.

32. La Porte County Public Library, "The Legend," p. 3; R. Jones, *Mammoth Book*, p. 232. For a detailed description of the difficulty of a servant's occupation tasks, see *Bedlam Asylum Crime Files*, "Belle Gunness," p. 3.

33. Kelleher and Kelleher, *Murder Most Foul*, p. 33; Newton, *The Encyclopedia*, p. 88.

34. La Porte County Public Library, "The Legend," p. 1.

35. Geringer, "Mrs. Sorenson," p. 1.

36. La Porte County Public Library, "The Legend," p. 1.

37. Kelleher and Kelleher, *Murder Most Foul*, p. 35.

38. R. Jones, *Mammoth Book*, p. 233; A. Jones, *Women Who Kill*, p. 129.

39. Wilson and Wilson, *Killers Among Us*, p. 164; R. Jones, *Mammoth Book*, p. 233; and Geringer, "Mrs. Sorenson," p. 1.

40. Geringer, "Premonition," p. 1; Wilson and Wilson, *Killers Among Us*, p. 153; R. Jones, *Mammoth Book*, p. 238; and A. Jones, *Women Who Kill*, p. 134. However, a different version of events has Belle leaving all of her assets to her children. See *Bedlam Asylum Crime Files*, "Belle Gunness," p. 11.

41. Troy Taylor, "Come Prepared to Stay Forever: Belle Gunness—Lady Bluebeard," *Dead Men Do Tell Tales* (2004). http://www.prairieghosts.com/belle.html, p. 1. Accessed on October 31, 2008.

42. Geringer, "Women of Bad Luck," *The Crime Library*, p. 1.

43. Charles Montaldo, "Belle Gunness," *About.com* (n.d.). http://crime.about.com/od/murder/p/gunness.htm, p. 1. Accessed on October 31, 2008; Niplie Pictures, "Belle Gunness" (May 15, 2008). http://niplie.blogspot.com/2008/05/belle-gunness.html, p. 1. Accessed on October 31, 2008.

44. *Bedlam Asylum Crime Files*, "Belle Gunness," p. 7; Timothy Sexton, "Belle Gunness: America's First Female Serial Killer," *Associated Content* (2008). http://www.associatedcontent.com/pop_print.shtml?content_type=ar..., p. 1. Accessed on October 31, 2008;

45. R. Jones, *Mammoth Book*, p. 238; A. Jones, *Women Who Kill*, p. 138.

46. Taylor, "Come Prepared," p. 1; Kelleher and Kelleher, *Murder Most Foul*, p. 32.

47. Geringer, "More Lovers," *The Crime Library*, p. 1.

48. A. Jones, *Women Who Kill*, p. 131; Wilson and Wilson, *Killers Among Us*, pp. 158–59.

49. R. Jones, *Mammoth Book*, p. 238.

50. *Bedlam Asylum Crime Files*, "Belle Gunness," p. 2.

51. La Porte County Public Library, "The Legend," p. 1.

52. Geringer, "Premonition," *The Crime Library*, p. 1.

53. *Biography Channel*, "Belle Gunness," p. 2.

54. Katherine Ramsland, *The Human Predator: A Historical Chronicle of Serial Murder and Forensic Investigation* (New York: Berkley Books, 2005), p. 102; Wilson and Wilson, *Killers Among Us*, p. 157; and *Biography Channel*, "Belle Gunness," p. 1.

55. Newton, *The Encyclopedia*, p. 88; *Bedlam Asylum Crime Files*, "Belle Gunness," p. 3. Also see La Porte County Public Library, "The Legend," pp. 3–4.

56. Kelleher and Kelleher, *Murder Most Foul*, p. 33; R. Jones, *Mammoth Book*, p. 233; and Lane, *Butchers*, p. 112.

57. R. Jones, *Mammoth Book*, p. 233; Lane, *Butchers*, p. 112.

58. Kelleher and Kelleher, *Murder Most Foul*, p. 34; *Bedlam Asylum Crime Files*, "Belle Gunness," p. 3; and the La Porte County Public Library, "The Legend," p. 4.

59. Geringer, "Mrs. Sorenson," p. 1.

60. Lyons, "DNA Tests," p. 1; Lane, *Butchers*, p. 113; and Newton, *The Encyclopedia*, p. 89.

61. La Porte County Public Library, "The Legend," p. 2.

62. La Porte County Public Library, "The Legend," p. 2; Wilson and Wilson, *Killers Among Us*, p. 156; and Taylor, "Come Prepared," p. 2.

63. Newton, *The Encyclopedia*, p. 89; Kelleher and Kelleher, *Murder Most Foul*, pp. 33, 36.

64. Publications International Ltd., *Murder and Mayhem* (Lincolnwood, Illinois: Publications International Ltd., 1991), p. 110.

65. Wilson and Wilson, *Killers Among Us*, p. 165; *INDYSTAR.COM*, "Notorious Hoosiers," p. 1.

66. Kelleher and Kelleher, *Murder Most Foul*, p. 36; *Biography Channel*, "Belle Gunness," p. 2; La Porte County Historical Society, "La Porte's 'Lady Bluebeard,'" p. 2; and *Bedlam Asylum Crime Files*, "Belle Gunness," p. 14.

67. Sexton, "America's First," p. 1; *Serial Killer Database*, "Belle Gunness," p. 1; and *Bedlam Asylum Crime Files*, "Belle Gunness," p. 17.

68. Newton, *The Encyclopedia*, p. 90; Montaldo, "Belle Gunness," p. 1; and *Niplie Pictures*, "Belle Gunness," p. 1.

69. Healthy Communities of La Porte County, "Belle Gunness" (2008). http://www.laportecounty.net/history/belle_gunness.html, p. 1. Accessed on October 31, 2008.

70. Sexton, "America's First," p. 1.

71. *Bedlam Asylum Crime Files*, "Belle Gunness," p. 16; La Porte County Public Library, "The Legend," p. 6.

72. *Fortune City*, "Belle Gunness" (n.d.). http://www.fortunecity.com/roswell.hammer/73/gunness.html, p. 1. Accessed on October 31, 2008; Lyons, "DNA Tests," p. 1; Lane, *Butchers*, p. 116; and *Bedlam Asylum Crime Files*, "Belle Gunness," pp. 3, 17.

73. *Serial Killer Database*, "Belle Gunness," p. 1; Sexton, "America's First," p. 1.

74. A. Jones, *Women Who Kill*, p. 132; Lane, *Butchers*, p. 114.

75. Lane, *Butchers*, p. 116; La Porte County Public Library, "The Legend," p. 7.

76. Eric Hickey, *Serial Murderers and Their Victims* (Belmont, California: Wadsworth Publishing Company, 1997) pp. 74–75; A. Jones, *Women Who Kill*,

p. 137; Kelleher and Kelleher, *Murder Most Foul*, p. 33; and R. Jones, *Mammoth Book*, p. 232.

77. *INDYSTAR.COM*, "Notorious Hoosiers," p. 1; *Bedlam Asylum Crime Files*, "Belle Gunness," p. 4; and Geringer, "Mrs. Sorenson," p. 1.

78. A. Jones, *Women Who Kill*, p. 130; Lane, *Butchers*, p. 112; La Porte County Historical Society, "La Porte's 'Lady Bluebeard,'" p. 1; La Porte County Public Library, "The Legend," p. 4; Ramsland, *Human Predator*, p. 102; and Wilson and Wilson, *Killers Among Us*, p. 156. Her actual insurance payout was $8,000, not $8,500. See La Porte County Historical Society, "La Porte's 'Lady Bluebeard,'" p. 1.

79. A. Jones, *Women Who Murder*, p. 130; *Biography Channel*, "Belle Gunness," p. 2; La Porte County Public Library, "The Legend," p. 4; Geringer, "Executioner," p. 1; and *Bedlam Asylum Crime Files*, "Belle Gunness," p. 3.

80. La Porte County Public Library, "The Legend," p. 5; *Bedlam Asylum Crime Files*, "Belle Gunness," p. 5.

81. La Porte County Public Library, "The Legend," p. 5; *Bedlam Asylum Crime Files*, "Belle Gunness," p. 5; and A. Jones, *Women Who Kill*, pp. 130–31.

82. *Biography Channel*, "Belle Gunness," p. 2; La Porte County Public Library, "The Legend," p. 4; and Wilson and Wilson, *Killers Among Us*, p. 167.

83. *Bedlam Asylum Crime Files*, "Belle Gunness," pp. 7, 14; A. Jones, *Women Who Kill*, pp. 132–33; and La Porte County Public Library, "The Legend," p. 1.

84. *Bedlam Asylum Crime Files*, "Belle Gunness," pp. 8, 14; Wilson and Wilson, *Killers Among Us*, p. 154; A. Jones, *Women Who Kill*, pp. 131–32; Geringer, "So Many Disappeared," *The Crime Library*, p. 1; and Sexton, "America's First," p. 1.

85. Wilson and Wilson, *Killers Among Us*, p. 166.

86. Ramsland, *Human Predator*, p. 101; R. Jones, *Mammoth Book*, p. 236; and Taylor, "Come Prepared," p. 2.

87. Geringer, "Gold Digger," *The Crime Library*, p. 1.

88. Healthy Communities, "Belle Gunness," p. 1; *Bedlam Asylum Crime Files*, "Belle Gunness," p. 17.

89. Montaldo, "Belle Gunness," p. 1; Taylor, "Come Prepared," p. 2; and Wilson and Wilson, *Killers Among Us*, p. 165.

90. Newton, *The Encyclopedia*, p. 90; Kelleher and Kelleher, *Murder Most Foul*, p. 37; Sexton, "America's First," p. 1; and *Dead Silence: The Serial Killer Blog*, "Female Serial Killer: Belle Gunness" (2006). http://deadsilence.wordpress.com/2006/08/02/female-serial-killer-be..., p. 1. Accessed on October 31, 2008.

91. *Bedlam Asylum Crime Files*, "Belle Gunness," p. 17.

92. Kelleher and Kelleher, *Murder Most Foul*, p. 35.

93. Newton, *The Encyclopedia*, p. 89; *Serial Killer Database*, "Belle Gunness," p. 1; Lyons, "DNA Tests," p. 1; INDYSTAR.COM, "Notorious Hoosiers," p. 1; and Publications International Ltd., *Murder and Mayhem*, p. 109.

94. *Serial Killer Database*, "Belle Gunness," p. 4; *Bedlam Asylum Crime Files*, "Belle Gunness," p. 6.

95. La Porte County Public Library, "The Legend," p. 1.

96. Healthy Communities, "Belle Gunness," p. 1; Wilson and Wilson, *Killers Among Us*, p. 159.

97. R. Jones, *Mammoth Book*, p. 234; Geringer, "Gold Digger," p. 1.

98. Newton, *The Encyclopedia*, p. 89; Taylor, "Come Prepared," p. 2; Ramsland, *Human Predator*, p. 102; Wilson and Wilson, *Killers Among Us*, p. 154; and La Porte County Public Library, "The Legend," p. 1.

99. Sexton, "America's First," p. 1.

100. *Bedlam Asylum Crime Files*, "Belle Gunness," p. 8.

101. Belle Gunness. Personal communication (n.d.); Lane, *Butchers*, p. 113.

CHAPTER 4

1. Harold Schechter, *The Serial Killer Files* (New York: Ballantine Books, 2003), p. 211; Summer Banks, "The Butcher of Hanover: The Life of Serial Killer Fritz Haarmann," Associated Content (2008). http://www.associatedcontent.com/pop_print.shtml?content_type=ar..., p. 1. Accessed on November 10, 2008.

2. Banks, "The Butcher of Hanover," p. 1; *Monstropedia*, "Fritz Haarmann" (n.d.). http://www.monstropedia.org/index.php?title=Fritz_Haarmann, p. 1. Accessed on November 10, 2008; and *Onpedia*, "Fritz Haarmann" (2008). http://www.onpedia.com/encyclopedia/fritz-haarmann, p. 1. Accessed on November 10, 2008.

3. Colin Wilson and Donald Seaman, *The Serial Killers: A Study in the Psychology of Violence* (New York: Carol Publishing Group, 1992), p. 175.

4. Michael Newton, *The Encyclopedia of Serial Killers* (New York: Checkmark Books, 2000), p. 92; Alexander Gilbert, "Incarceration," *The Crime Library* (n.d.). http://trutv.com/library/crime/serial_killers/history/haarmann/2b..., p. 1. Accessed on November 10, 2008; and Gilbert, "Reign of Terror," *The Crime Library*, p. 1. Accessed on November 10, 2008.

5. Steven Morris, "Fritz Haarmann—Werewolf in Hannover [*sic*]," *New Criminologist* (September 20, 2007). http://www.newcriminologist.com/article.asp?cid=107&nid=19, p. 3. Accessed on November 10, 2008; Banks, "The Butcher of Hanover," p. 1; and *Monstropedia*, "Fritz Haarmann," p. 1.

6. Katherine Ramsland, *The Human Predator: A Historical Chronicle of Serial Murder and Forensic Investigation* (New York: Berkley Books, 2005), p. 115.

7. Colin Wilson and Damon Wilson, *The Killers Among Us: Sex, Madness & Mass Murder* (New York: Warner Books, 1995), p. 110.

8. Wilson and Wilson, *Killers Among Us*, p. 110; Morris, "Fritz Haarmann—Werewolf," p. 1; and Newton, *The Encyclopedia*, p. 91.

9. Morris, "Fritz Haarmann—Werewolf," p. 5; Gilbert, "The Making of a Killer," *The Crime Library*, p. 1; *FritzHaarmann@Everything2.com*, "Fritz

Haarmann" (n.d.). http://everything2.com/e2node/Fritz%2520Haarmann, p. 1. Accessed on November 10, 2008; and Banks, "The Butcher of Hanover," p. 1.

10. Banks, "The Butcher of Hanover," p. 1; Morris, "Fritz Haarmann—Werewolf," p. 5; *FritzHaarmann@Everything2.com*, "Fritz Haarmann," p. 1; and Gilbert, "The Making of a Killer," p. 1.

11. Gilbert, "The Making of a Killer," p. 1; Banks, "The Butcher of Hanover," p. 1; and Morris, "Fritz Haarmann—Werewolf," p. 5.

12. Gilbert, "The Making of a Killer," p. 1; Morris, "Fritz Haarmann—Werewolf," p. 5.

13. Morris, "Fritz Haarmann—Werewolf," p. 6; Gilbert, "The Making of a Killer," p. 1; Brian Lane, *The Butchers: A Casebook of Macabre Crimes and Forensic Detection*. Kettering, U.K.: Index House, 1994), p. 97; and *FritzHaarmann@Everything2.com*, "Fritz Haarmann," p. 1.

14. Wilson and Wilson, *Killers Among Us*, p. 110.

15. Morris, "Fritz Haarmann—Werewolf," p. 6; Gilbert, "The Making of a Killer," p. 1.

16. Ramsland, *Human Predator*, p. 114; *FritzHaarmann@Everything2.com*, "Fritz Haarmann," p. 1.

17. Morris, "Fritz Haarmann—Werewolf," p. 6; Gilbert, "The Making of a Killer," p. 1.

18. Morris, "Fritz Haarmann—Werewolf," p. 6; Gilbert, "The Making of a Killer," p. 1.

19. Wilson and Wilson, *Killers Among Us*, p. 111; Lane, *Butchers*, p. 97; and Banks, "The Butcher of Hanover," p. 1.

20. David Lester, *Serial Killers: The Insatiable Passion* (Philadelphia: The Charles Press, Publishers, 1995), p. 21; Brian Lane and Wilfred Gregg, *The Encyclopedia of Serial Killers* (New York: Berkley Books, 1995), p. 192; and Wilson and Wilson, *Killers Among Us*, p. 112.

21. Katherine Ramsland, "A Most Vicious Vampire," *Vampire Killers* (2008). http://www.trutv.com/library/crime/serial_killers/weird/vampires/11..., p. 1. Accessed on November 10, 2008; Lane, *Butchers*, p. 97; Ramsland, *Human Predator*, p. 114; and Wilson and Wilson, *Killers Among Us*, pp. 110–11.

22. Morris, "Fritz Haarmann—Werewolf," p. 8.

23. David Everitt, *Human Monsters: An Illustrated Encyclopedia of the World's Most Vicious Murderers* (Chicago: Contemporary Books, 1993), p. 85.

24. Ramsland, "A Most Vicious Vampire," p. 1.

25. Wilson and Wilson, *Killers Among Us*, p. 109.

26. Morris, "Fritz Haarmann—Werewolf," p. 26.

27. Everitt, *Human Monsters*, p. 86.

28. Morris, "Fritz Haarmann—Werewolf," p. 3; Lane and Gregg, *The Encyclopedia*, p. 192; Wilson and Wilson, *Killers Among Us*, p. 111; and Gilbert, "First Finds," *The Crime Library*, p. 1.

29. Schechter, *Serial Killer Files*, p. 212; Newton, *The Encyclopedia*, p. 91; and Wilson and Wilson, *Killers Among Us*, p. 111.

30. Gilbert, "Young Adulthood," p. 1.

31. Lane, *Butchers*, p. 97; Gilbert, "Young Adulthood," p. 1.
32. Schechter, *Serial Killer Files*, pp. 242–43; Everitt, *Human Monsters*, p. 35.
33. Ramsland, *Human Predator*, p. 114.
34. *FritzHaarmann@Everything2.com*, "Fritz Haarmann," p. 1.
35. Wilson and Wilson, *Killers Among Us*, p. 107.
36. Lane and Gregg, *The Encyclopedia*, p. 192; *Fortune City*, "Fritz Haarmann" (n.d.). http://www.fortunecity.com/roswell/stysreiber/273/haarmann_mo.htm, p. 1. Accessed on November 10, 2008; Peter Vronsky, *Serial Killers: The Method and Madness of Monsters* (New York: Berkley Books, 2005), p. 68; and Morris, "Fritz Haarmann—Werewolf," p. 11.
37. Philip Jenkins, *Using Murder: The Social Construction of Serial Homicide* (New York: Aldine de Gruyter, 1994), p. 183; Schechter, *Serial Killer Files*, p. 212.
38. Newton, *The Encyclopedia*, p. 91; Wilson and Wilson, *Killers Among Us*, p. 107.
39. Wilson and Wilson, *Killers Among Us*, p. 110.
40. Morris, "Fritz Haarmann—Werewolf," p. 6; Gilbert, "Inside the Mind of Haarmann," *The Crime Library*, p. 1; and Wilson and Wilson, *Killers Among Us*, p. 107.
41. Lane, *Butchers*, p. 97; *Fortune City*, "Fritz Haarmann," p. 1; Morris, "Fritz Haarmann—Werewolf," p. 7; and Gilbert, "Making of a Killer," p. 1.
42. Wilson and Wilson, *Killers Among Us*, p. 111.
43. Ramsland, "A Most Vicious Vampire," p. 1.
44. Wilson and Wilson, *Killers Among Us*, p. 111.
45. Newton, *The Encyclopedia*, p. 91.
46. Wilson and Wilson, *Killers Among Us*, p. 112.
47. Ramsland, *Human Predator*, p. 114.
48. *FritzHaarmann@Everything2.com*, "Fritz Haarmann," p. 1.
49. Wilson and Wilson, *Killers Among Us*, p. 107.
50. Gilbert, "The First Finds," *The Crime Library*, p. 1.
51. Gilbert, "The First Finds," p. 1; Morris, "Fritz Haarmann—Werewolf," p. 2.
52. Schechter, *Serial Killer Files*, p. 6; Wilson and Wilson, *Killers Among Us*, p. 107.
53. Everitt, *Human Monsters*, p. 85; Schechter, *Serial Killer Files*, p. 102; Morris, "Fritz Haarmann—Werewolf," p. 16; Ramsland, *Human Predator*, p. 114; and *Angelfire*, "Fritz Haarmann" (n.d.). http://www.angelfire.com/ca/serialmurder/FritzHaarmann.html, p. 1. Accessed on November 10, 2008.
54. Lane and Gregg, *The Encyclopedia*, p. 192; Morris, "Fritz Haarmann—Werewolf," p. 16; Lane, *Butchers*, p. 98; and *Knowledgerush.com*, "Fritz Haarmann" (n.d.). http://www.knowledgerush.com/kr/encyclopedia/Fritz_Haarmann/, p. 1. Accessed on November 10, 2008.
55. *Fortune City*, "Fritz Haarmann," p. 1; Everitt, *Human Monsters*, p. 85; Schechter, *Serial Killer Files*, p. 212; and Banks, "The Butcher of Hanover," p. 1.

56. Everitt, *Human Monsters*, p. 85; Schechter, *Serial Killer Files*, p. 212; *Monstropedia*, "Fritz Haarmann," p. 1; and *Onpedia*, "Fritz Haarmann," p. 1.

57. Wilson and Wilson, *Killers Among Us*, p. 114; Ramsland, *Human Predator*, p. 114; and Morris, "Fritz Haarmann—Werewolf," p. 14.

58. Lane, *Butchers*, p. 98; *FritzHaarmann@Everything2.com*, "Fritz Haarmann," p. 1; and Lane and Gregg, *The Encyclopedia*, p. 194.

59. Gilbert, "The End," *The Crime Library*, pp. 1–2.

60. *Onpedia*, "Fritz Haarmann," p. 1; *Monstropedia*, "Fritz Haarmann," p. 1; and Banks, "The Butcher of Hanover," p. 1.

61. Lane, *Butchers*, p. 96; Newton, *The Encyclopedia*, p. 91; Wilson and Wilson, *Killers Among Us*, p. 113; and Lane and Gregg, *The Encyclopedia*, p. 194.

62. Lane and Gregg, *The Encyclopedia*, p. 193;Lane, *Butchers*, p. 98.

63. Wilson and Wilson, *Killers Among Us*, p. 114; Gilbert, "Conclusion," *The Crime Library*, p. 1.

64. Newton, *The Encyclopedia*, p. 91; Gilbert, "Deadly Combination," *The Crime Library*, p. 1.

65. Morris, "Fritz Haarmann—Werewolf," p. 15; Wilson and Wilson, *Killers Among Us*, p. 109; Lane, *Butchers*, p. 98; and Gilbert, "Inside the Mind," p. 1.

66. Lane, *Butchers*, p. 97; Morris, "Fritz Haarmann—Werewolf," p. 9; and Gilbert, "Young Adulthood," p. 1.

67. Everitt, *Human Monsters*, p. 85; Newton, *The Encyclopedia*, p. 91; and Lane and Gregg, *The Encyclopedia*, p. 192.

68. Schechter, *Serial Killer Files*, p. 212; Newton, *The Encyclopedia*, p. 91; *Angelfire*, "Fritz Haarmann," p. 1; and *FritzHaarmann@Everything2.com*, "Fritz Haarmann," p. 1.

69. Lester, *Insatiable Passion*, p. 21; Jenkins, *Using Murder*, p. 193; and Lane and Gregg, *The Encyclopedia*, p. 192.

70. Wilson and Wilson, *Killers Among Us*, p. 112; Morris, "Fritz Haarmann —Werewolf," p. 9; and Banks, "The Butcher of Hanover," p. 1.

71. Wilson and Wilson, *Killers Among Us*, p. 112; Schechter, *Serial Killer Files*, p. 212.

72. Gilbert, "Young Adulthood," p. 1; Morris, "Fritz Haarmann—Werewolf," p. 9; and Newton, *The Encyclopedia*, p. 91.

73. Everitt, *Human Monsters*, p. 85; Morris, "Fritz Haarmann—Werewolf," p. 10; and Newton, *The Encyclopedia*, p. 91.

74. Lester, *Insatiable Passion*, p. 21; *Fortune City*, "Fritz Haarmann," p. 1; Lane and Gregg, *The Encyclopedia*, p. 192; Gilbert, "Reign of Terror," p, 1; and Morris, "Fritz Haarmann—Werewolf," p. 11.

75. Jenkins, *Using Murder*, p. 38; Vronsky, *Serial Murder: Method*, p. 68; *Angelfire*, "Fritz Haarmann," p. 1; *Fortune City*, "Fritz Haarmann," p. 1; Newton, *The Encyclopedia*, p. 92; *FritzHaarmann@Everything2com.*, "Fritz Haarmann," p. 1; *Onpedia*, "Fritz Haarmann," p. 1; *Monstropedia*, "Fritz Haarmann," p. 1; Banks, "The Butcher of Hanover," p. 1; Lane, *Butchers*, 98; Wilson and Wilson, *Killers Among Us*, p. 107; Gilbert, "First Finds," p. 1; and Morris, "Fritz Haarmann—Werewolf," p. 16.

76. Jenkins, *Using Murder*, p. 183; Schechter, *Serial Killer Files*, p. 212; Lane, *Butchers*, p. 96; *Fortune City*, "Fritz Haarmann," p. 1; Lane and Gregg, *The Encyclopedia*, p. 194;Eric Hickey, *Serial Murderers and their Victims* (Belmont, California: Wadsworth Publishing Company, 1997), p. 248; Newton, *The Encyclopedia*, p. 92; and Wilson and Wilson, *Killers Among Us*, p. 115.

77. Wilson and Seaman, *The Serial Killers*, p. 11; Ramsland, "A Most Vicious Vampire," p. 1; Schechter, *Serial Killer Files*, p. 147; *Angelfire*, "Fritz Haarmann," p. 1; Lane and Gregg, *The Encyclopedia*, p. 192; *Knowledgerush*, "Fritz Haarmann," p. 1; Everitt, *Human Monsters*, p. 86; and Ramsland, *Human Predator*, p. 114.

78. Gilbert, "Deadly Combination," p. 1; *FritzHaarmann@Everything2.com*, "Fritz Haarmann," p. 1; Lane, *Butchers*, p. 97; Newton, *The Encyclopedia*, p. 91; and Wilson and Wilson, *Killers Among Us*, p. 115.

79. Lane and Gregg, *The Encyclopedia*, p. 193.

80. Lane, *Butchers*, p. 97; Everitt, *Human Monsters*, pp. 84–85; and *Knowledgerush*, "Fritz Haarmann," p. 1.

81. *Monstropedia*, "Fritz Haarmann," p. 1; Lane, *Butchers*, p. 96.

82. Morris, "Fritz Haarmann—Werewolf," p. 11.

83. Ramsland, "A Most Vicious Vampire," p. 1; Gilbert, "Reign of Terror," p. 1.

84. Ramsland, "A Most Vicious Vampire," p. 1; Gilbert, "Reign of Terror," p. 1.

85. Lester, *Insatiable Passion*, p. 21.

86. Lane and Gregg, *The Encyclopedia*, p. 192; Everitt, *Human Monsters*, p. 85; *Knowledgerush*, "Fritz Haarmann," p. 1; and *Onpedia*, "Fritz Haarmann," p. 1.

87. Lane, *Butchers*, p. 97, Morris, "Fritz Haarmann—Werewolf," p. 10; and *FritzHaarmann@Everything2.com*, "Fritz Haarmann," p. 1.

88. Vronsky, *Serial Killers: Methods*, p. 68; Jenkins, *Using Murder*, p. 43.

89. Lester, *Insatiable Passion*, p. 21; *Fortune City*, "Fritz Haarmann," p. 1.

90. Lane, *Butchers*, p. 97; Lane and Gregg, *The Encyclopedia*, p. 192.

91. Schechter, *Serial Killer Files*, p. 212.

92. Morris, "Fritz Haarmann—Werewolf," p. 11; Gilbert, "Making of Killer," p. 1.

93. Lane, *Butchers*, p. 98.

94. Gilbert, "Conclusion," p. 1; Newton, *The Encyclopedia*, p. 91; and Lane, *Butchers*, p. 97.

95. Everitt, *Human Monsters*, p. 85; *Fortune City*, "Fritz Haarmann," p. 1; Gilbert, "Reign of Terror," p. 1; and *FritzHaarmann@Everything2.com*, "Fritz Haarmann," p. 1.

96. Lester, *Insatiable Passion*, p. 21; Newton, *The Encyclopedia*, p. 91.

97. Vronsky, *Serial Killers: Methods*, p. 68; Everitt, *Human Monsters*, p. 85. *Angelfire*, "Fritz Haarmann," p. 1; *Knowledgerush*, "Fritz Haarmann," p. 1.

98. *Monstropedia*, "Fritz Haarmann," p. 1; Banks, "The Butcher of Hanover," p. 1; and Ramsland, *Human Predator*, p. 114.

99. Everitt, *Human Monsters*, p. 86; Newton, *The Encyclopedia*, p. 91; *Angelfire*, "Fritz Haarmann," p. 1; Lane, *Butchers*, p. 98; Morris, "Fritz Haarmann—Werewolf," p. 15; Gilbert, "Reign of Terror," p. 1; and *Knowledgerush*, "Fritz Haarmann," p. 1.

100. *Fortune City*, "Fritz Haarmann," p. 1; Morris, "Fritz Haarmann—Werewolf," p. 14; and Banks, "The Butcher of Hanover," p. 1; and *Monstropedia*, "Fritz Haarmann," p. 1.

101. Wilson and Seaman, *Serial Killers*, p. 11; Gilbert, "Reign of Terror," p. 1.

102. Lane, *Butchers*, p. 98, Wilson and Wilson, *Killers Among Us*, p. 108; *Angelfire*, "Fritz Haarmann," p. 1; and Ramsland, "A Most Vicious Vampire," p. 1.

103. Gilbert, "Incarceration," *The Crime Library*, p. 1; Morris, "Fritz Haarmann—Werewolf," p. 4.

CHAPTER 5

1. Peter Vronsky, *Serial Killers: The Method and Madness of Monsters* (New York: Berkley Books, 2004), p. 33.

2. Anne Commire, *Women In World History: A Bibliographical Encyclopedia* (Waterford, Connecticut: Yorkin Publications, 1999), p. 343.

3. *Nationmaster.com*, "Encyclopedia—Marie Becker" (2005). http://www.nationmaster.com/encyclopedia/Marie-Becker, p. 1. Accessed on January 3, 2009.

4. *AllExperts.com*, "Marie Becker—Encyclopedia" (n.d.). http://en.allexperts.com/e/m/ma/marie_becker.htm, p. 1. Accessed on January 3, 2009.

5. Jay Robert Nash, *Encyclopedia of World Crime* (Wilmette, Illinois: Crime Books Inc., 1990), p. 309.

6. *Bedlam Asylum Crime Files*, "Marie Becker" (n.d.). http://usersites.horrorfind.com/home/horror/bedlambound/library/b..., p. 3. Accessed on January 3, 2009.

7. Michael Kelleher and C.L. Kelleher, *Murder Most Rare: The Female Serial Killer* (New York: Dell Publishing, 1999), p. 59.

8. *Bedlam Asylum Crime Files*, "Marie Becker," p. 3.

9. Brian Lane and Wilfred Gregg, *The Encyclopedia of Serial Killers* (New York: Berkley Books, 1995), p. 44.

10. Nash, *Encyclopedia of World Crime*, p. 310.

11. Kerry Seagrave, *Women Serial and Mass Murderers: A Worldwide Reference, 1580 Through 1990* (Jefferson, North Carolina: McFarland & Company, 1992), p. 33.

12. Commire, *Women*, p. 343.

13. Lane and Gregg, *The Encyclopedia*, p. 44.

14. Bernard O'Donnell, *The World's Worst Women* (London: Allen, 1953), pp. 163–72. Also see Nash, *Encyclopedia of World Crime*, p. 309.

15. O'Donnell, *World's Worst*, pp. 163–72. Also see *Bedlam Asylum Crime Files*, "Marie Becker," p. 3.

16. Seagrave, *Women Serial*, p. 34.

17. *Moerder in Serie*, "Marie Alexandrine Becker," *SerienKiller* (2003). http://www.moerder-in-serie.de/marie-alexandrine-becker.php, p. 1. Accessed on January 3, 2009.

18. Commire, *Women*, p. 343.

19. Kelleher and Kelleher, *Murder Most*, p. 58.

20. *Bedlam Asylum Crime Files*, "Marie Becker," p. 1.

21. Seagrave, *Women Serial*, p. 32.

22. *Crime Museum UK*, "Lady Killers," *Discovery Channel* (2008). http://www.discoverychannel.co.uk/web/crime-museum-uk/episode-..., p. 1. Accessed on January 3, 2009.

23. Queenie, "Marie Alexandrine Becker," *Serial Killers A-Z* (n.d.). http://www.geocities.com/verbal_plainfield/a-h/becker.html?20093, p. 1. Accessed on January 3, 2009.

24. Seagrave, *Women Serial*, p. 32.

25. Commire, *Women*, p. 343. Charles Becker was described as being "honest but unromantic and unimaginative." See Lane and Gregg, *The Encyclopedia*, p. 43.

26. *Bedlam Asylum Crime Files*, "Marie Becker," p. 1.

27. Seagrave, *Women Serial*, p. 32.

28. Seagrave, *Women Serial*, p. 32.

29. Nash, *Encyclopedia of World Crime*, p. 310.

30. Lane and Gregg, *The Encyclopedia*, p. 44.

31. Seagrave, *Women Serial*, p. 32.

32. Seagrave, *Women Serial*, p. 33.

33. Nash, *Encyclopedia of World Crime*, p. 310.

34. Kelleher and Kelleher, *Murder Most*, p. 58.

35. *Bedlam Asylum Crime Files*, "Marie Becker," p. 2.

36. *Bedlam Asylum Crime Files*, "Marie Becker," p. 1.

37. Seagrave, *Women Serial*, p. 32.

38. Commire, *Women*, p. 343.

39. *AllExperts.com*, "Marie Becker—Encyclopedia," p. 1.

40. Seagrave, *Women Serial*, p. 32.

41. Seagrave, *Women Serial*, p. 34.

42. Seagrave, *Women Serial*, p. 32.

43. Kelleher and Kelleher, *Murder Most*, p. 58. However, a number of other authorities contend that Becker was fifty-three years of age when she began to kill. The reference work on women in history refers to "the 53-year-old Marie Becker." See Commire, *Women*, p. 343. Lane and Gregg refer to Becker's needs "after fifty-three years." See Lane and Gregg, *The Encyclopedia*, p. 43. Similarly, *Bedlam Asylum Crime Files* suggested that Becker was fifty-three years old when her affair began. See *Bedlam Asylum Crime Files*, "Marie Becker," p. 1. Also in agreement were Ramsland, *Human Predator*, p. 124, and Queenie, "Marie Alexandrine Becker," p. 1.

44. Seagrave, *Women Serial*, p. 32.

45. *Crime Museum UK*, "Lady Killers," p. 1.
46. *Nationmaster.com*, "Encyclopedia—Marie Becker," p. 1.
47. *AllExperts.com*, "Marie Becker—Encyclopedia," p. 1.
48. Nash, *Encyclopedia of World Crime*, p. 309. Becker's idea of dancing was not a sedate waltz, but a nineteenth century version of dirty dancing. *Bedlam Asylum Crime Files* described her "performing erotic dances in Liege nightclubs." See *Bedlam Asylum Crime Files*, "Marie Becker," p. 3.
49. Lane and Gregg, *The Encyclopedia*, p. 43.
50. *Nationmaster.com*, "Encyclopedia—Marie Becker," p. 1.
51. *AllExperts.com*, "Marie Becker—Encyclopedia," p. 1.
52. Queenie, "Mary Alexandrine Becker," p. 1.
53. Nash, *Encyclopedia of World Crime*, p. 309.
54. *Bedlam Asylum Crime Files*, "Marie Becker," p. 1.
55. Lane and Gregg, *The Encyclopedia*, pp. 43–44.
56. Queenie, "Marie Alexandrine Becker," p. 1.
57. Nash, *Encyclopedia of World Crime*, p. 309.
58. *Bedlam Asylum Crime Files*, "Marie Becker," p. 2.
59. Seagrave, *Women Serial*, p. 32.
60. *Bedlam Asylum Crime Files*, "Marie Becker," p. 1.
61. Lane and Gregg, *The Encyclopedia*, pp. 43–44.
62. Nash, *Encyclopedia of World Crime*, p. 309.
63. There is disagreement among authorities as to the spelling of Becker's infamous lover's name. Most sources spell it Beyer, including Commire, *Women*, p. 343; Seagrave, *Women Serial*, p. 32; Nash, *Encyclopedia of World Crime*, p. 309; *Nationmaster.com*, "Encyclopedia—Marie Becker," p. 1; Kelleher and Kelleher, *Murder Most*, p. 58; and *Bedlam Asylum Crime Files*, "Marie Becker," p. 1. However, at least two respected sources disagree. Lane and Gregg and *Serial Killer A-Z* (Queenie) both spell the name Bayer. See Lane and Gregg, *The Encyclopedia*, p. 43; and Queenie, "Marie Alexandrine Becker," p. 1.
64. Commire, *Women*, p. 343.
65. *Nationmaster.com*, "Encyclopedia—Marie Becker," p. 1.
66. Kelleher and Kelleher, *Murder Most*, p. 58.
67. Lane and Gregg, *The Encyclopedia*, p. 43.
68. Queenie, "Marie Alexandrine Becker," p. 1.
69. Nash, *Encyclopedia of World Crime*, p. 309.
70. *Bedlam Asylum Crime Files*, "Marie Becker," pp. 1–2.
71. Seagrave, *Women Serial*, p. 32.
72. Seagrave, *Women Serial*, p. 32.
73. Seagrave, *Women Serial*, p. 32.
74. Seagrave, *Women Serial*, p. 33.
75. Seagrave, *Women Serial*, p. 33.
76. Seagrave, *Women Serial*, p. 34.
77. Nash, *Encyclopedia of World Crime*, p. 309.
78. *Bedlam Asylum Crime Files*, "Marie Becker," p. 3.
79. *Crime Museum UK*, "Lady Killers," p. 1.

80. *SerienKiller*, "Marie Alexandrine Becker," p. 1.
81. Kelleher and Kelleher, *Murder Most*, p. 59.
82. Katherine Ramsland, *The Human Predator: A Historical Chronicle of Serial Murder and Forensic Investigation* (New York: Berkley Books, 2005), p. 124.
83. Kelleher and Kelleher, *Murder Most*, p. 58.
84. Seagrave, *Women Serial*, p. 32.
85. Peter Vronsky, *Female Serial Killers: How and Why Women Become Monsters* (New York: Berkley Books, 2007), p. 439.
86. Nash, *Encyclopedia of World Crime*, p. 309.
87. *Bedlam Asylum Crime Files*, "Marie Becker," p. 3.
88. Lane and Gregg, *The Encyclopedia*, p. 45.
89. The Society of Toxicology of Canada, "STC: News/Nouvelles" (October, 1997). Volume XVI, No. 3, p. 1.
90. Ramsland, *Human Predator*, p. 124.
91. *Crime Museum UK*, "Lady Killers," p. 1.
92. Kelleher and Kelleher, *Murder Most*, pp. 58–59.
93. Queenie, "Marie Alexandrine Becker," p. 1.
94. Nash, *Encyclopedia of World Crime*, p. 309.
95. Seagrave, *Women Serial*, p. 32.
96. *Bedlam Asylum Crime Files*, "Marie Becker," p. 2.
97. *Crime Museum UK*, "Lady Killers," p. 1.
98. Nash, *Encyclopedia of World Crime*, p. 309.
99. Seagrave, *Women Serial*, p. 33.
100. Nash, *Encyclopedia of World Crime*, p. 309.
101. *Crime Museum UK*, "Lady Killers," p. 1.
102. *Bedlam Asylum Crime Files*, "Marie Becker," p. 2.
103. Lane and Gregg, *The Encyclopedia*, p. 44.
104. O'Donnell, *World's Worst*, pp. 163–72.
105. Queenie, "Marie Alexandrine Becker," p. 1.
106. The Society of Toxicology of Canada, "STC News," p. 1.
107. Lane and Gregg, *The Encyclopedia*, p. 45.
108. Seagrave, *Women Serial*, p. 32.
109. The Society of Toxicology of Canada, "STC News," p. 1.
110. The Society of Toxicology of Canada, "STC News," p. 1.
111. *Bedlam Asylum Crime Files*, "Marie Becker," p. 2.
112. Lane and Gregg, *The Encyclopedia*, p. 44.
113. Queenie, "Marie Alexandrine Becker," p. 1.
114. Ramsland, *Human Predator*, p. 124.
115. *Bedlam Asylum Crime Files*, "Marie Becker," p. 2.
116. *Crime Museum UK*, "Lady Killers," p. 1.
117. Nash, *Encyclopedia of World Crime*, p. 309.
118. *Bedlam Asylum Crime Files*, "Marie Becker," p. 2.
119. Commire, *Women*, p. 343.
120. *AllExperts.com*, "Marie Becker—Encyclopedia," p. 1.

121. *Nationmaster.com*, "Encyclopedia—Marie Becker," p. 1.
122. Kelleher and Kelleher, *Murder Most*, p. 58.
123. Commire, *Women*, p. 343.
124. *Crime Museum UK*, "Lady Killers," p. 1.
125. Ramsland, *Human Predator*, p. 124.
126. *SerienKiller*, "Marie Alexandrine Becker," p. 1.
127. Kelleher and Kelleher, *Murder Most*, p. 58.
128. Lane and Gregg, *The Encyclopedia*, p. 45.
129. Seagrave, *Women Serial*, p. 32.
130. Seagrave, *Women Serial*, p. 33.
131. Seagrave, *Women Serial*, p. 32.
132. *Court Museum UK*, "Lady Killers," p. 1.
133. Kelleher and Kelleher, *Murder Most*, p. 58.
134. *Bedlam Asylum Crime Files*, "Marie Becker," p. 3.
135. Robert Hale and Anthony Bolin, "The Female Serial Killer," in Ronald M. Holmes and Stephen T. Holmes (Eds.), *Contemporary Perspectives on Serial Murder* (Thousand Oaks, California: Sage Publications, 1998), p. 46.
136. *SerienKiller*, "Marie Alexandrine Becker," p. 1.
137. Commire, *Women*, p. 343.
138. Ramsland, *Human Predator*, p. 124.
139. *AllExperts.com*, "Marie Becker—Encyclopedia," p. 1.
140. *Nationmaster.com*, "Encyclopedia—Marie Becker," p. 1.
141. Lane and Gregg, *The Encyclopedia*, p. 44.
142. Nash, *Encyclopedia of World Crime*, p. 309.
143. *Bedlam Asylum Crime Files*, "Marie Becker," p. 2.
144. Seagrave, *Women Serial*, p. 32.
145. Kelleher and Kelleher, *Murder Most*, p. 58.
146. *Bedlam Asylum Crime Files*, "Marie Becker," p. 1.
147. Seagrave, *Women Serial*, p. 32.
148. *Bedlam Asylum Crime Files*, "Marie Becker," p. 1.
149. Queenie, "Mary Alexandrine Becker," p. 1.
150. Seagrave, *Women Serial*, p. 33.
151. Seagrave, *Women Serial*, p. 33.
152. Seagrave, *Women Serial*, p. 33.
153. The Society of Toxicology of Canada, "STC News," p. 1. Kelleher and Kelleher also noted the general lifestyle dimension of Becker's expenses. See Kelleher and Kelleher, *Murder Most*, p. 59.
154. Lane and Gregg, *The Encyclopedia*, p. 44.
155. Kelleher and Kelleher, *Murder Most*, p. 58.
156. Ramsland, *Human Predator*, p. 124.
157. Queenie, "Marie Alexandrine Becker," p. 1.
158. *Bedlam Asylum Crime Files*, "Marie Becker," p. 2.
159. Seagrave, *Women Serial*, p. 32.
160. Lane and Gregg, *The Encyclopedia*, p. 44.
161. Queenie, "Marie Alexandrine Becker," p. 1.

162. *Bedlam Asylum Crime Files*, "Marie Becker," p. 3.
163. Seagrave, *Women Serial*, p. 34.
164. Seagrave, *Women Serial*, pp. 33–34.
165. Seagrave, *Women Serial*, p. 34.
166. Seagrave, *Women Serial*, p. 34; Nash, *Encyclopedia of World Crime*, p. 309; and *Serienkiller*, "Mary Alexandrine Becker," p. 1.

CHAPTER 6

1. Derek Bickerton, *The Murders of Boysie Singh* (London: Arthur Baker Limited, 1962), p. 12.
2. Anne Hilton, "Boysie Singh 20th Century Pirate of the Caribbean," *Trinidad & Tobago's Newsday* (August 7, 2005). http://newsday.co.tt/people/print.0.29353.html, p. 3. Accessed on December 18, 2008; Bickerton, *The Murders*, pp. 10, 220.
3. Brian Lane and Wilfred Gregg, *The Encyclopedia of Serial Killers* (New York: Berkley Books, 1995), p. 313.
4. *TripAtlas.com*, "Boysie Singh—A 20th Century Pirate" (n.d.). http://tripatlas.com/Piracy_in_the_Caribbean, p. 8. Accessed on January 16, 2009.
5. *Piracy in the Caribbean*, "Boysie Singh—A 20th Century Pirate" (n.d.). http://www.experiencefestival.com/piracy_in_the_Caribbean-boys..., p. 2. Accessed on December 18, 2008.
6. *Larry's View*, "Pirates of the Caribbean" (n.d.). http://larry50.wordpress.com/2008/01/16, p. 1. Accessed on December 18, 2008.
7. Bickerton, *The Murders*, p. 120.
8. Lane and Gregg, *The Encyclopedia*, p. 313.
9. *AbsoluteAstronomy.com*, "Piracy in the Caribbean" (2008). http://www.absoluteastronomy.com/topics/Piracy_in_the_Caribbean, p. 19. Accessed on January 16, 2009.
10. *Time*, "Blood & Plunder" (May 29, 1950). http://www.time.com/time/printout/0.8816.888806.00.html, p. 1. Accessed on December 18, 2008.
11. Bickerton, *The Murders*, p. 200.
12. Bickerton, *The Murders*, p. 205.
13. Selwyn R. Cudjoe, "De True, True Story," *Trinicenter.com* (June 7, 2004). http://www.trinicenter.com/Cudjoe/2004/0706.htm, p. 6. Accessed on December 18, 2008.
14. Cudjoe, "De True, True Story," p. 6.
15. Cudjoe, "De True, True Story," p. 6.
16. David Brewster, "Badjohn 'Mastife' Dies at 79," *Trinidad & Tobago News Bulletin Board* (December 11, 2002), p. 1.
17. Cudjoe, "De True, True Story," p. 5.
18. Hilton, "Boysie Singh," p. 1.
19. Bickerton, *The Murders*, p. 13.
20. Bickerton, *The Murders*, p. 14.
21. Bickerton, *The Murders*, p. 14.

22. Lane and Gregg, *The Encyclopedia*, p. 313. Singh's parents were part of a migration pattern from India to the Caribbean between 1845 and 1917. See Central Intelligence Agency, "Trinidad and Tobago," *The World Factbook* (December 8, 2008). http://www.cia.gov/library/publications/the-world-factbook/geos/td.html, pp. 1–2. Accessed on January 16, 2009.
23. Hilton, "Boysie Singh," p. 1.
24. Cudjoe, "De True, True Story," p. 6.
25. Bickerton, *The Murders*, pp. 13–14.
26. Bickerton, *The Murders*, p. 24.
27. Bickerton, *The Murders*, pp. 14–15. It is believed that she was "a more enterprising character than her husband," because she kept cows to supplement their meager income. See Bickerton, *The Murders*, p. 14.
28. Bickerton, *The Murders*, p. 15.
29. Bickerton, *The Murders*, pp. 14–15.
30. Bickerton, *The Murders*, p. 14.
31. Bickerton, *The Murders*, p. 14.
32. Bickerton, *The Murders*, pp. 14–15.
33. Bickerton, *The Murders*, p. 15.
34. Lane and Gregg, *The Encyclopedia*, p. 313.
35. *Sepia Mutiny*, "Pirates of the Caribbean" (January 14, 2006). http://www.sepiamutiny.com/sepia/archives/002842.html, p. 2. Accessed on December 18, 2008.
36. Bickerton, *The Murders*, pp. 27–30.
37. Hilton, "Boysie Singh," p. 1.
38. Bickerton, *The Murders*, p. 15.
39. Bickerton, *The Murders*, p. 217.
40. *Time*, "Blood and Plunder," p. 1.
41. Bickerton, *The Murders*, p. 28.
42. Bickerton, *The Murders*, p. 20.
43. Bickerton, *The Murders*, p. 18.
44. Bickerton, *The Murders*, pp. 18–19, 218.
45. Bickerton, *The Murders*, p. 17.
46. Bickerton, *The Murders*, p. 20.
47. Bickerton, *The Murders*, pp. 61–62.
48. Bickerton, *The Murders*, p. 212.
49. Bickerton, *The Murders*, p. 152.
50. *Magnoy's Samsara*, "Piracy in the Caribbean" (January 16, 2006). http://magnoysamsara.blogspot.com/2006/01/piracy-in-the-caribbean.html, p. 2. Accessed on December 18, 2008.
51. *Socialcritic.net*.,"Success and Blackbeard—Facial Hair Not a Factor" (February 19, 2007). http://www.socialcritic.net/blackbeard/, p. 3. Accessed on December 18, 2008.
52. *Sepia Mutiny*, "Pirates of," p. 2.
53. Bickerton, *The Murders*, pp. 102, 160.
54. Bickerton, *The Murders*, p. 121.

55. Bickerton, *The Murders*, pp. 34, 57.
56. Bickerton, *The Murders*, p. 192.
57. *Socialcritic.net.*, "Success and Blackbeard," p. 3.
58. Bickerton, *The Murders*, pp. 16–17.
59. Bickerton, *The Murders*, p. 17.
60. Bickerton, *The Murders*, pp. 15–16, 26.
61. Bickerton, *The Murders*, p. 219.
62. Bickerton, *The Murders*, p. 17.
63. Bickerton, *The Murders*, p. 20.
64. *Socialcritic.net.*, "Success and Blackbeard," p. 3.
65. Brewster, "Badjohn Mastife," pp. 1–2.
66. Bickerton, *The Murders*, pp. 45–46.
67. Bickerton, *The Murders*, pp. 60–66.
68. Bickerton, *The Murders*, pp. 69, 92–93.
69. Bickerton, *The Murders*, pp. 21, 70.
70. Bickerton, *The Murders*, p. 56.
71. Bickerton, *The Murders*, pp. 172–73.
72. *Time*, "Blood and Plunder," p. 1.
73. Bickerton, *The Murders*, p. 57.
74. Bickerton, *The Murders*, pp. 24, 26.
75. Bickerton, *The Murders*, p. 26.
76. Bickerton, *The Murders*, p. 30.
77. Bickerton, *The Murders*, p. 36.
78. Bickerton, *The Murders*, p. 42.
79. *Sepia Mutiny*, "Pirates of," p. 2.
80. *AbsoluteAstronomy*, "Piracy in the Caribbean," p. 19.
81. Hilton, "Boysie Singh," p. 2; Raffique Shah, "Badjohns Who Spawned Today's Criminals" (November 23, 2003). http://www.trinicenter.com/Raffique/2003/Nov/232003.htm, p. 2. Accessed on January 16, 2009.
82. Hilton, "Boysie Singh," p. 2.
83. Shah, "Badjohns Who Spawned," p. 2.
84. Brewster, "Badjohn Mastife," p. 1.
85. Shah, "Badjohns Who Spawned," p. 2.
86. Bickerton, *The Murders*, p. 24.
87. Bickerton, *The Murders*, pp. 16, 19.
88. Bickerton, *The Murders*, p. 24.
89. Bickerton, *The Murders*, p. 16.
90. Bickerton, *The Murders*, p. 18.
91. Bickerton, *The Murders*, pp. 165–66.
92. Bickerton, *The Murders*, p. 47.
93. Bickerton, *The Murders*, p. 50.
94. Bickerton, *The Murders*, p. 140.
95. Bickerton, *The Murders*, p. 174.
96. Bickerton, *The Murders*, p. 182.
97. Hilton, "Boysie Singh," p. 2.

98. Cudjoe, "De True, True Story," p. 5.
99. Lane and Gregg, *The Encyclopedia*, p. 314.
100. Bickerton, *The Murders*, pp. 170, 223.
101. Bickerton, *The Murders*, pp. 164–66.
102. Bickerton, *The Murders*, p. 11.
103. Bickerton, *The Murders*, pp. 17, 23, 89.
104. Bickerton, *The Murders*, p. 24.
105. Bickerton, *The Murders*, p. 16.
106. *Larry's View*, "Pirates of the Caribbean," p. 1.
107. *Piracy in the Caribbean*, "Boysie Singh," p. 2.
108. Cudjoe, "De True, True Story," p. 5.
109. Lane and Gregg, *The Encyclopedia*, p. 314.
110. Cudjoe, "De True, True Story," p. 5; Bickerton, *The Murders*, pp. 86–88.
111. *Sepia Mutiny*, "Pirates of," p. 2;Bickerton, *The Murders*, p. 16.
112. Hilton, "Boysie Singh," p. 1.
113. Hilton, "Boysie Singh," p. 1.
114. Lane and Gregg, *The Encyclopedia*, pp. 313–14.
115. Bickerton, *The Murders*, pp. 53–54.
116. Hilton, "Boysie Singh," p. 2.
117. Bickerton, *The Murders*, p. 56.
118. *Sepia Mutiny*, "Pirates of," p. 2.
119. *TripAtlas.com*, "Boysie Singh," p. 8.
120. *AbsoluteAstronomy*, "Piracy in the Caribbean," p. 19.
121. *Socialcritic.net.*, "Success and Blackbeard," p. 3.
122. *Larry's View*, "Pirates of the Caribbean," p. 1.
123. Bickerton, *The Murders*, pp. 102, 106.
124. *Piracy in the Caribbean*, "Boysie Singh," p. 2.
125. Shah, "Badjohns Who Spawned," p. 2.
126. Terry Joseph, "Those Good Ol' Days," *Terry-J at "I" Level* (June 20, 2003). http://www.trinicenter.com/Terryj/2003/June/202003.htm, p. 2. Accessed on December 18, 2008.
127. Bickerton, *The Murders*, p. 9.
128. Bickerton, *The Murders*, p. 9.
129. Bickerton, *The Murders*, p. 97.
130. Hilton, "Boysie Singh," p. 2.
131. *Samsara*, "Piracy," p. 2.
132. Hilton, "Boysie Singh," p. 3; Bickerton, *The Murders*, p. 224.
133. Bickerton, *The Murders*, pp. 107, 109–11.
134. *TripAtlas.com*, "Boysie Singh," p. 8.
135. Joseph, "Those Good Ol' Days," p. 2.
136. Hilton, "Boysie Singh," p. 2.
137. Bickerton, *The Murders*, p. 105.
138. Lane and Gregg, *The Encyclopedia*, p. 313.
139. Lane and Gregg, *The Encyclopedia*, pp. 313–14.
140. *TripAtlas.com*, "Boysie Singh," p. 8.

141. Bickerton, *The Murders*, p. 98.
142. Lane and Gregg, *The Encyclopedia*, p. 313.
143. Hilton, "Boysie Singh," p. 2.
144. *WordIQ*, "Piracy" (2008). http://www.wordiq.com/definition/Piracy, p. 1. Accessed on January 16, 2009.
145. Bickerton, *The Murders*, p. 211.
146. Bickerton, *The Murders*, p. 210.
147. Bickerton, *The Murders*, p. 188.
148. Lane and Gregg, *The Encyclopedia*, p. 314.
149. *TripAtlas.com*, "Boysie Singh," p. 8.
150. Hilton, "Boysie Singh," p. 2.
151. *Samsara*, "Piracy," pp. 1–2.
152. Bickerton, *The Murders*, p. 70.
153. Hilton, "Boysie Singh," p. 2.
154. *Time*, "Blood and Plunder," p. 1.
155. Bickerton, *The Murders*, p. 106.
156. Bickerton, *The Murders*, p. 114.
157. Bickerton, *The Murders*, pp. 83–84.
158. *Sepia Mutiny*, "Pirates of," p. 2.
159. Hilton, "Boysie Singh," p. 2.
160. *Time*, "Blood and Plunder," pp. 1–2.
161. Bickerton, *The Murders*, p. 163.
162. *Trinbagopan.com*, "Neville Jules and Sonny Roach" (March 1, 2005). http://www.trinbagopan.com/darway/0103058.htm, p. 2. Accessed on December 18, 2008.
163. Brewster, "Badjohn Mastife," p. 1.
164. *Sepia Mutiny*, "Pirates of," p. 2.
165. *TripAtlas.com*, "Boysie Singh," p. 8.
166. Bickerton, *The Murders*, p. 48.
167. Bickerton, *The Murders*, p. 37.
168. Bickerton, *The Murders*, pp. 15–16.
169. Bickerton, *The Murders*, pp. 34, 39.
170. Lane and Gregg, *The Encyclopedia*, p. 315.

CHAPTER 7

1. Mike Mayo, *American Murder: Criminals, Crime and the Media* (Canton, Missouri: Visible Ink Press, 2008), p. 25.
2. Mark Gado, "Raymond Fernandez," *The Lonely Hearts Killers* (n.d.). http://www.trutv.com/library/crime/serial_killers/partners/fernandez..., p. 1. Accessed on December 1, 2008. Gado added that "Their murder trial took place during the scorching hot summer of 1949 in Bronx Criminal Court where the salacious testimony of 'abnormal sex practices' caused a near-riot among spectators." See Gado, "The Lonely Hearts Killers," *The Lonely Hearts Killers* (n.d.). http://www.trutv.com/library/crime/serial_killers/partners/fernandez..., p. 2. Accessed on December 1, 2008.

3. Richard Glyn Jones, *The Mammoth Book of Women Who Kill* (New York: Carroll & Graf, 2002), p. 73.

4. "Raymond Fernandez," *The Biography Channel* (2008). http://www.biography.com/notorious/crimefiles.do?action=view&c..., p. 2. Accessed on December 1, 2008.

5. Brian Lane and Wilfred Gregg, *The Encyclopedia of Serial Killers* (New York: Berkley Books, 1995), p. 42. See *Nationmaster.com*, "Raymond Fernandez" (n.d.). http://www.nationmaster.com/encyclopedia/Raymond-Fernandez, p. 1. Accessed on December 1, 2008.

6. Publications International Ltd., *Murder and Mayhem* (Lincolnwood, Illinois: Publications International Ltd., 1991), p. 76.

7. Gado, "Raymond Fernandez," p. 1; *Biography Channel*, "Raymond Fernandez," p. 2.

8. Colin Wilson and Donald Seaman, *The Serial Killers: A Study in the Psychology of Violence* (New York: Carol Publishing Group, 1992), p. 231.

9. Gado, "Raymond Fernandez," p. 1.

10. Gado, "Raymond Fernandez," p. 1. Lane and Gregg noted that Fernandez was raised in Connecticut. See Lane and Gregg, *The Encyclopedia*, p. 42.

11. Wilson and Seaman, *Serial Killers*, pp. 231–32.

12. *Biography Channel*, "Raymond Fernandez," p. 2.

13. Gado, "Raymond Fernandez," p. 1.

14. Lane and Gregg, *The Encyclopedia*, p. 42.

15. Mayo, *American Murder*, p. 25.

16. Gado, "Raymond Fernandez," p. 1.

17. Gado, "Raymond Fernandez," p. 1.

18. Lane and Gregg, *The Encyclopedia*, p. 42.

19. Gado, "Raymond Fernandez," p. 1.

20. Lane and Gregg, *The Encyclopedia*, p. 42.

21. Robin Odell and Wilfred Gregg, *Murderers Row: An International Murderers' Who's Who* (Phoenix Mill, U.K.: Sutton Publishing, 2006), pp. 25–26.

22. Wilson and Seaman, *Serial Killers*, p. 231.

23. Mayo, *American Murder*, p. 25.

24. Gado, "Raymond Fernandez," p. 1.

25. *Biography Channel*, "Raymond Fernandez," p. 2.

26. Lane and Gregg, *The Encyclopedia*, p. 42.

27. Mayo, *American Murder*, p. 25.

28. Publications International Ltd., *Murder and Mayhem*, p. 77.

29. Gado, "Raymond Fernandez," p. 1.

30. Publications International Ltd., *Murder and Mayhem*, p. 77.

31. Gado, "Lonely Hearts Killers," p. 1.

32. Gado, "Raymond Fernandez," p. 1.

33. Gado, "Lonely Hearts Killers," p. 1.

34. Wilson and Seaman, *Serial Killers*, p. 231.

35. Publications International Ltd., *Murder and Mayhem*, p. 77.

36. Jones, *Women Who Kill*, p. 72.

37. Everitt, *Human Monsters*, p. 139.
38. Mayo, *American Murder*, p. 26.
39. Mayo, *American Murder*, p. 25.
40. *Biography Channel*, "Raymond Fernandez," p. 2.
41. Gado, "Lonely Hearts Killers," p. 1.
42. Lane and Gregg, *The Encyclopedia*, p. 42.
43. Odell and Gregg, *Murderers Row*, pp. 25–26.
44. Mayo, *American Murder*, p. 25.
45. Jones, *Women Who Kill*, p. 73.
46. Gado, "Lonely Hearts Killers," p. 1.
47. Jones, *Women Who Kill*, p. 73.
48. Gado, "Martha," p. 1.
49. Lane and Gregg, *The Encyclopedia*, p. 41.
50. Jones, *Women Who Kill*, p. 79.
51. Lane and Gregg, *The Encyclopedia*, p. 41.
52. Gado, "Martha," p. 1.
53. Mayo, *American Murder*, p. 26.
54. Jones, *Women Who Kill*, p. 72.
55. Gado, "Martha," p. 1.
56. Odell and Gregg, *Murderers Row*, p. 25.
57. Gado, "Martha," p. 1.
58. Gado, "Martha," p. 1.
59. Ramsland, *Human Predator*, p. 141; Everitt, *Human Monsters*, p. 139. In terms understandable to the British, Martha weighed approximately fourteen stone. See Wilson and Seaman, *Serial Killers*, p. 231.
60. *CrimeLife.com*, "Martha Beck" (n.d.). http://www.crimelife.com/killers/beck.html, p. 1. Accessed on September 6, 2006.
61. Odell and Gregg, *Murderers Row*, p. 25.
62. Mayo, *American Murder*, p. 25.
63. Jones, *Women Who Kill*, p. 72.
64. Lane and Gregg, *The Encyclopedia*, p. 41.
65. Gado, "Martha," p. 1.
66. Odell and Gregg, *Murderers Row*, p. 25.
67. Gado, "Martha," p. 1.
68. Mayo, *American Murder*, p. 25.
69. Jones, *Women Who Kill*, p. 73.
70. Gado, "Martha," p. 1.
71. Lane and Gregg, *The Encyclopedia*, p. 42.
72. Everitt, *Human Monsters*, p. 139.
73. Jones, *Women Who Kill*, p. 73.
74. Gado, "Martha," p. 1.
75. Gado, "Martha," p. 1; Lane and Gregg, *The Encyclopedia*, p. 42.
76. Lane and Gregg, *The Encyclopedia*, p. 42; Everitt, *Human Monsters*, p. 139.
77. Jones, *Women Who Kill*, p. 73.

78. Lane and Gregg, *The Encyclopedia*, p. 41.
79. Odell and Gregg, *Murderers Row*, p. 25; Everitt, *Human Monsters*, p. 139.
80. Ramsland, *Human Predator*, p. 141.
81. Jones, *Women Who Kill*, p. 73.
82. Gado, "Martha," p. 1.
83. Everitt, *Human Monsters*, p. 139.
84. *Biography Channel*, "Raymond Fernandez," p. 2.
85. Mayo, *American Murder*, p. 26.
86. Jones, *Women Who Kill*, p. 73.
87. *CrimeLife.com*, "Martha Beck," p. 1.
88. *Serial Killers A-Z*, "Martha Beck and Raymond Fernandez" (n.d.). http://www.geocities.com/verbal_plainfield/a-h/beckfernandez.html..., p. 1. Accessed on December 1, 2008.
89. Ramsland, *Human Predator*, p. 141.
90. Odell and Gregg, *Murderers Row*, p. 25.
91. Wilson and Seaman, *Serial Killers*, p. 231.
92. Everitt, *Human Monsters*, p. 139.
93. Jones, *Women Who Kill*, p. 73.
94. *Biography Channel*, "Raymond Fernandez," p. 2.
95. Lane and Gregg, *The Encyclopedia*, p. 42.
96. Mayo, *American Murder*, p. 25.
97. *CrimeLife.com*, "Martha Beck," p. 1.
98. Wilson and Seaman, *Serial Killers*, p. 231.
99. Everitt, *Human Monsters*, p. 139.
100. Jones, *Women Who Kill*, pp. 73, 77.
101. Lane and Gregg, *The Encyclopedia*, pp. 42–43.
102. *Serial Killers A-Z*, "Martha Beck," p. 1.
103. Lane and Gregg, *The Encyclopedia*, p. 42.
104. Everitt, *Human Monsters*, p. 139.
105. *CrimeLife.com*, "Martha Beck," p. 1.
106. Jones, *Women Who Kill*, p. 73.
107. *Serial Killers A-Z*, "Martha Beck," p. 1.
108. Jones, *Women Who Kill*, pp. 72–73, 75.
109. Everitt, *Human Monsters*, p. 109.
110. Wilson and Seaman, *Serial Killers*, pp. 231–32.
111. Wilson and Seaman, *Serial Killers*, p. 231.
112. *Biography Channel*, "Raymond Fernandez," p. 2.
113. Wilson and Seaman, *Serial Killers*, p. 232.
114. Everitt, *Human Monsters*, p. 138.
115. Mayo, *American Murder*, p. 25.
116. Odell and Gregg, *Murderers Row*, p. 25.
117. Wilson and Seaman, *Serial Killers*, p. 231.
118. Jones, *Women Who Kill*, p. 73.
119. Everitt, *Human Monsters*, p. 138.

120. *Biography Channel*, "Raymond Fernandez," p. 2.

121. Ramsland, *Human Predator*, p. 141; Lane and Gregg, *The Encyclopedia*, p. 42.

122. Jones, *Women Who Kill*, p. 73.

123. *Biography Channel*, "Raymond Fernandez," p. 2.

124. Ramsland, *Human Predator*, p. 141; Wilson and Seaman, *Serial Killers*, p. 231.

125. Lane and Gregg, *The Encyclopedia*, p. 43; Odell and Gregg, *Murderers Row*, p. 26.

126. Ramsland, *Human Predator*, p. 141; Everitt, *Human Monsters*, p. 139.

127. *CrimeLife.com*, "Martha Beck," p. 1; *Serial Killers A-Z*, "Martha Beck," p. 1.

128. Ronald M. Holmes and Stephen T. Holmes, *Serial Murder* (Thousand Oaks, California: Sage Publications, 1998), p. 154; *Nationmaster.com*, "Raymond Fernandez," p. 1; and Publications International Ltd., *Murder and Mayhem*, p. 78.

129. *CrimeLife.com*, "Martha Beck," p. 1.

130. Wilson and Seaman, *Serial Killers*, p. 231.

131. *Biography Channel*, "Raymond Fernandez," p. 2.

132. Mayo, *American Murder*, p. 25.

133. Publications International Ltd., *Murder and Mayhem*, p. 78.

134. Mayo, *American Murder*, p. 26.

135. Publications International Ltd., *Murder and Mayhem*, p. 78.

136. Holmes and Holmes, *Serial Murder*, p. 154.

137. Ramsland, *Human Predator*, p. 141.

138. Odell and Gregg, *Murderers Row*, p. 26. See also Everitt, *Human Monsters*, p. 139; *CrimeLife.com*, "Martha Beck," p. 1; and Ramsland, *Human Predator*, p. 141.

139. Publications International Ltd., *Murder and Mayhem*, p. 79. See also Lane and Gregg, *The Encyclopedia*, p. 42; Everitt, *Human Monsters*, p. 139; and Jones, *Women Who Kill*, p. 78.

140. Mayo, *American Murder*, p. 26. See also Everitt, *Human Monsters*, p. 140; Publications International Ltd., *Murder and Mayhem*, p. 78; and Jones, *Women Who Kill*, p. 75.

141. Publications International Ltd., *Murder and Mayhem*, p. 78.

142. Jones, *Women Who Kill*, p. 78. See also Mayo, *American Murder*, p. 26; Wilson and Seaman, *Serial Killers*, p. 231; Odell and Gregg, *Murderers Row*, p. 26; Everitt, *Human Monsters*, p. 138; and Publications International Ltd., *Murder and Mayhem*, pp. 77, 79.

143. Mayo, *American Murder*, p. 25; Jones, *Women Who Kill*, p. 79.

144. Wilson and Seaman, *Serial Killers*, p. 231; Odell and Gregg, *Murderers Row*, p. 26.

145. Odell and Gregg, *Murderers Row*, p. 26.

146. Everitt, *Human Monsters*, p. 139.

147. Mayo, *American Murder*, p. 25.

148. Publications International Ltd., *Murder and Mayhem*, p. 78.
149. Mayo, *American Murder*, p. 25.
150. *Biography Channel*, "Raymond Fernandez," p. 2.
151. Lane and Gregg, *The Encyclopedia*, p. 42.
152. Odell and Gregg, *Murderers Row*, p. 26.
153. Everitt, *Human Monsters*, p. 139.
154. Publications International Ltd., *Murder and Mayhem*, p. 79.
155. Jones, *Women Who Kill*, p. 77.
156. Jones, *Women Who Kill*, p. 75.
157. Everitt, *Human Monsters*, p. 140.
158. Mayo, *American Murder*, p. 26.
159. Lane and Gregg, *The Encyclopedia*, p. 43.

CHAPTER 8

1. Jim Schutze, *Preacher's Girl: The Life and Crimes of Blanche Taylor Moore* (New York: Avon Books, 1993), p. 3.
2. Schutze, *Preacher's Girl*, p. 357.
3. Schutze, *Preacher's Girl*, pp. 343–45.
4. Jay Ashley, "Blanche," *TheTimes.News.com* (March 24, 2007). http://www.thetimesnews.com/onset?id=146&template=article.html, p. 1. Accessed on November 21, 2008.
5. Schutze, *Preacher's Girl*, p. 315.
6. North Carolina Department of Correction, Public Information Access System. "Blanche Moore" (November 20, 2008). http://webapps6.doc.state.nc.us/apps/offender/offend1?DOCNUM..., p. 1. Accessed on November 21, 2008.
7. *Serial Killer Central*, "Blanche Moore" (n.d.). http://skcentral.com/readarticle.php?article_id=422, p. 1. Accessed on November 11, 2008.
8. North Carolina Department of Correction, "Blanche Moore," p. 1.
9. Schutze, *Preacher's Girl*, pp. 10–11.
10. Schutze, *Preacher's Girl*, p. 11.
11. Schutze, *Preacher's Girl*, p. 11.
12. Schutze, *Preacher's Girl*, p. 12.
13. Ashley, "Blanche," p. 3; Schutze, *Preacher's Girl*, pp. 1–2, 10.
14. Schutze, *Preacher's Girl*, p. 2. Kiser's gambling losses were substantial and repetitive. Kelleher and Kelleher referred to them as "perennial gambling debts." See Michael Kelleher and C.L. Kelleher, *Murder Most Rare: The Female Serial Killer* (New York: Dell Publishing, 1998), p. 71.
15. Charles Montaldo, "Women on Death Row—Blanche Moore," *About.com* (n.d.). http://crime.about.com/od/female_offenders.p/deathrow-women3.htm, p. 1. Accessed on November 21, 2008.
16. *Serial Killer Central*, "Blanche Moore," p. 1.
17. Joseph Geringer, "The Most Aggressive New Breed," *The Crime Library* (2008). http://www.trutv.com/library/crime/criminal_mind/psychology/mid..., p. 6. Accessed on November 21, 2008.

18. Kelleher and Kelleher, *Murder Most Rare*, p. 70.
19. Schutze, *Preacher's Girl*, p. 2.
20. Schutze, *Preacher's Girl*, p. 16. The divorce was a mere formality, however, since P.D. had run out on his family and abandoned them shortly before Christmas, 1984. See Schutze, *Preacher's Girl*, p. 52.
21. Kelleher and Kelleher, *Murder Most Rare*, p. 71.
22. Schutze, *Preacher's Girl*, p. 10. "The dysfunctional home life" in the Kiser home was recalled by Geringer. See Geringer, "Aggressive New Breed," p. 6.
23. Geringer, "Aggressive New Breed," p. 6.
24. Kelleher and Kelleher, *Murder Most Rare*, p. 71; Geringer, "Aggressive New Breed," p. 6. An Internet study also concluded that Blanche left home at the earliest opportunity, and that marriage seemed to be her easiest option. See *Serial Killer Central*, "Blanche Moore," p. 1.
25. Kelleher and Kelleher, *Murder Most Rare*, p. 71. Several sources suggest that Blanche's marriage to Taylor was a happy one for some time. See Geringer, "Aggressive New Breed," p. 6.
26. Schutze, *Preacher's Girl*, p. 17.
27. Schutze, *Preacher's Girl*, pp. 27–29, 36–37.
28. *Serial Killer Central*, "Blanche Moore," p. 1.
29. Geringer, "Aggressive New Breed," p. 6.
30. Kelleher and Kelleher, *Murder Most Rare*, p. 72.
31. Schutze, *Preacher's Girl*, p. 13. See also Kelleher and Kelleher, *Murder Most Rare*, p. 72.
32. Schutze, *Preacher's Girl*, p. 13; Kelleher and Kelleher, *Murder Most Rare*, p. 71.
33. Schutze, *Preacher's Girl*, pp. 20, 36.
34. Schutze, *Preacher's Girl*, p. 9.
35. Schutze, *Preacher's Girl*, p. 10.
36. Geringer, "Aggressive New Breed," p. 6.
37. Kelleher and Kelleher, *Murder Most Rare*, p. 72.
38. Ashley, "Blanche," p. 3.
39. Schutze, *Preacher's Girl*, p. 52.
40. Schutze, *Preacher's Girl*, p. 52.
41. Ashley, "Blanche," p. 3; *Serial Killer Central*, "Blanche Moore," p. 1.
42. *Serial Killer Central*, "Blanche Moore," p. 1.
43. Schutze, *Preacher's Girl*, pp. 55–56.
44. Schutze, *Preacher's Girl*, p. 59.
45. Kelleher and Kelleher, *Murder Most Rare*, pp. 41, 45.
46. Ashley, "Blanche," pp. 3–4.
47. Schutze, *Preacher's Girl*, pp. 14–15. The jury determined that Moore was a "good mother and a churchgoer." See Schutze, *Preacher's Girl*, p. 370.
48. Kelleher and Kelleher, *Murder Most Rare*, p. 71.
49. Schutze, *Preacher's Girl*, p. 14.
50. Schutze, *Preacher's Girl*, p. 14.
51. Schutze, *Preacher's Girl*, pp. 17, 24.

52. Schutze, *Preacher's Girl*, p. 20. The ladies of Burlington, North Carolina, referred to Tupperware as "Tumbleware." See Schutze, *Preacher's Girl*, p. 20.
53. Schutze, *Preacher's Girl*, pp. 341–42.
54. Kelleher and Kelleher, *Murder Most Rare*, p. 72.
55. *Serial Killer Central*, "Blanche Moore," p. 1.
56. Schutze, *Preacher's Girl*, p. 324.
57. Schutze, *Preacher's Girl*, p. 356.
58. Schutze, *Preacher's Girl*, p. 259.
59. Schutze, *Preacher's Girl*, pp. 251, 258.
60. Schutze, *Preacher's Girl*, p. 203.
61. Schutze, *Preacher's Girl*, pp. 208–9.
62. Schutze, *Preacher's Girl*, p. 55.
63. Schutze, *Preacher's Girl*, p. 135.
64. Schutze, *Preacher's Girl*, p. 165.
65. Schutze, *Preacher's Girl*, pp. 188–89.
66. Schutze, *Preacher's Girl*, p. 198.
67. Schutze, *Preacher's Girl*, p. 73.
68. Schutze, *Preacher's Girl*, p. 196.
69. Schutze, *Preacher's Girl*, pp. 170–72.
70. Schutze, *Preacher's Girl*, pp. 185, 190.
71. *Serial Killer Central*, "Blanche Moore," p. 1.
72. Geringer, "Aggressive New Breed," p. 6.
73. Kelleher and Kelleher, *Murder Most Rare*, p. 72.
74. Schutze, *Preacher's Girl*, pp. 20, 55.
75. Montaldo, "Women on Death Row," p. 1.
76. *Serial Killer Central*, "Blanche Moore," p. 1.
77. Kelleher and Kelleher, *Murder Most Rare*, pp. 71–72.
78. *Serial Killer Central*, "Blanche Moore," p. 1.
79. Kelleher and Kelleher, *Murder Most Rare*, p. 70.
80. Schutze, *Preacher's Girl*, pp. 52–56.
81. Schutze, *Preacher's Girl*, pp. 16–18, 43, 46. *Serial Killer Central* also reported this suspicion about Moore. "Blanche soon purchased a new home in Burlington, fostering suspicions that she may have tapped the till at work." See *Serial Killer Central*, "Blanche Moore," p. 1.
82. Schutze, *Preacher's Girl*, pp. 81–92.
83. Schutze, *Preacher's Girl*, p. 152.
84. Schutze, *Preacher's Girl*, pp. 235–36, 253.
85. Montaldo, "Women on Death Row," p. 1.
86. Wikipedia, "Blanche Taylor Moore" (November 8, 2008). http://en.wikipedia.org/wiki/Blanche_Taylor_Moore, p. 1. Accessed on November 21, 2008.
87. Kelleher and Kelleher, *Murder Most Rare*, p. 70.
88. *Unsolved Mysteries*, "Female Serial Killers' True Crimes" (November 11, 2001). http://www.unsolvedmysteries.com/usm189366.html, p. 1. Accessed on November 21, 2008.

89. Wikipedia, "Blanche Taylor Moore," p. 1.
90. Schutze, *Preacher's Girl*, pp. 202, 209–10.
91. Ashley, "Blanche," p. 1.
92. Montaldo, "Women on Death Row," p. 1.
93. Scott Michels, "Moore Requesting New Trial: Attorneys for Blanche Taylor Moore Say Prosecutors Did Not Disclose a Witness Whose Testimony May Have Helped Her," *The News & Record* (January 23, 2004). http://www.encyclopedia.com/doc/1G1-112494674.html, p. 1. Accessed on November 21, 2008.
94. *Unsolved Mysteries*, "Female Serial Killers," p. 1.
95. *Serial Killer Central*, "Blanche Moore," p. 1.
96. Schutze, *Preacher's Girl*, p. 365.
97. *Serial Killer Central*, "Blanche Moore," p. 1.
98. Kelleher and Kelleher, *Murder Most Rare*, p. 72.
99. *Serial Killer Central*, "Blanche Moore," p. 1.
100. Kelleher and Kelleher, *Murder Most Rare*, p. 73.
101. *Serial Killer Central*, "Blanche Moore," p. 1.
102. Kelleher and Kelleher, *Murder Most Rare*, p. 75.
103. Schutze, *Preacher's Girl*, pp. 117, 120, 122, 138–40, 254.
104. Schutze, *Preacher's Girl*, p. 41.
105. *Serial Killer Central*, "Blanche Moore," p. 1.
106. Geringer, "Aggressive New Breed," p. 6.
107. Kelleher and Kelleher, *Murder Most Rare*, p. 73. Kelleher and Kelleher added that Moore may have had a secondary motive, "A few of the murders were committed for revenge." See Kelleher and Kelleher, *Murder Most Rare*, p. 73.
108. Schutze, *Preacher's Girl*, p. 325.
109. *Serial Killer Central*, "Blanche Moore," p. 1.
110. Geringer, "Aggressive New Breed," p. 6.
111. Kelleher and Kelleher, *Murder Most Rare*, p. 73.
112. Schutze, *Preacher's Girl*, p. 287.
113. Schutze, *Preacher's Girl*, p. 287.
114. Schutze, *Preacher's Girl*, p. 370.
115. Schutze, *Preacher's Girl*, p. 167.
116. Geringer, "Aggressive New Breed," p. 6; Kelleher and Kelleher, *Murder Most Rare*, p. 76.
117. *Serial Killer Central*, "Blanche Moore," p. 1.
118. *Serial Killer Central*, "Blanche Moore," p. 1; Schutze, *Preacher's Girl*, p. 153.
119. Schutze, *Preacher's Girl*, pp. 136, 154.
120. Schutze, *Preacher's Girl*, p. 136.
121. Kelleher and Kelleher, *Murder Most Foul*, pp. 75–76.
122. *Serial Killer Central*, "Blanche Moore," p. 1; Schutze, *Preacher's Girl*, pp. 144–46.
123. Geringer, "Aggressive New Breed," p. 6.
124. Schutze, *Preacher's Girl*, pp. 257, 355.

125. Schutze, *Preacher's Girl*, p. 152.
126. Schutze, *Preacher's Girl*, p. 155.
127. Schutze, *Preacher's Girl*, p. 167.
128. Schutze, *Preacher's Girl*, p. 253.
129. Schutze, *Preacher's Girl*, p. 152.
130. Schutze, *Preacher's Girl*, p. 178.
131. Schutze, *Preacher's Girl*, p. 156.
132. Geringer, "Aggressive New Breed," p. 6.
133. Schutze, *Preacher's Girl*, p. 225.
134. Schutze, *Preacher's Girl*, p. 177.
135. Schutze, *Preacher's Girl*, p. 253.
136. *Crime and Investigation*, "Deadly Women: Revenge" (n.d.). http://www.crimeandinvestigation.co.uk.tv_programme/297/Deadl..., p. 2. Accessed on November 21, 2008.
137. Schutze, *Preacher's Girl*, p. 330.

CHAPTER 9

1. Jane Caputi, *The Age of Sex Crime* (Bowling Green, Ohio: Bowling Green State University Popular Press, 1987), pp. 106–7. Caputi noted that "Friends reported that he was obsessed with the satanic themes on a 1979 album by AC/DC called *Highway to Hell*." See Caputi, *Age of Sex Crime*, pp. 106–7.
2. James Alan Fox and Jack Levin, *Extreme Killing: Understanding Serial and Mass Murder* (Thousand Oaks, California: Sage Publications, 2005), p. 134.
3. Publications International Ltd., *Murder and Mayhem* (Lincolnwood, Illinois: Publications International Ltd., 1991), p. 219.
4. Philip Carlo, *The Night Stalker: The Life and Crimes of Richard Ramirez* (New York: Kensington Publishing Corporation, 1996), p. 236.
5. Brian Lane and Wilfred Gregg, *The Encyclopedia of Serial Killers* (New York: Berkley Books, 1995), p. 296.
6. *IMDb*, "Biography for Richard Ramirez" (1990–2008). http://www.imdb.com/name/nm0708368, p. 1. Accessed on December 10, 2008.
7. Carlo, *Night Stalker*, p. 115.
8. Anthony Bruno, "Full-Blown Rampage," *The Night Stalker: Serial Killer Richard Ramirez* (n.d.). http://www.trutv.com/library/crime/serial_killers/notorious/ramirez/..., p. 1. Accessed on December 10, 2008.
9. *The History Channel*, "Richard Ramirez: The Night Stalker" (2004). http://www.thehistorychannel.co.uk/site/features/richard_ramirez:1..., p. 1. *Serial Killers A-Z* agreed, "Richard Ramirez struck pure terror into the Los Angeles area in 1984–85." See *Serial Killers A-Z*, "Richard Ramirez" (n.d.). http://www.geocities.com/verbal_plainfield/q-z/ramirez_html?200810, p. 1. Accessed on December 10, 2008.
10. *The Serial Killer Database*, "Richard Ramirez" (n.d.). http://www.serialkillerdatabase.net/richardramirez.html, p. 1. Accessed on December 10, 2008.

11. Charles Montaldo, "Richard Ramirez—The Night Stalker" (n.d.). http://crime.about.com/od/serial/p/nightstalker.htm, p. 1. Accessed on December 10, 2008.
12. Time-Life Books, *True Crime: Serial Killers* (Alexandria, Virginia: Time Life Books, 1992), p. 114; *IMDb*, "Biography for Richard Ramirez," p. 1.
13. Montaldo, "The Night Stalker," p. 1; Carlo, *Night Stalker*, p. 177.
14. Carlo, *Night Stalker*, pp. 177–78.
15. Carlo, *Night Stalker*, pp. 196–98.
16. Peter Vronsky, *Serial Killers: The Method and Madness of Monsters* (New York: Berkley Books, 2004), p. 143.
17. Carlo, *Night Stalker*, pp. 177–78.
18. Carlo, *Night Stalker*, pp. 179.
19. Carlo, *Night Stalker*, p. 197.
20. Vronsky, *Serial Killers: Method*, p. 143.
21. Harold Schechter, *The Serial Killer Files* (New York: Ballantine Books, 2003), p. 104.
22. Time-Life Books, *True Crime*, p. 114.
23. Bruno, "A Good Boy," *The Night Stalker: Serial Killer Richard Ramirez*, p. 1.
24. Carlo, *Night Stalker*, p. 177.
25. Carlo, *Night Stalker*, pp. 191–92, 194.
26. Carlo, *Night Stalker*, pp. 209–10.
27. Vronsky, *Serial Killers: Method*, p. 143; Carlo, *Night Stalker*, p. 239.
28. Carlo, *Night Stalker*, pp. 239–41.
29. Carlo, *Night Stalker*, pp. 235, 246.
30. Carlo, *Night Stalker*, p. 194.
31. Carlo, *Night Stalker*, p. 199.
32. Carlo, *Night Stalker*, p. 202.
33. Time-Life Books, *True Crime*, p. 114;Carlo, *Night Stalker*, p. 205.
34. Carlo, *Night Stalker*, p. 205.
35. Carlo, *Night Stalker*, p. 202; Schechter, *Serial Killer Files*, p. 104.
36. Carlo, *Night Stalker*, p. 203.
37. Carlo, *Night Stalker*, p. 206.
38. Carlo, *Night Stalker*, p. 217.
39. Bruno, "Good Boy," p. 1.
40. Fox and Levin, *Extreme Killing*, p. 134. Interestingly, law enforcement officials doubted Ramirez's Satanic sincerity. See Time-Life Books, *True Crime*, p. 115.
41. David Lester, *Serial Killers: The Insatiable Passion* (Philadelphia: The Charles Press, Publishers, 1995), p. 167.
42. Eric Hickey, *Serial Murderers and Their Victims* (Belmont, California: Wadsworth Publishing Company, 1997), p. 42.
43. Katherine Ramsland, *Human Predator: A Historical Chronicle of Serial Murder and Forensic Investigation* (New York: Berkley Books, 2005), p. 220.
44. *History Channel*, "Richard Ramirez," p. 1.

45. Philip Jenkins, *Using Murder: The Social Construction of Serial Homicide* (New York: Aldine de Gruyter, 1994), p. 199.

46. Vronsky, *Serial Killers: Method*, p. 145. In fact, Ramirez was so inspired by La Vey's work that he stole a vehicle and went to San Francisco. There he met La Vey, and for a while studied under him. See Carlo, *Night Stalker*, p. 237.

47. Schechter, *Serial Killer Files*, p. 104.

48. Bruno, "Good Boy," p. 1.

49. Robin Odell and Wilfred Gregg, *Murderers Row: An International Murderers' Who's Who* (Phoenix Mill, U.K.: Sutton, 2006), p. 357.

50. Ramsland, *Human Predator*, p. 221.

51. Bruno, "I Love Satan," *The Night Stalker: Serial Killer Richard Ramirez*, p. 1.

52. Carlo, *Night Stalker*, pp. 124, 142–43, 147, 162–63.

53. Publications International Ltd., *Murder and Mayhem*, p. 217.

54. Fox and Levin, *Extreme Killing*, p. 133.

55. Michael Newton, *The Encyclopedia of Serial Killers* (New York: Checkmark Books, 2000), p. 194.

56. *AllSerialKillers.com*, "Richard Ramirez" (n.d.). http://www.allserialkillers.com/richard_ramirez.htm, p. 1. Accessed on December 10, 2008.

57. *History Channel*, "Richard Ramirez," p. 1.

58. *Serial Killer Database*, "Richard Ramirez," p. 1.

59. Time-Life Books, *True Crime*, p. 15.

60. Publications International Ltd., *Murder and Mayhem*, p. 219.

61. Montaldo, "The Night Stalker," p. 1.

62. Vronsky, *Serial Killers: Method*, pp. 143–45.

63. Schechter, *Serial Killer Files*, p. 104.

64. Newton, *The Encyclopedia*, p. 195.

65. Carlo, *Night Stalker*, pp. 15, 158, 170, 208–9, 213, 220, 235–37.

66. Carlo, *Night Stalker*, pp. 229–31.

67. Carlo, *Night Stalker*, p. 236.

68. Carlo, *Night Stalker*, pp. 60, 158.

69. Carlo, *Night Stalker*, pp. 128, 223.

70. Fox and Levin, *Extreme Killing*, p. 12.

71. *History Channel*, "Richard Ramirez," p. 1.

72. Schechter, *Serial Killer Files*, p. 104.

73. Fox and Levin, *Extreme Killing*, p. 2; *History Channel*, "Richard Ramirez," p. 1.

74. Montaldo, "The Night Stalker," p. 1.

75. Bruno, "Good Boy," p. 1.

76. *IMDb*, "Biography for Richard Ramirez," p. 1; Ramsland, *Human Predator*, p. 220.

77. Vronsky, *Serial Killers: Method*, p. 144.

78. Carlo, *Night Stalker*, p. 200.

79. Carlo, *Night Stalker*, p. 195.

80. Vronsky, *Serial Killers: Method*, pp. 144, 275. Ramirez was five years of age when the playground accident occurred. See Carlo, *Night Stalker*, p. 200.
81. Carlo, *Night Stalker*, pp. 291–92.
82. Vronsky, *Serial Killers: Method*, p. 143.
83. Vronsky, *Serial Killers: Method*, p. 144.
84. Vronsky, *Serial Killers: Method*, p. 144.
85. Carlo, *Night Stalker*, p. 202.
86. Carlo, *Night Stalker*, p. 135.
87. Carlo, *Night Stalker*, pp. 76, 79, 126, 143.
88. Montaldo, "The Night Stalker," p. 1.
89. Carlo, *Night Stalker*, pp. 15, 104.
90. Carlo, *Night Stalker*, p. 75.
91. Carlo, *Night Stalker*, p. 107.
92. Carlo, *Night Stalker*, p. 131.
93. Fox and Levin, *Extreme Killing*, p. 134.
94. Hickey, *Serial Murderers*, p. 36.
95. *IMDb*, "Biography for Richard Ramirez," p. 1.
96. Carlo, *Night Stalker*, p. 60.
97. Carlo, *Night Stalker*, p. 61.
98. bela.black, "Richard Ramirez 'The Night Stalker,' " *American Serial Killers* (November 27, 2006). http://americanserialkillers.com/articles/richard-ramirez-the -night..., p. 1. Accessed on December 10, 2008.
99. Vronsky, *Serial Killers: Method*, p. 144.
100. Carlo, *Night Stalker*, pp. 210–11, 213.
101. *IMDb*, "Biography for Richard Ramirez," p. 1.
102. Carlo, *Night Stalker*, pp. 223–25.
103. Carlo, *Night Stalker*, p. 228.
104. Time-Life Books, *True Crime*, p. 114.
105. Publications International Ltd., *Murder and Mayhem*, p. 219.
106. Newton, *The Encyclopedia*, p. 195.
107. *AllSerialKillers.com*, "Richard Ramirez," p. 1.
108. Colin Wilson and Donald Seaman, *The Serial Killers: A Study in the Psychology of Violence* (New York: Carol Publishing Group, 1992), p. 116.
109. *Serial Killers A-Z*, "Richard Ramirez," p. 1.
110. *IMDb*, "Biography for Richard Ramirez," p. 1.
111. Newton, *The Encyclopedia*, p. 195.
112. Bruno, "Good Boy," p. 1.
113. Publications International Ltd., *Murder and Mayhem*, p. 219.
114. Carlo, *Night Stalker*, p. 220.
115. Bruno, "Good Boy," p. 1.
116. Montaldo, "The Night Stalker," p. 1.
117. *Serial Killers A-Z*, "Richard Ramirez," p. 1.
118. Carlo, *Night Stalker*, pp. 51, 64, 71, 75, 124, 143, 155, 163.
119. *Serial Killers A-Z*, "Richard Ramirez," p. 1.
120. Lester, *Insatiable Passion*, p. 167.

121. Time-Life Books, *True Crime*, p. 114.
122. Odell and Gregg, *Murderers Row*, p. 357.
123. Wilson and Seaman, *Serial Killers*, p. 306.
124. *History Channel*, "Richard Ramirez," p. 1.
125. bela.black, "Richard Ramirez," p. 1.
126. Publications International Ltd., *Murder and Mayhem*, p. 216.
127. Ramsland, *Human Predator*, p. 221.
128. *IMDb*, "Richard Ramirez," p. 1.
129. Publications International Ltd., *Murder and Mayhem*, p. 217.
130. Caputi, *Age of Sex Crime*, p. 29; Newton, *The Encyclopedia*, p. 194.
131. *Serial Killer Database*, "Richard Ramirez," p. 1.
132. Vronsky, *Serial Killers: Method*, pp. 142–43.
133. Newton, *The Encyclopedia*, p. 195.
134. Caputi, *Age of Sex Crime*, p. 29. Also see Odell and Gregg, *Murderers Row*, p. 357, Lane and Gregg, *The Encyclopedia*, p. 296, and Publications International Ltd., *Murder and Mayhem*, p. 217.
135. Wilson and Seaman, *Serial Killers*, p. 116.
136. *IMDb*, "Richard Ramirez," p. 1.
137. Fox and Levin, *Extreme Killing*, p. 133.
138. Time-Life Books, *True Crime*, p. 114.
139. *History Channel*, "Richard Ramirez," p. 1.
140. Odell and Gregg, *Murderers Row*, p. 357.
141. Bruno, "If You Look at Me Again, I'll Shoot You," *The Night Stalker: Serial Killer Richard Ramirez*, p. 1.
142. *AllSerialKillers.com*, "Richard Ramirez," p. 1.
143. Bruno, "Full-Blown," p. 1.
144. Bruno, "Good Boy," p. 1.
145. Carlo, *Night Stalker*, p. 21.
146. Carlo, *Night Stalker*, p. 119.
147. Wilson and Seaman, *Serial Killers*, p. 116.
148. Carlo, *Night Stalker*, p. 127.
149. *History Channel*, "Richard Ramirez," p. 1.
150. Carlo, *Night Stalker*, p. 101.
151. Carlo, *Night Stalker*, pp. 16, 165.
152. Vronsky, *Serial Killers: Method*, p. 143.
153. *History Channel*, "Richard Ramirez," p. 1.
154. Carlo, *Night Stalker*, p. 25.
155. Time-Life Books, *True Crime*, p. 114.
156. Wilson and Seaman, *Serial Killers*, p. 116.
157. Bruno, "Good Boy," p. 2.
158. *Serial Killer Database*, "Richard Ramirez," p. 1.
159. *Serial Killer Database*, "Richard Ramirez," p. 1.
160. Montaldo, "The Night Stalker," p. 1.
161. Bruno, "I Love Satan,"*Night Stalker: Serial Killer Richard Ramirez*, p. 2.
162. Bruno, "Good Boy," p. 1.

163. Carlo, *Night Stalker*, p. 20.
164. Carlo, *Night Stalker*, p. 50.
165. Carlo, *Night Stalker*, p. 51.
166. Carlo, *Night Stalker*, p. 64.
167. Carlo, *Night Stalker*, p. 71.
168. Carlo, *Night Stalker*, p. 91.
169. Carlo, *Night Stalker*, p. 106.
170. Carlo, *Night Stalker*, p. 121.
171. Carlo, *Night Stalker*, pp. 124–25.
172. Carlo, *Night Stalker*, pp. 141–42.
173. Carlo, *Night Stalker*, p. 155.
174. Fox and Levin, *Extreme Killing*, p. 134.
175. Odell and Gregg, *Murderers Row*, p. 357.
176. Bruno, "I Love Satan," p. 2.
177. Carlo, *Night Stalker*, p. 52.
178. Carlo, *Night Stalker*, p. 166.
179. Carlo, *Night Stalker*, p. 167.
180. Vronsky, *Serial Killers: Method*, p. 143.
181. Bruno, "I Love Satan," p. 1.
182. Carlo, *Night Stalker*, p. 48.
183. Newton, *The Encyclopedia*, p. 194.
184. *AllSerialKillers.com*, "Richard Ramirez," p. 1.
185. Bruno, "Full-Blown," p. 2.

CHAPTER 10

1. Irene Pence, *Buried Memories: The Chilling True Story of Betty* [*sic*] *Lou Beets, the Texas Black Widow* (New York: Kensington Publishing Company, 2001), pp. 42–45, 264.
2. Pence, *Buried Memories*, pp. 51, 174.
3. Pence, *Buried Memories*, pp. 10–11, 15, 185–86, 222–23.
4. *Beets v. Collins*, 986 F.2d, 1478. United States Court of Appeals, Fifth Circuit (March 18, 1993). No. 91-4606, p. 4.
5. Pence, *Buried Memories*, pp. 223, 225, 309.
6. Pence, *Buried Memories*, p. 178.
7. Charles Zewe, "Texas Authorities Prepare to Execute Betty [*sic*] Lou Beets; Bush, Supreme Court Refuse to Delay Execution," *CNN.com* (February 24, 2000). http://transcripts.cnn.com/TRANSCRIPTS/00002/24/bn.03.html, pp. 5–6. Accessed on December 3, 2008.
8. "Betty [*sic*] Lou Beets" (n.d.). http://www.clarkprosecutor.org/html/death/US/beets616.htm, p. 9. Accessed on December 3, 2008.
9. Pence, *Buried Memories*, pp. 299–300.
10. Pence, *Buried Memories*, pp. 303–4.
11. Pence, *Buried Memories*, p. 29.
12. Pence, *Buried Memories*, p. 29.

13. Pence, *Buried Memories*, p. 29.

14. Bettie Lou Beets, "A Battered Woman's Story from Texas Death Row," *Canadian Coalition Against the Death Penalty* (April 25, 2005). http://www.ccadp.org/bettiebeets.htm, p. 4. Accessed on December 3, 2008.

15. Pence, *Buried Memories*, p. 32.

16. Pence, *Buried Memories*, p. 32.

17. Pence, *Buried Memories*, pp. 29–30.

18. Pence, *Buried Memories*, p. 31.

19. Beets, "A Battered Woman's," p. 4; Pence, *Buried Memories*, p. 32.

20. Beets, "A Battered Woman's," p. 4.

21. Pence, *Buried Memories*, p. 31.

22. Pence, *Buried Memories*, pp. 30–31.

23. *Business Wire*, "Texas Board of Pardons Denies Betty [*sic*] Lou Beets' Request for Stay of Execution" (February 22, 2000). http://findarticles.com/p/articles/mi_m0EIN/is_2000_Feb_22/ai_59..., p. 1. Accessed on December 3, 2008.

24. European Coalition to Abolish the Death Penalty, "In Memorium—Betty [*sic*] Lou Betts" (n.d.). http://www.clarkprosecutor.org/html/death/US/beets616.htm, p. 9. Accessed on December 3, 2008.

25. *Beets v. Collins*, p. 28.

26. Pence, *Buried Memories*, p. 295.

27. Pence, *Buried Memories*, p. 207.

28. Pence, *Buried Memories*, p. 188.

29. Pence, *Buried Memories*, pp. 94, 105.

30. Pence, *Buried Memories*, p. 26.

31. Pence, *Buried Memories*, p. 38.

32. Pence, *Buried Memories*, pp. 34, 49.

33. Pence, *Buried Memories*, p. 37.

34. *The Evil Divas*, "Betty [*sic*] Lou Beets." (n.d.). http://www.divasthesite.com/Evil_Divas/Evil_Diva>Betty_Lou_Bee..., p. 1. Accessed on December 3, 2008; Pence, *Buried Memories*, p. 34.

35. Pence, *Buried Memories*, pp. 38, 49.

36. Pence, *Buried Memories*, p. 182.

37. Pence, *Buried Memories*, p. 81.

38. Pence, *Buried Memories*, p. 187.

39. Pence, *Buried Memories*, p. 29.

40. Pence, *Buried Memories*, p. 30.

41. Pence, *Buried Memories*, p. 30.

42. European Coalition to Abolish the Death Penalty, "In Memorium," p. 9.

43. *Beets v. Collins*, p. 28.

44. Pence, *Buried Memories*, pp. 296, 299.

45. Pence, *Buried Memories*, p. 297.

46. Pence, *Buried Memories*, p. 33.

47. Pence, *Buried Memories*, p. 33.

48. *About.com*, "BETTY [*sic*] LOU BEETS: Grandmotherly Victim, or 'Black Widow'?" (n.d.). http://www.clarkprosecutor.org/hmtl/death/US/beets616.htm, p. 5. Accessed on December 3, 2008.
49. Pence, *Buried Memories*, p. 297.
50. Pence, *Buried Memories*, p. 297.
51. Pence, *Buried Memories*, p. 296.
52. Pence, *Buried Memories*, pp. 38–39.
53. Pence, *Buried Memories*, p. 39.
54. Beets, "A Battered Woman's," pp. 5–6.
55. Beets, "A Battered Woman's," p. 7.
56. *About.com*, "Grandmotherly Victim," p. 5.
57. European Coalition to Abolish the Death Penalty, "In Memoriam," p. 9.
58. Michael Graczyk, "Texas Woman Executed for Killing Her Husband," *The Independent* (February 25, 2000). http://www.independent.co.uk/news/world/Americas/texas-woman-e..., p. 1. Accessed on December 3, 2008.
59. *WIRED*, "Betty [*sic*] Lou Beets, 62, Executed" (February 2, 2000). http://www.wired.com/print/culture/lifestyle/news/2000/02/34569, p. 1. Accessed on December 3, 2008.
60. *Business Wire*, "Texas Board of Pardons," p. 1.
61. David Carson, "Betty [*sic*] Beets," *Texas Execution Information Center* (June 13, 2002). http://www.txexecutions.org/reports/208.asp, p. 1. Accessed on December 3, 2008.
62. *Beets v. Collins*, pp. 28–29.
63. Beets, "A Battered Woman's," p. 6.
64. Beets, "A Battered Woman's," p. 6.
65. Pence, *Buried Memories*, pp. 51–54.
66. Pence, *Buried Memories*, p. 297.
67. *CNN.com*, "Texas Executes Betty [*sic*] Lou Beets for Husband's Murder" (February 24, 2000). http://www.clarkprosecutor.org/html/death/US/beets616.htm, p. 4. Accessed on December 3, 2008.
68. Beets, "A Battered Woman's," p. 4.
69. Beets, "A Battered Woman's," p. 4; Pence, *Buried Memories*, pp. 32–33.
70. Beets, "A Battered Woman's," p. 4; Pence, *Buried Memories*, p. 34.
71. *The Evil Divas*, "Betty [*sic*] Lou Beets," p. 1.
72. *About.com*, "Grandmotherly Victim," p. 5.
73. Pence, *Buried Memories*, pp. 36–37.
74. Pence, *Buried Memories*, p. 45.
75. Pence, *Buried Memories*, pp. 285–86.
76. Pence, *Buried Memories*, p. 298.
77. Beets, "A Battered Woman's," p. 4.
78. European Coalition to Abolish the Death Penalty, "In Memoriam," p. 9.
79. *Beets v. Collins*, p. 28.
80. Pence, *Buried Memories*, p. 29.
81. Pence, *Buried Memories*, p. 37.
82. Beets, "A Battered Woman's," p. 6.

83. Beets, "A Battered Woman's," p. 6.
84. Pence, *Buried Memories*, p. 181.
85. Pence, *Buried Memories*, p. 187.
86. Pence, *Buried Memories*, pp. 194–95.
87. Pence, *Buried Memories*, p. 252.
88. Daughter Shirley and son Robby's complicity was discussed in Pence, *Buried Memories*, pp. 66–67, 70–71, 111–15, 196–98. Also see Carson, "Betty [*sic*] Beets," p. 1.
89. Pence, *Buried Memories*, p. 48.
90. Pence, *Buried Memories*, p. 49.
91. Pence, *Buried Memories*, p. 48.
92. Pence, *Buried Memories*, pp. 49, 180.
93. Pence, *Buried Memories*, pp. 125, 193.
94. Pence, *Buried Memories*, pp. 156, 185.
95. Texas Attorney General's Office, "Media Advisory: Betty [*sic*] Lou Beets Scheduled to be Executed" (February 11, 2000). http://www.clarkprosecutor.org/html/death/US/beets616.htm, p. 3. Accessed on December 3, 2008.
96. Pence, *Buried Memories*, p. 54.
97. Pence, *Buried Memories*, p. 270.
98. Texas Attorney General, "Media Advisory," p. 3.
99. *CNN.com*, "Texas Executes," p. 4.
100. *About.com*, "Grandmotherly Victim," p. 5.
101. *Beets v. State*, 767 S.W., .2d 711 (Tex, Cr.App, 1987) (Direct Appeal). p. 10.
102. *Beets v. Collins*, p. 3.
103. Pence, *Buried Memories*, pp. 88, 138–39, 143.
104. Pence, *Buried Memories*, pp. 163–64, 271.
105. *Beets v. State*, p. 14.
106. Pence, *Buried Memories*, p. 132.
107. Pence, *Buried Memories*, pp. 241–42.
108. Pence, *Buried Memories*, pp. 267–68.
109. Pence, *Buried Memories*, p. 174.
110. Carson, "Betty [*sic*] Beets," p. 1.
111. *The Evil Divas*, "Betty [*sic*] Lou Beets," p. 1.
112. Texas Attorney General, "Media Advisory," pp. 1–2.
113. *ProDeathPenalty.com* (n.d.). Untitled. http://www.clarkprosecutor.org/html/death/US/beets616.htm, p. 3. Accessed on December 3, 2008.
114. *Beets v. State*, p. 12.
115. *Beets v. Collins*, p. 4.
116. Geraldine Sealy, "'Black Widow' Executed. Great-Grandmother is 4th Female Inmate to Die in U.S. Since 1976," *ABCNews.com* (2000). http://www.clarkprosecutor.org/html/death/US/beets616.htm, p. 6. Accessed on December 3, 2008.
117. *CNN.com*, "Texas Executes," p. 5.
118. Pence, *Buried Memories*, pp. 70, 110, 184.

119. Graczyk, "Texas Woman Executed," p. 1.
120. Michael Simonich, "States Have Executed 11 Women Since '84," *Pittsburgh Post-Gazette* (September 24, 2005). http://www.post-gazette.com/pg/06267/724622-stm, p. 1. Accessed on December 3, 2008.
121. Carson, "Betty [*sic*] Beets," p. 1.
122. *The Global Ethic Project*, "#121 Betty [*sic*] Beets" (November 16, 2000). https://listserv.temple.edu/cgi-bin/wa?A2=ind0011&L=g-ethic&P=7998, p. 2. Accessed on December 3, 2008.
123. *The Evil Divas*, "Betty [*sic*] Lou Beets," p. 1.
124. *Pro-DeathPenalty.com*, Untitled, p. 3.
125. *About.com*, "Grandmotherly Victim," p. 5.
126. Pence, *Buried Memories*, p. 278.
127. Texas Attorney General, "Media Advisory," p. 2.
128. *Beets v. Collins*, p. 5.
129. Pence, *Buried Memories*, p. 200.
130. *Beets v. State*, p. 10.
131. Pence, *Buried Memories*, p. 206.
132. Sealy, "Black Widow," pp. 7–8.
133. Office of the Attorney General, State of Texas, "Betty [*sic*] Lou Beets" (February 11, 2000). http://www.clarkprosecutor.org/html/death/US/beets616.htm, p. 1. Accessed on December 3, 2008.
134. Pence, *Buried Memories*, p. 106.
135. *Beets v. State*, p. 13; Pence, *Buried Memories*, p. 74.
136. Pence, *Buried Memories*, p. 271.
137. *Beets v. Collins*, p. 6; Pence, *Buried Memories*, p. 122.
138. Pence, *Buried Memories*, p. 144.
139. *Beets v. State*, p. 14.
140. Carson, "Betty [*sic*] Beets," p. 1.
141. Zewe, "Texas Authorities," p. 5.
142. Pence, *Buried Memories*, p. 205.
143. *Beets v. Collins*, pp. 7, 16–17.
144. Pence, *Buried Memories*, p. 230.
145. *Beets v. Collins*, pp. 5–6, 34; *Beets v. State*, p. 10.
146. Pence, *Buried Memories*, pp. 120–21.
147. Pence, *Buried Memories*, p. 275.
148. *Beets v. Collins*, p. 7; Pence, *Buried Memories*, p. 144.
149. *Beets v. State*, p. 14; Pence, *Buried Memories*, p. 171.
150. *Beets v. State*, p. 14.
151. Pence, *Buried Memories*, pp. 95–98, 241–42; *Beets v. State*, pp. 14, 163.
152. Texas Attorney General, "Media Advisory," p. 2.
153. *Beets v. State*, p. 14.
154. Pence, *Buried Memories*, pp. 132, 174, 247.
155. Pence, *Buried Memories*, pp. 132, 144–45, 205.
156. Pence, *Buried Memories*, p. 124.

157. Pence, *Buried Memories*, pp. 126–31, 191.
158. Pence, *Buried Memories*, pp. 126–31.

CHAPTER 11

1. Tom Miller, *The Copeland Killings: The Bizarre True Account of Ray and Faye Copeland, the Oldest Couple Ever Sentenced to Death in America* (New York: Windsor Publishing Corporation, 1993), p. 228. The distinction that McCormick sought to make was that bums never work, while tramps are merely unemployed at the moment.
2. "Rural Intrigue Is Unearthed with 5 Bodies," *New York Times* (November 25, 1989). http://query-nytimes.com/gst/fullpage.html?res=950DE6DB163FF..., p. 1. Accessed on December 10, 2008; and David Lohr, "Trials and Verdicts," *The Crime Library* (2008). http://www.trutv.com/library/crime/serial_killers/partners/copelands..., p. 1. Accessed on December 10, 2008.
3. Ronald M. Holmes and Stephen T. Holmes, *Serial Murder* (Thousand Oaks, California: Sage Publications, 1998), p. 121.
4. Lohr, "Downward Spiral," *The Crime Library*, p. 1.
5. Miller, *Copeland Killings*, pp. 14, 45–46.
6. Miller, *Copeland Killings*, pp. 297–99.
7. Miller, *Copeland Killings*, pp. 257–61, 281–87.
8. Miller, *Copeland Killings*, p. 24.
9. Miller, *Copeland Killings*, pp. 16, 166–68.
10. *The Serial Killer Database*, "The Copelands" (n.d.). http://www.serialkillerdatabase.net/thecopelands.html, p. 1. Accessed on December 10, 2008.
11. *Serial Killer Database*, "The Copelands," p. 1; Lohr, "Early Years," *The Crime Library*, p. 1.
12. Miller, *Copeland Killings*, p. 27.
13. Lohr, "Early Years," p. 1.
14. Miller, *Copeland Killings*, p. 25.
15. Lohr, "Early Years," p. 1.
16. Miller, *Copeland Killings*, p. 26.
17. Lohr, "Early Years," p. 1.
18. *The Prairie Chicken*, "Ray and Faye Copeland: The Elderly Murderers" (October 5, 2008). http://prairiechicken.blogspot.com/2008/10/ray-and-faye-copeland..., p. 1. Accessed on December 10, 2008.
19. Lohr, "Early Years," p. 1.
20. Miller, *Copeland Killings*, p. 14.
21. Miller, *Copeland Killings*, p. 26.
22. Miller, *Copeland Killings*, p. 26.
23. Miller, *Copeland Killings*, p. 26.
24. Miller, *Copeland Killings*, p. 26.
25. Miller, *Copeland Killings*, p. 15.
26. Miller, *Copeland Killings*, p. 43.
27. Lohr, "Downward Spiral," p. 1.

28. Miller, *Copeland Killings*, p. 28.
29. Miller, *Copeland Killings*, p. 26.
30. Miller, *Copeland Killings*, p. 28.
31. *Prairie Chicken*, "The Elderly Murderers," p. 1.
32. Charles Montaldo, "Serial Killers Couple Ray and Faye Copeland," *About.com* (n.d.). http://crime.about.com/od/murder/p/copelands.htm, p. 2. Accessed on December 10, 2008.
33. Lohr, "Downward Spiral," p. 1.
34. Miller, *Copeland Killings*, p. 36.
35. Miller, *Copeland Killings*, pp. 54, 275.
36. Miller, *Copeland Killings*, p. 54.
37. Miller, *Copeland Killings*, pp. 54, 275.
38. Miller, *Copeland Killings*, p. 275.
39. Miller, *Copeland Killings*, p. 275.
40. *Prairie Chicken*, "The Elderly Murderers," p. 1.
41. Montaldo, "Serial Killers Couple," p. 1. Also see *bonka's mom*, "Ray and Faye Copeland: The Elderly Murderers" (2008). Associated Content. http://www.associatedcontent.com/pop_print.shtml?content_type=ar..., p. 1. Accessed on December 10, 2008.
42. "Faye Copeland, 82; Convicted of Killing 5 Men in Missouri," *Los Angeles Times* (January 1, 2004). http://articles.latimes.com/2004.jan/01/local/me-passings1.3, p. 1. Accessed on December 10, 2008.
43. Lohr, "Early Years," p. 1.
44. Miller, *Copeland Killings*, p. 166.
45. *Serial Killer Database*, "The Copelands," p. 1.
46. *Serial Killer Database*, "The Copelands," p. 1.
47. Miller, *Copeland Killings*, p. 30.
48. Miller, *Copeland Killings*, p. 30.
49. Lohr, "Early Years," p. 1.
50. Miller, *Copeland Killings*, p. 30.
51. Miller, *Copeland Killings*, p. 191.
52. Miller, *Copeland Killings*, p. 216.
53. Miller, *Copeland Killings*, p. 292.
54. Miller, *Copeland Killings*, p. 30.
55. Miller, *Copeland Killings*, p. 49.
56. Miller, *Copeland Killings*, p. 49.
57. Miller, *Copeland Killings*, p. 215.
58. Miller, *Copeland Killings*, p. 49.
59. Lohr, "Downward Spiral," p. 1.
60. Miller, *Copeland Killings*, pp. 15, 48.
61. Miller, *Copeland Killings*, pp. 15, 48.
62. Miller, *Copeland Killings*, pp. 28–29.
63. *geocities*, "Copeland, Ray and Faye" (n.d.). http://www.geocities.com/serialkillers101.copeland.html?200810, p. 1. Accessed on December 10, 2008.

64. Public Interest Litigation Clinic, "Faye Copeland" (1999–2000). http://www.pilc.net/clients4.html, p. 2. Accessed on December 10, 2008.
65. Public Interest Litigation Clinic, "Faye Copeland," p. 1.
66. *Investigation Discovery*, "Ten: Ray and Faye Copeland" (n.d.). http://investigation.discovery.com/tv/wicked-attraction/deadly-duos-..., p. 1. Accessed on December 10, 2008.
67. *Los Angeles Times*, "Faye Copeland," p. 1.
68. Miller, *Copeland Killings*, p. 13.
69. Miller, *Copeland Killings*, p. 240.
70. Miller, *Copeland Killings*, p. 183.
71. *The Finer Times*, "The Oldest Serial Killers" (n.d.). http://www.thefinertimes.com/Serial-Killers/the-oldest-serial-killers/..., p. 1. Accessed on December 10, 2008.
72. Holmes and Holmes, *Serial Murder*, p. 122.
73. *Investigation Discovery*, "Ten: Ray and Faye," p. 1.
74. Public Interest Law Clinic, "Faye Copeland," p. 1.
75. *bonka's mom*, "Ray and Faye," p. 1.
76. *Serial Killers A-Z*, "Ray Copeland" (n.d.). http://www.geocities.com/verbal_plainfield/a-h/copeland.html?200810, p. 1. Accessed on December 10, 2008.
77. Miller, *Copeland Killings*, pp. 79, 87–88, 139–40, 143, 234.
78. *geocities*, "Copeland, Ray and Faye," p. 1.
79. United States Court of Appeals for the Eighth Circuit. *Faye D. Copeland, Appellee, v. James Washington, Appellant: Appeals From the United States District Court for the Western District of Missouri.* No. 99-3693 (September 13, 2000).
80. *Finer Times*, "The Oldest," p. 1.
81. *New York Times*, "Real Intrigue," p. 1.
82. *Serial Killers A-Z*, "Ray Copeland," p. 1.
83. *Serial Killer Database*, "The Copelands," p. 1.
84. *geocities*, "Copeland, Ray and Fay," p. 1.
85. *Finer Times*, "The Oldest," p. 1.
86. *bonka's mom*, "Ray and Faye," p. 1.
87. Lohr, "No Deal," p. 1.
88. *Prairie Chicken*, "The Elderly Murderers," p. 2.
89. Lohr, "Early Years," p. 1.
90. Miller, *Copeland Killings*, p. 29.
91. Miller, *Copeland Killings*, p. 30.
92. Lohr, "Early Years," p. 1.
93. Miller, *Copeland Killings*, p. 30.
94. Lohr, "Epilogue," *The Crime Library*, p. 1.
95. Miller, *Copeland Killings*, p. 299.
96. Miller, *Copeland Killings*, pp. 217–18, 248–49.
97. *Prairie Chicken*, "The Elderly Murderers," p. 2.
98. Public Interest Law Clinic, "Faye Copeland," p. 2.

99. Miller, *Copeland Killings*, p. 38.
100. Miller, *Copeland Killings*, p. 292.
101. Miller, *Copeland Killings*, p. 292.
102. Lohr, "Downward Spiral," p. 1.
103. Miller, *Copeland Killings*, p. 33.
104. Miller, *Copeland Killings*, p. 32.
105. Miller, *Copeland Killings*, pp. 54–55.
106. Lohr, "Epilogue," p. 1.
107. Miller, *Copeland Killings*, p. 242.
108. Miller, *Copeland Killings*, p. 37.
109. Miller, *Copeland Killings*, p. 54.
110. Miller, *Copeland Killings*, pp. 299–300.
111. Miller, *Copeland Killings*, p. 38.
112. Miller, *Copeland Killings*, p. 14.
113. Miller, *Copeland Killings*, p. 15.
114. Miller, *Copeland Killings*, p. 15.
115. Miller, *Copeland Killings*, p. 15.
116. Miller, *Copeland Killings*, p. 20.
117. Lohr, "Early Years," p. 1.
118. Miller, *Copeland Killings*, pp. 27–28.
119. Lohr, "Early Years," p. 1. Also see Lohr, "Downward Spiral," p. 1.
120. Lohr, "Early Years," p. 1.
121. Miller, *Copeland Killings*, p. 31.
122. Miller, *Copeland Killings*, p. 28.
123. *Prairie Chicken*, "The Elderly Murderers," p. 2.
124. Lohr, "Early Years," p. 1; Lohr, "Downward Spiral," p. 1.
125. Lohr, "Downward Spiral," p. 1.
126. Miller, *Copeland Killings*, pp. 33–34.
127. Miller, *Copeland Killings*, p. 18.
128. Stephen Egger, *The Need to Kill: Inside the World of the Serial Killer* (Upper Saddle River, New Jersey: Prentice-Hall, 2003), p. 12; Lohr, "Rare Breed," *The Crime Library*, p. 1; *Los Angeles Times*, "Faye Copeland," p. 1; and *Investigation Discovery*, "Ten: Ray and Faye," p. 1.
129. *Serial Killers A Z*, "Ray Copeland," p. 1.
130. *New York Times*, "Real Intrigue," p. 1.
131. *New York Times*, "Real Intrigue," p. 1.
132. Miller, *Copeland Killings*, p. 142.
133. Lohr, "Trial and Verdicts," *The Crime Library*, p. 1.
134. Miller, *Copeland Killings*, pp. 51–52.
135. Miller, *Copeland Killings*, pp. 302–3.
136. Miller, *Copeland Killings*, pp. 89, 123.
137. *Nationmaster.com*, "Encyclopedia—Faye Copeland" (2003–05). http://www.nationmaster.com.encyclopedia/Faye-Copeland, p. 1. Accessed on December 10, 2008.
138. Miller, *Copeland Killings*, p. 266.

139. Lohr, "No Deal," p. 1; *Serial Killer Database*, "The Copelands," p. 1.

140. Egger, *Need to Kill*, p. 12; *Investigation Discovery*, "Ten: Ray and Faye," p. 1; *Finer Times*, "The Oldest," p. 1; and *geocities*, "Copeland, Ray and Faye," p. 1.

141. Holmes and Holmes, *Serial Murder*, p. 112; *New York Times*, "Real Intrigue," p. 1; and Miller, *Copeland Killings*, pp. 21–23.

142. *geocities*, "Copelands, Ray and Faye," p. 1.

143. Egger, *Need to Kill*, p. 12; *Serial Killer Database*, "The Copelands," p. 1.

144. *Nationmaster.com*, "Encyclopedia—Faye Copeland," p. 1.

145. U.S. Court of Appeals, "Faye D. Copeland, Appellee," p. 3.

146. Miller, *Copeland Killings*, pp. 243–44.

147. Miller, *Copeland Killings*, p. 276.

148. Miller, *Copeland Killings*, pp. 143–44.

149. Miller, *Copeland Killings*, pp. 172–73.

150. *Los Angeles Times*, "Faye Copeland," p. 1.

151. *Investigation Discovery*, "Ten: Ray and Faye," p. 1.

152. U.S. Court of Appeals, "Faye D. Copeland, Appellee," p. 3.

153. Lohr, "The Unsophisticated Swindler," *The Crime Library*, p. 1.

154. Lohr, "Unsophisticated," p. 1.

155. Miller, *Copeland Killings*, pp. 50–51.

156. Miller, *Copeland Killings*, pp. 52–53.

157. Miller, *Copeland Killings*, p. 53.

158. Miller, *Copeland Killings*, pp. 62, 81.

159. Miller, *Copeland Killings*, p. 78.

160. Miller, *Copeland Killings*, p. 81.

161. Miller, *Copeland Killings*, p. 83.

162. Miller, *Copeland Killings*, p. 303.

163. Miller, *Copeland Killings*, pp. 16, 246, 304.

164. *Serial Killers Database*, "Ray Copeland," p. 1.

165. Miller, *Copeland Killings*, pp. 38–39.

CHAPTER 12

1. Steven A. Egger, *The Need to Kill: Inside the World of the Serial Killer* (Upper Saddle River, New Jersey: Prentice-Hall, 2003), p. 15.

2. "Female Serial Killer, Dana Sue Gray," *Crimeshots True Crime Forums* (May 17, 2004). http://www.crimeshots.com/forums/showthread.php?t=129, p. 2. Accessed on December 3, 2008.

3. Kathy Braidhill, *To Die For: The Shocking True Story of Female Serial Killer Dana Sue Gray* (New York: St. Martin's Press, 2000), p. 121.

4. Katherine Ramsland, "Giving In," *The Crime Library* (2008). http://www.trutv.com/library/crime/notorious_murders/women/dan..., pp. 1–2.

5. Braidhill, *To Die For*, pp. 36, 41.

6. Ramsland, "Home Alone," *The Crime Library*, p. 2. Also see Braidhill, *To Die For*, p. 15.

7. *Crimeshots*, "Female Serial Killer," p. 3.
8. Braidhill, *To Die For*, pp. 232, 290.
9. *Crimeshots*, "Female Serial Killers," pp. 2, 6.
10. Ramsland, "Attacking the Vulnerable," *The Crime Library*, p. 2.
11. Ramsland, "Home Alone," p. 2.
12. Braidhill, *To Die For*, pp. 54, 72, 124.
13. Braidhill, *To Die For*, p. 73.
14. Braidhill, *To Die For*, p. 101.
15. Braidhill, *To Die For*, p. 195.
16. *Crimeshots*, "Female Serial Killer," p. 4.
17. Braidhill, *To Die For*, p. 225.
18. *Crimeshots*, "Female Serial Killer," p. 4.
19. Braidhill, *To Die For*, pp. 194–95.
20. Braidhill, *To Die For*, pp. 195–96.
21. Braidhill, *To Die For*, pp. 197–200.
22. *Reference.com*, "Dana Sue Gray" (n.d.). http://www.reference.com/browse/Dana+Sue+Gray, p. 1. Accessed on January 15, 2009.
23. *Reference.com*, "Dana Sue Gray," p. 1.
24. *Crimeshots*, "Female Serial Killer," p. 4.
25. Ramsland, "Crazy Over Cash," *The Crime Library*, p. 2.
26. Braidhill, *To Die For*, p. 200.
27. *Reference.com*, "Dana Sue Gray," p. 1.
28. Braidhill, *To Die For*, pp. 195–96.
29. Braidhill, *To Die For*, pp. 210–16.
30. Braidhill, *To Die For*, pp. 196–97.
31. Braidhill, *To Die For*, p. 197. Ironically, *Crimeshots* asserted that "Unlike many serial killers, she apparently never tortured animals." See *Crimeshots*, "Female Serial Killer," p. 4.
32. Braidhill, *To Die For*, pp. 101, 200–01.
33. *Reference.com*, "Dana Sue Gray," p. 1.
34. *Wikipedia*, "Dana Sue Gray" (January 12, 2009). http://en.wikipedia.org/wiki/Dana_Sue_Gray, p. 1. Accessed on January 15, 2009.
35. Braidhill, *To Die For*, p. 206.
36. *Crimeshots*, "Female Serial Killer," p. 4.
37. *Wikipedia.com*, "Dana Sue Gray," p. 2.
38. Braidhill, *To Die For*, p. 223.
39. Braidhill, *To Die For*, pp. 194–96.
40. *Crimeshots*, "Female Serial Killer," p. 4.
41. Braidhill, *To Die For*, pp. 147, 194–95.
42. Braidhill, *To Die For*, p. 149.
43. Braidhill, *To Die For*, p. 191.
44. Braidhill, *To Die For*, p. 217.
45. Braidhill, *To Die For*, p. 253.
46. Braidhill, *To Die For*, p. 231.
47. *Crimeshots*, "Female Serial Killer," p. 3.

48. Braidhill, *To Die For*, p. 221.
49. *Crimeshots*, "Female Serial Killer," p. 5. At sixteen years of age, here is how Gray was described, "disarmingly light blue eyes, sun-kissed good looks and a figure that turned heads." See Braidhill, *To Die For*, p. 201.
50. Braidhill, *To Die For*, p. 31.
51. Ramsland, "Cagey Customer," *The Crime Library*, p. 1.
52. *Crimeshots*, "Female Serial Killer," p. 6.
53. Braidhill, *To Die For*, pp. 65, 83.
54. Braidhill, *To Die For*, p. 95.
55. Braidhill, *To Die For*, p. 194.
56. Braidhill, *To Die For*, pp. 183–84, 187.
57. Braidhill, *To Die For*, p. 74.
58. Ramsland, "Crazy Over Cash," p. 1.
59. Braidhill, *To Die For*, p. 197.
60. Braidhill, *To Die For*, pp. 201–06.
61. Braidhill, *To Die For*, p. 75.
62. Braidhill, *To Die For*, p. 189.
63. Braidhill, *To Die For*, p. 217.
64. Ramsland, "A Wrench in the Works," p. 1.
65. *Crimeshots*, "Female Serial Killer," pp. 2, 5.
66. *Reference.com*, "Dana Sue Gray," p. 1.
67. Braidhill, *To Die For*, pp. 210, 220.
68. Braidhill, *To Die For*, p. 220.
69. Braidhill, *To Die For*, pp. 154–55.
70. Braidhill, *To Die For*, p. 201.
71. Braidhill, *To Die For*, p. 185.
72. *Crimeshots*, "Female Serial Killer," p. 5.
73. Braidhill, *To Die For*, p. 202.
74. Braidhill, *To Die For*, p. 205.
75. Braidhill, *To Die For*, p. 217.
76. Ramsland, "Crazy Over Cash," p. 1.
77. Braidhill, *To Die For*, p. 140.
78. Braidhill, *To Die For*, pp. 212, 221.
79. Braidhill, *To Die For*, p. 184.
80. *Crimeshots*, "Female Serial Killer," p. 7.
81. Ramsland, "Evolution of a Serial Killer," *The Crime Library*, p. 1.
82. Ramsland, "Giving In," pp. 1–2.
83. Braidhill, *To Die For*, p. 102.
84. Braidhill, *To Die For*, pp. 184–85.
85. Braidhill, *To Die For*, p. 200.
86. Braidhill, *To Die For*, p. 222.
87. Braidhill, *To Die For*, pp. 150–51, 211.
88. Braidhill, *To Die For*, p. 281.
89. Braidhill, *To Die For*, pp. 280–89. "She also told each of the three experts a different rendition of events." See Ramsland, "A Wrench in the Works," p. 1.

90. Braidhill, *To Die For*, p. 291.
91. Braidhill, *To Die For*, p. 201.
92. *Reference.com*, "Dana Sue Gray," p. 1.
93. Braidhill, *To Die For*, p. 198.
94. Braidhill, *To Die For*, p. 230.
95. Ramsland, "Crazy Over Cash," p. 1.
96. Ramsland, "Crazy Over Cash," p. 1.
97. Braidhill, *To Die For*, p. 106.
98. Braidhill, *To Die For*, pp. 195–97.
99. Braidhill, *To Die For*, pp. 213, 217.
100. Braidhill, *To Die For*, p. 223.
101. *Crimeshots*, "Female Serial Killer," p. 4.
102. Braidhill, *To Die For*, p. 216. According to one account, Dana and her Great-Aunt walked through the elderly woman's house, with her niece pointing out the items she wanted, "When you die, I want this Chinese cup." See *Crimeshots*, "Female Serial Killer," p. 5.
103. *Reference.com*, "Dana Sue Gray," p. 1.
104. Braidhill, *To Die For*, pp. 209, 213.
105. *Crimeshots*, "Female Serial Killer," p. 7.
106. Braidhill, *To Die For*, p. 234.
107. *Crimeshots*, "Female Serial Killer," p. 5.
108. Braidhill, *To Die For*, p. 221.
109. Braidhill, *To Die For*, p. 239.
110. Braidhill, *To Die For*, p. 221.
111. *Crimeshots*, "Female Serial Killer," p. 3.
112. Ramsland, "Giving In," p. 1.
113. Braidhill, *To Die For*, p. 17.
114. *Reference.com*, "Dana Sue Gray," p. 1.
115. Ramsland, "Crazy Over Cash," p. 2.
116. Braidhill, *To Die For*, p. 194. When the policeman left, Beverly pointedly told Dana, "Don't get *caught* again!" See Braidhill, *To Die For*, p. 194.
117. Braidhill, *To Die For*, pp. 198–99.
118. Braidhill, *To Die For*, p. 202.
119. *Crimeshots*, "Female Serial Killer," p. 5.
120. *Reference.com*, "Dana Sue Gray," p. 1.
121. Braidhill, *To Die For*, pp. 222–24.
122. *Crimeshots*, "Female Serial Killer," p. 1.
123. *Crimeshots*, "Female Serial Killer," p. 3; *Crimeshots: Psychology of Crime* (n.d.). http://crimeshots.com/Psychology.html, p. 2. Accessed on January 15, 2009.
124. Egger, *Need to Kill*, p. 14.
125. *Crimeshots*, "Female Serial Killer," p. 5; Ramsland, "Tragic Anniversary," *The Crime Library*, p. 1.
126. *SKCentral*, "Galleries" (n.d.). http://gallery.skcentral.com/index.php?cat=6, p. 1. Accessed on January 15, 2009; *Reference.com*, "Dana Sue Gray," p. 1.

127. Ramsland, "Surviving Witness," *The Crime Library*, p. 2.

128. *Crimeshots*, "Female Serial Killer," p. 7.

129. *Crimeshots*, "Female Serial Killer," p. 3. In fact, Gray's confession ended investigation of the murder of elderly female victims in San Diego and Newport Beach; police suspected she was responsible. See *Crimeshots*, "Female Serial Killers," p. 3.

130. Braidhill, *To Die For*, p. 76.

131. Egger, *Need to Kill*, p. 14. Also see *Crimeshots*, "Female Serial Killer," pp. 2, 6; Ramsland, "Cagey Customer," pp. 1–2; and Ramsland, "Surviving Witnesses," p. 1.

132. Braidhill, *To Die For*, pp. 275, 277.

133. Ramsland, "A Wrench in the Works," p. 2.

134. *Crimeshots*, "Female Serial Killer," p. 2.

135. Braidhill, *To Die For*, p. 1.

136. Braidhill, *To Die For*, pp. 31–32.

137. Ramsland, "Home Alone," p. 2.

138. Egger, *Need to Kill*, p. 14. Also see Braidhill, *To Die For*, p. 40; *Crimeshots*, "Female Serial Killer," p. 1; Ramsland, "Attacking the Vulnerable," *The Crime Library*, pp. 1–2.

139. Egger, *Need to Kill*, p. 14. Also see *Crimeshots*, "Female Serial Killer," p. 2; Braidhill, *To Die For*, p. 189; and Ramsland, "Tragic Anniversary," *The Crime Library*, p. 1.

140. Ramsland, "Home Alone," p. 2; Braidhill, *To Die For*, p. 15.

141. Ramsland, "Home Alone," p. 2.

142. Ramsland, "Attacking the Vulnerable," p. 2.

143. *Crimeshots*, "Female Serial Killer," p. 1.

144. Ramsland, "Attacking the Vulnerable," p. 1.

145. Braidhill, *To Die For*, p. 92.

146. Ramsland, "Tragic Anniversary," p. 1; Braidhill, *To Die For*, pp. 125, 212.

147. *Crimeshots*, "Female Serial Killer," p. 2; Ramsland, "Tragic Anniversary," p. 1; and Braidhill, *To Die For*, pp. 125–26.

148. Egger, *Need to Kill*, p. 14; Braidhill, *To Die For*, p. 12.

149. Braidhill, *To Die For*, pp. 187, 297.

150. *Crimeshots*, "Female Serial Killer," p. 3.

151. Egger, *Need to Kill*, p. 14.

152. *SKCentral*, "Galleries," p. 1.

153. Frank Logue, "Turn Away From Running After the Gods of Advertising" (n.d.). http://www.kingofpeace.org/religioncolumn/071505.htm, p. 1. Accessed on January 15, 2009.

154. *Reference.com*, "Dana Sue Gray," p. 1.

155. *Crimeshots*, "Female Serial Killer," p. 1.

156. *Crimeshots*, "Female Serial Killer," p. 3.

157. *Crimeshots*, "Female Serial Killer," p. 5.

158. Braidhill, *To Die For*, p. 295; *Crimeshots*, "Female Serial Killer," p. 2.

159. Ramsland, "A Wrench in the Works," p. 1.
160. Ramsland, "Home Alone," p. 2.
161. Braidhill, *To Die For*, p. 19.
162. Braidhill, *To Die For*, pp. 26–27.
163. *Wikipedia*, "Dana Sue Gray," p. 2.
164. Braidhill, *To Die For*, p. 33.
165. Braidhill, *To Die For*, pp. 57–58.
166. Braidhill, *To Die For*, p. 35.
167. Braidhill, *To Die For*, pp. 14, 45–48.
168. *Crimeshots*, "Female Serial Killer," p. 1; Braidhill, *To Die For*, pp. 33–34.
169. Ramsland, "Crazy Over Cash," p. 2; Crimeshots, "Female Serial Killer," p. 1.
170. Ramsland, "Unusual Suspect," p. 1.
171. Ramsland, "Crazy Over Cash," p. 2.
172. Ramsland, "Unusual Suspect," p. 1.
173. Braidhill, *To Die For*, p. 43.
174. Ramsland, "Surviving Witness," p. 1.
175. Braidhill, *To Die For*, pp. 67, 286.
176. Braidhill, *To Die For*, pp. 180, 265.
177. Braidhill, *To Die For*, p. 128.
178. *Crimeshots*, "Female Serial Killer," p. 6. There is reason to believe that Gray unsuccessfully tried to withdraw another $2,000 from Beebe's bank account later that day. See Ramsland, "Unusual Suspect," p. 1.
179. Ramsland, "Attacking the Vulnerable," p. 2.
180. Braidhill, *To Die For*, p. 18.
181. Braidhill, *To Die For*, p. 68.
182. Ramsland, "Unusual Suspect," p. 1.
183. Ramsland, "Unusual Suspect," p. 1.
184. Ramsland, "A Wrench in the Works," p. 1.
185. Ramsland, "A Wrench in the Works," p. 1.
186. *Reference.com*, "Dana Sue Gray," p. 1.
187. Braidhill, *To Die For*, p. 164.
188. Braidhill, *To Die For*, p. 141.
189. Braidhill, *To Die For*, p. 159.
190. Braidhill, *To Die For*, p. 2.
191. Braidhill, *To Die For*, p. 141.
192. Ramsland, "Addicted to Luxury," *The Crime Library*, p. 1.

Select Bibliography

BOOKS

Adleman, Robert H. *The Bloody Benders*. New York: Stein & Day, 1970.

Bickerton, Derek. *The Murders of Boysie Singh*. London: Arthur Baker Limited, 1962.

Braidhill, Kathy. *To Die For: The Shocking True Story of Female Serial Killer Dana Sue Gray*. New York: St. Martin's Press, 2000.

Carlo, Philip. *The Night Stalker: The Life and Crimes of Richard Ramirez*. New York: Kensington Publishing Corporation, 1996.

Commire, Anne. (Ed). *Women in World History: A Biographical Encyclopedia*. Waterford, Connecticut: Yorkin Publications, 1999.

Everitt, David. *Human Monsters: An Illustrated Encyclopedia of the World's Most Vicious Murderers*. Chicago: Contemporary Books, 1993.

Holmes, Ronald M., and Holmes, Stephen T. *Contemporary Perspectives on Serial Murder*. Thousand Oaks, California: Sage Publications, 1998.

Holmes, Ronald M., and Holmes, Stephen T. *Serial Murder*. Thousand Oaks, California: Sage Publications, 1998.

Jenkins, Philip. *Using Murder: The Social Construction of Serial Homicide*. New York: Aldine de Gruyter, 1994.

Jones, Ann. *Women Who Kill*. New York: Fawcett Columbine, 1980.

Jones, Richard Gwyn. *The Mammoth Book of Women Who Kill*. New York: Carroll & Graf, 2002.

Kelleher, Michael D., and Kelleher, C.L. *Murder Most Rare: The Female Serial Killer*. New York: Dell Books, 1998.

Lane, Brian, and Gregg, Wilfred. *The Encyclopedia of Serial Killers*. New York: Berkley Books, 1995.

Miller, Tom. *The Copeland Killings: The Bizarre True Account of Ray and Faye Copeland, the Oldest Couple Ever Sentenced to Death in America*. New York: Windsor Publishing Corporation, 1993.

Nash, Jay Robert. *Encyclopedia of World Crime*. Wilmette, Illinois: Crime Books, Inc., 1990.

Newton, Michael. *The Encyclopedia of Serial Killers*. New York: Checkmark Books, 2000.

Pence, Irene. *Buried Memories: The Chilling True Story of Betty* [*sic*] *Lou Beets, the Texas Black Widow*. New York: Kensington Publishing Company, 2001.

Ramsland, Katherine. *The Human Predator: A Historical Chronicle of Serial Murder and Forensic Investigation*. New York: Berkley Books, 2005.

Schechter, Harold. *Depraved: The Shocking True Story of America's First Serial Killer*. New York: Simon and Schuster, 1994.

Schechter, Harold. *The Serial Killer Files*. New York: Ballantine Books, 2003.

Schutze, Jim. *Preacher's Girl: The Life and Crimes of Blanche Taylor Moore*. New York: Avon Books, 1993.

Seagrave, Kerry. *Women Serial and Mass Murderers: A Worldwide Reference, 1580 Through 1990*. Jefferson, North Carolina: McFarland & Company, 1992.

Seltzer, Mark. *Serial Killers: Death and Life in America's Wound Culture*. New York: Routledge, 1998.

Wilson, Colin, and Seaman, Donald, *The Serial Killers: A Study in the Psychology of Violence*. New York: Carol Publishing Group, 1992.

BOOK CHAPTERS

Bolitho, William. "Old Man Bender's Orchard." In Jonathan Goodman (Ed.), *Masterpieces of Murder*. London: Magpie Books, 2004.

Hale, Robert, and Bolin, Anthony. "The Female Serial Killer." In Ronald M. Holmes and Stephen T. Holmes (Eds.), *Contemporary Perspectives on Serial Murder*. Jefferson, North Carolina: McFarland & Company, 1992.

Jones, Richard G. "Kate Bender: Bumps in the Night," *The Mammoth Book of Women Who Kill*. New York: Carroll & Graf, 2002.

PERIODICALS

"Blood & Plunder."*Time* (May 29, 1950).

"Rural Intrigue Is Unearthed with 5 Bodies." *New York Times* (November 25, 1989).

INTERNET SOURCES

Bedlam Asylum Crime Files. "Marie Becker" (n.d.). http://usersites.horrorfind.com/home/horror/bedlambound/library/b. Accessed on January 3, 2009.

Bruno, Anthony. "Full-Blown Rampage." *The Night Stalker: Serial Killer Richard Ramirez* (n.d.). http://www.trutv.com/library/crime/serial_killers/notorious/ramirez/. Accessed on December 10, 2008.

CrimeLife.com. "H.H. Holmes" (n.d.). http://www.crimelife.com/killers/holmes.html. Accessed on September 6, 2006.

CrimeLife.com. "Martha Beck" (n.d.). http://www.crimelife.com/killers/beck.html. Accessed on September 6, 2006.

Crimeshots True Crime Forums. "Female Serial Killer, Dana Sue Gray"(May 17, 2004). http://www.crimeshots.com/forums/showthread.php?t=129. Accessed on December 3, 2008.

Gado, Mark. "Raymond Fernandez." *The Lonely Hearts Killers* (n.d.). http://www.trutv.com/library/crime/serial_killers/partners/fernandez. Accessed on December 1, 2008.

Geringer, Joseph. "The Most Aggressive New Breed." *The Crime Library* (2008). http://www.trutv.com/library/crime/criminal_mind/psychology/mid. Accessed on November 21, 2008.

Geringer, Joseph. "Mrs. Sorenson." *The Crime Library* (n.d.). http://www.trutv.com/library/crime/serial_killers/history/gunness/4. Accessed on October 31, 2008.

Gilbert, Alexander. "Incarceration." *The Crime Library* (n.d.). http://trutv.com/library/crime/serial_killers/history/haarmann/2b. Accessed on November 10, 2008.

Hilton, Anne. "Boysie Singh 20th Century Pirate of the Caribbean." *Trinidad & Tobago's Newsday* (August 7, 2005). http://newsday.co.tt/people/print.0.29353.html. Accessed on December 18, 2008.

Hinch, Ronald, and Hepburn, Crystal. "Researching Serial Murder: Methodological and Definitional Problems." *Electronic Journal of Sociology* (1998). http://www.sociology.org/content.vol003.002/hinch.html. Accessed on January 13, 2003.

Internet Crime Archive. "The Bender Family" (n.d.). http://www.mayhem.net/Crime/serial2.html. Accessed on August 29, 2006.

La Porte County Historical Society. "Belle Gunness, La Porte's 'Lady Bluebeard' " (1999). http://www.laportecountyhistory.org/belleg1.htm. Accessed on October 31, 2008.

La Porte County Public Library. "The Legend of Belle Gunness" (n.d.). http://www.alco.org/libraries/lepl/belle.html. Accessed on October 31, 2008.

Lohr, David. "Trials and Verdicts." *The Crime Library* (2008). http://www.trutv.com/library/crime/serial_killers/partners/copelands. Accessed on December 10, 2008.

Morris, Steven. "Fritz Haarmann—Werewolf in Hannover [*sic*]." *New Criminologist* (September 20, 2007). http://www.newcriminologist.com/article.asp?cid=107&nid=19. Accessed on November 10, 2008.

The Prairie Chicken. "Ray and Faye Copeland: The Elderly Murderers" (October 5, 2008). http://prairiechicken.blogspot.com/2008/10/ray-and-faye-copeland. Accessed on December 10, 2008.

Queenie. "Marie Alexandrine Becker."*Serial Killers A–Z* (n.d.). http://www.gwocities.com/verbal_plainfield/a-h/becker.html?20093. Accessed on January 3, 2009.

Ramsland, Katherine. "Giving In." *The Crime Library* (2008). http://www.trutv.com/library/crime/notorious_murders/women/dan. Accessed on December 10, 2008.

Ramsland, Katherine. "H.H. Holmes: Master of Illusion: Swindler." *Court TV Crime Library* (2006). http://www.crimelibrary.com/features/fea_printPage.asp?curPage=&thisFile=serial_killers/. Accessed on September 4, 2006.

Zewe, Charles. "Texas Authorities Prepare to Execute Betty [*sic*] Lou Beets; Bush, Supreme Court Refuse to Delay Execution." *CNN.com* (February 24, 2000). http://transcripts.cnn.com/TRANSCRIPTS/00002/24/bn.03.html. Accessed on December 3, 2008.

COURT DOCUMENTS

Beets v. Collins. 986 F.2d, 1478. United States Court of Appeals, Fifth Circuit (March 18, 1993). No. 91-4606.

Beets v. State. 767 S.W., .2d 711 (Tex, Cr.App, 1987) (Direct Appeal).

Public Interest Litigation Clinic. "Faye Copeland" (1999–2000). http://www.pilc.net/clients4.html. Accessed on December 10, 2008.

United States Court of Appeals for the Eighth Circuit. *Faye D. Copeland, Appellee, v. James Washington, Appellant: Appeals From the United States District Court for the Western District of Missouri*. No. 99-3693 (September 13, 2000).

GOVERNMENT DOCUMENTS

"Betty [*sic*] Lou Beets" (n.d.). http://www.clarkprosecutor.org/html/death/US/beets616.htm. Accessed on December 3, 2008.

Central Intelligence Agency. "Trinidad and Tobago." *The World Factbook* (December 8, 2008). http://www.cia.gov/library/publications/the-world-factbook/geos/td.html.

North Carolina Department of Correction, Public Information Access System. "Blanche Moore" (November 20, 2008). http://webapps6.doc.state.nc.us/apps/offender/offend1?DOCNUM. Accessed on November 21, 2008.

State of Kansas, Executive Department. "Governor's Proclamation: $2,000 Reward" (May 17, 1878).

Texas Attorney General's Office. "Media Advisory: Betty [*sic*] Lou Beets Scheduled to be Executed" (February 11, 2000). http://www.clarkprosecutor.org/html/death/US/beets616.htm. Accessed on December 3, 2008.

Index

About the Author

DIRK C. GIBSON has recently served as an expert source for a number of print and electric broadcast media outlets. His book, *Clues from Killers: Serial Murder and Crime Scene Messages* (Westport, CT: Praeger, 2004) describes ten cases of serial murderer communication in detail. The sequel, *Serial Murder and Media Circuses*, was published by Praeger in 2006, and analyzes the interrelationships between the four main serial murder stakeholders: the killer, the police, the media, and the public.

Related research has been published in *Public Relations Quarterly*, *Public Relations Review*, the *Journal of Visual Literacy*, the *Lambda Alpha Epsilon Honorary Journal of Law Enforcement*, and the *Journal of Travel & Tourism Marketing*.

Several refereed convention papers have been produced from this research. One paper, on the Ripper correspondence, won the Top Paper in Mass Communication award from the Western States Communication Association. Gibson's serial killer communication scholarship has been accepted by the Western States Criminology Association, the National Communication Association, the Western States Communication Association, the Rocky Mountain Communication Association, and the Southwest Symposium on Journalism and Mass Communication for conference presentations.

Gibson has been interviewed about serial murder on CNN, Fox News, and *ABC.com*, as well as local TV and radio outlets in the United States and Canada, and by print media such as *Pravda*, *USA Today*, and the Associated Press.

www.ingramcontent.com/pod-product-compliance
Lightning Source LLC
LaVergne TN
LVHW011751200926
848484LV00003B/667